SEXUAL POLITICS
IN MODERN IRELAND

To all the Women's History Association
of Ireland members, past and present

SEXUAL POLITICS
IN MODERN IRELAND

EDITORS

JENNIFER REDMOND
SONJA TIERNAN
SANDRA McAVOY
MARY McAULIFFE

IRISH ACADEMIC PRESS

First published in 2015 by Irish Academic Press
8 Chapel Lane
Sallins
Co. Kildare, Ireland

British Library Cataloguing in Publication Data
An entry can be found on request

978-07165-3284-2 (paper)
978-07165-3285-9 (cloth)
978-07165-3286-6 (PDF)

Library of Congress Cataloging in Publication Data
An entry can be found on request

Printed in Ireland by Sprint-print Ltd.

Contents

Acknowledgements

The editors wish to thank all those within the Women's History Association of Ireland and at University College Cork who helped to organise and host the 2011 conference on which this volume is based. The Women's History Association of Ireland's annual conferences are lively, stimulating and thought-provoking events that engage the scholarly community working in women's and gender history and reach out to the public interested in this work. They have always been an important forum for the exchange of ideas on the history of modern Ireland.

We also wish to thank all the contributors to this volume for their hard work and stimulating contributions, and on their behalf, the libraries, archives and research participants who have made these chapters possible.

LIST OF CONTRIBUTORS

EDITORS

Dr Jennifer Redmond is Lecturer in Twentieth-Century Irish History at Maynooth University. She was formerly Women's History Association of Ireland (WHAI) Treasurer (2008–11), International Secretary and Ireland representative to the International Federation for Research in Women's History (2011–14) and its current President (2014–17). She is also a member of the Royal Irish Academy Committee for Historical Studies. Her research is primarily on Irish social history, including gendered aspects of migration from Ireland in the twentieth century, the Irish diaspora and the history of women's education. She completed her PhD at Trinity College Dublin and has held postdoctoral fellowships from the Irish Research Council (IRC) at Maynooth University and the Council on Library and Information Resources (CLIR) in digital humanities at Bryn Mawr College, USA, where she was also Director of The Albert M. Greenfield Digital Center for the History of Women's Education. Jennifer is the author of numerous chapters and journal articles in women's history, and her monograph on Irish women's migration to England in the post-Independence period, *Moving Histories*, is currently being prepared for publication.

Dr Sonja Tiernan is a Senior Lecturer in Modern History at Liverpool Hope University. She specialises in Irish and British social and political history of the nineteenth and twentieth centuries. Sonja received her PhD from University College Dublin and has held fellowships at the National Library of Ireland, Trinity College Dublin and at the University of Notre Dame. Her recent publications include *Eva Gore-Booth: An Image of Such Politics* published by Manchester University Press. Her next book, *The Political Writings of Eva*

Gore-Booth, will be published by Manchester University Press in 2015. She is a contributor to the Dictionary of Irish Biography and is currently writing the history of the marriage equality campaign in Ireland. Sonja was Secretary of the Women's History Association of Ireland (WHAI) 2011–2013 and WHAI Executive Committee Member 2008–2011.

Dr Sandra McAvoy coordinates Women's Studies in University College Cork. She is a historian whose research focuses on the history of sexuality and the politics of reproductive rights issues in Ireland and on the history of the women's movement. Recent publications include: "'Bring forth abundantly in the earth, and multiply therein": aspects of Irish discourse on contraception (1837-1908)', in M. Leane and E. Kiely (eds), *Sexualities & Irish Society: A Reader* (Dublin: Orpen Press, 2013), and 'Vindicating women's rights in a foetocentric state: the longest Irish journey', in Noreen Giffney and Margrit Shildrick (eds), *Theory on the Edge* (New York: Palgrave Macmillan, 2013).

Dr Mary McAuliffe holds a PhD in history from the School of History and Humanities, Trinity College, Dublin. She currently lectures on the UCD Women's Studies programmes at UCD. Her research interests include gender and Irish history, memory and history, and oral history. She is a committee member and past President (2011–14) of the WHAI, and is on the committee of the Irish Association of Professional Historians. Her latest publication was a re-issue, with a new introduction, of the mid-nineteenth-century travelogue by Frances Taylor, *Irish Homes and Irish Hearts* (Dublin: UCD Press Classics Series, 2013).

COVER IMAGE ARTIST

Joy Ní Dhomhnaill is a painter living and working in Dublin. She was born in 1977 and studied Animation at the Irish School of Animation in Ballyfermot College. Prior to this Joy taught Art through a number of innovative educational projects including the City of Dublin VEC, the Rehab Group and for the City of Dublin Youth Service Board. Joy recently exhibited her work at The Copper House Gallery in Dublin 2 and donated paintings from this exhibition to causes close to her heart; the Irish Marriage Equality campaign and Gay Switchboard Ireland. Joy's first solo exhibition was in 2011 and in 2014 she compiled her latest solo exhibition Pride -v- Prejudice which premiered in The Front Lounge, Dublin in 2014. Joy's work is publicly displayed at various venues on an ongoing basis, most recently at Jam Art Factory in Patrick Street, Dublin 2, The Chocolate Factory, Dublin and at Jingles in Naas, Co. Kildare.

ESSAYISTS

John Johnston-Kehoe completed his doctoral thesis on the history of women in policing in Ireland at the Centre for Contemporary Irish History, Trinity College, Dublin, where he was a Government of Ireland Post-graduate Scholar funded by the Irish Research Council. His research interests include autobiography, vaudeville, women's history, and activism for the unemployed in Ireland.

Elizabeth Kiely, PhD, is a senior lecturer in social policy in the School of Applied Social Studies, University College Cork. She teaches and has published work in the fields of women's studies, youth policy and practice, sex and drug education. She is co-editor of *Youth and Community Work in Ireland, Critical Perspectives* (Dublin, Blackhall, 2009) and *Sexualities and Irish Society, A Reader* (Dublin: Orpen, 2014). She is co-author of *Irish Women at Work 1930–1960: An Oral History* (Dublin: Irish Academic Press, 2012). She was principal investigator on a Department of Children and Youth Affairs funded project on the commercialisation and sexualisation of children and on a National Youth Council of Ireland funded project on youth health inequalities completed in 2014.

Mary Muldowney is an independent scholar who is particularly interested in labour history. She uses oral history interviews extensively in her research. Currently Mary is engaged in a number of projects, including an oral history of the pro-choice movement in Ireland; a study of the post-memory of the First World War in a trade union community; exploration of the involvement of women workers in the Irish railway industry. She is the Director of the Alternative Visions Oral History Group who produced the book *100 Years Later: The Legacy of the 1913 Lockout* (Dublin: Seven Towers, 2013). The group is working on a history of Left activism in Ireland in the twentieth century, to be published next year.

Tanya Ní Mhuirthile is a Senior lecturer at Griffith College Dublin. Tanya's research investigates the impact which law's understanding of corporeality has on certain types of bodies. Her doctoral research, entitled *Intersex Individuals, Gender and the Limits of Law* was conducted under the joint supervision of Dr Mary Donnelly and Prof Siobhán Mullally at UCC. She is a legal consultant to the Transgender Equality Network Ireland and is a founder member of Intersex UK. An expert in the field of gender recognition, Tanya has written opinions for newspapers including the *Irish Times* and *Irish Examiner*, has been a guest on radio shows including *Today with Pat Kenny* and has been an expert consultant on a BBC/Oprah Winfrey Network documentary *Me, My Sex and I.*

Bláthnaid Nolan graduated her PhD from the School of Social Justice, UCD in December 2013. Her thesis title was *Power, Punishment and Penance: An Archival Analysis of the Transportation of Women from Grangegorman in Dublin to Hobart Town in Van Diemen's Land (Tasmania) 1844–1853.* She was awarded the Government of Ireland, IRCHSS, PhD Studentship in 2009, the Lord Edward Fitzgerald Memorial Travel Grant in 2010, and the MacCurtain/ Cullen History Essay Prize in 2011. She has been published in the Routledge Journal of Lesbian Studies, the Women and Gender Working Papers Series in the UCD Research Repository and there will be a forthcoming essay in a publication arising from the International Famine Conference held in 2013. She has presented at conferences in Ireland, the UK and Tasmania. Her research interests include the history of prisons, penal theory, nineteenth-century Ireland, history of criminology, convict transportation, colonial history, feminist and gender historiography and prosopography.

Maeve O'Riordan is an Irish Research Council Post-Doctoral Fellow at the Centre for the Study of Historic Irish Houses and Estates at Maynooth University. She has taught several gender and women's history modules at Maynooth and at University College Cork. She is the author of a number of articles on the history and status of elite women in nineteenth- and twentieth-century Ireland.

Conor Reidy holds an MA and a Ph.D from the Department of History at the University of Limerick. His first monograph, *Ireland's 'Moral Hospital': the Irish Borstal System 1906–1956* was published by Irish Academic Press in 2009. His research interests include crime and punishment in twentieth-century Ireland, the social history of deviance, the Irish borstal system, gender, drunkenness and crime in pre-Independence Ireland. He lectures in family and local history at the University of Limerick. His second monograph *Criminal Irish Drunkards: The Inebriate Reformatory System in Ireland, 1900–1920* was published by The History Press in 2014.

FOREWORD

Long regarded as marginal to mainstream history, the writing of Irish women's history over the last twenty years or so has changed how we understand our past and relate to our present. Recent revelations about Magdalen Asylums in Ireland and the role of mother and baby homes have, for instance, alerted the general public to hidden aspects of our history. Historians of women and gender have played an important role in government-established inquiries to detail the social, political, economic and religious contexts of these institutions.

As is clear from a look at any Irish newspaper, the Irish public has always been interested in sexuality and its many expressions. Over the last three centuries cases relating to seduction, breach of promise to marry, sexual assault, criminal conversation cases where the details of intimate lives were exposed to the public, infanticide and abortion were reported extensively in the Irish national and local press. There is much to learn about Irish society, gender relations and social norms when exploring these kinds of cases. For example, breach of promise to marry cases are full of human frailty, weakness, manipulation, calculation, ambition, as well as evidencing love and attachment.

All kinds of difficulties could, and did, present themselves to intending marriage partners. In breach of promise cases defendants often lost interest in plaintiffs and married someone else, even when a courtship had gone on for a long time. Less often the plaintiff lost interest in the defendant and married someone else. Some men used the promise of marriage as a means of persuading women into a sexual relationship, and then abandoned them months or even years later. Sometimes families interfered and parental permission for the marriage was not granted, or relatives, siblings, or children disapproved of the marriage because of a fear they might lose out in some way in relation to an inheritance, or perhaps in emotional affection.

Generally in Irish society in the post-Famine period premarital intercourse was seen as the road to ruin for women. It is still unclear how acceptable premarital intercourse was within courtship; that it took place is evident. Women were vulnerable to the real consequences of loss of reputation and premarital pregnancy. In cases where the couple engaged in premarital sex, the women claimed it was always within the context of a promise to marry. They also present themselves, or are presented by others, as passive actors in these instances. They are 'persuaded' or 'induced' into a sexual relationship. This kind of passivity elides any sense of sexual desire that these young women might have had for the men they thought to marry, and this, of course, is in keeping with the general belief that women had little sexual desire.

There were political campaigns around issues of sexuality in the nineteenth century, the most prominent being the attempt to repeal the contagious diseases acts, implemented between the 1860s and 1880s. The formation of the Irish branch of the Ladies' National Association for the Repeal of the Contagious diseases Acts in 1870 saw the first organised and extended campaign on a national scale based on a perception of sexual oppression. The contagious diseases acts attempted to control the spread of venereal diseases amongst soldiers and the blame for the spread of these diseases was laid firmly on women who worked as prostitutes. The acts thus targeted these women; if found to be infected, patients were forcibly confined to a hospital until cured. (There was no known cure for such diseases in this period.)

The politicisation of sexual behaviour had been a feature of Irish nationalism from the late nineteenth century, evident most strongly in the equation of the British garrison as a source of moral and physical contagion for Irish women. Problems were to arise when the British garrison was gone, but levels of sexual immorality appeared to rise rather than decrease in the new State. Regarding one form of vice, prostitution, Richard S. Devane, S.J., evangelical in his concern regarding sexual immorality, observed in 1924 that as long as the British garrison was 'in Dublin it was impossible to deal with prostitution effectively. Now a new order has opened up, and things can be done with comparative ease, quite impossible before'.[1] However, what was to emerge from the early 1920s was a belief, strongly evident in clerical and public discussion of sexuality, that the real threat to chastity and sexual morality resided in the bodies of women. Thus moral regulation, by Church and State, attempted to impose, particularly on women, standards of idealised conduct that would return the nation to purity.

Both the State and the Church emphatically presented women's place as being in the home, and the ideal role of the Irish woman was as mother. The idealisation of motherhood was a significant feature of the rhetoric of politicians in the new Irish State; the female body and the maternal body, particularly in its unmarried condition, became a central focus of concern to the State and the Catholic Church.

Unmarried motherhood has proved as problematic in Ireland as it has in most other European countries. Reflecting badly on the 'moral character' of the woman, unmarried motherhood carried a stigma that was almost impossible to shake. An unmarried mother's child was more likely than a legitimate child to die in infancy; the mother, once her status was known, found it difficult, if not impossible to find respectable employment and was often shunned by her family. As an issue unmarried motherhood had become firmly problematised in Ireland by the end of the nineteenth century. Representing possible immorality, a drain on public finances and someone in need not only of rescue, but also of institutionalisation, the unmarried mother had become, by the foundation of the Irish Free State in 1922, a symbol of unacceptable sexual activity and a problem that had the potential to blight the reputation not only of the family but of the nation.

It was not really until the 1960s that attitudes to unmarried mothers in Ireland began to change. The most evident change was perhaps in the greater levels of tolerance which were apparent towards unmarried mothers by the end of the twentieth century, and which allowed a context where legislation to benefit the unmarried mother and her child could be publicly discussed, and laws formulated which brought them some benefit. However, for decades the fate of the unmarried mother was a life overshadowed by shame and disgrace. From the foundation of the State until the 1970s unmarried mothers, while generally enjoying the benefits of citizenship as women, had, ironically in a state that applauded motherhood, no rights as mothers. Their children also had no rights and retained the stigma of illegitimacy. The opprobrium shown to unmarried mothers and illegitimate children preserved the sanctity of marriage, and perhaps just as important, the ownership of property.

The revival of the women's movement in the 1970s saw extensive campaigning and lobbying on issues relating to sexuality, among other things. There were campaigns on contraception, the legalisation of homosexuality, and there are continuing divisive and bitter campaigns on the issue of abortion. It was the era when sexuality in all its forms was politicised. Sexual desire and sexual practices are integral to how we create our identities, and shape our interactions with the world. The essays in this volume are a welcome addition to our knowledge of the history of sexuality and its relationship to politics. The contributors bring new evidence to light on subjects that have received little attention in Irish history and thus are opening up the field in innovative and exciting ways.

Maria Luddy, 2014
University of Warwick

NOTE

1. Evidence of R.S. Devane in 'VD in the Irish Free State', Department of the Taoiseach File, S4183, National Archives of Ireland, Dublin.

INTRODUCTION
POLITICISING SEXUALITY IN MODERN IRELAND

Jennifer Redmond, Sonja Tiernan,
Sandra McAvoy and Mary McAuliffe

Gender history in Ireland is now thriving after four decades of lively, diverse and interrogative scholarly research. This collection adds to the body of literature thus far produced on Irish women's and gender history by gathering materials related to conceptions of bodies as political terrain, in essence the politicisation of gender and sexuality, in various ways. *Sexual Politics in Modern Ireland* follows upon the tradition established in Irish women's history since 1978 with the ground-breaking publication of *Women in Irish Society: The Historical Dimension*, edited by Margaret Mac Curtain and Donnchadh Ó Corráin, in bringing together new research by established and emerging scholars in the field.[1] Building upon subsequent seminal collections, *Sexual Politics in Modern Ireland* offers new research on social and cultural aspects of women's experiences and conceptions of gender identity and sexuality in modern Ireland.

Focusing in the first chapters on the nineteenth and early twentieth century, an era in which women significantly expanded their public role yet faced many challenges in doing so, the book finishes with reflections on gender and the status of women in the public sphere in the late twentieth century. Continuity

1

in these experiences can be seen in the fact that women were (and indeed are still) protesting for the right to make decisions about their own bodies, with the additional dimension of considering how people who do not fit neatly into gender binaries have been treated. In all cases, the body and the primacy of sexuality has been paramount in understanding how men and women, and intersex people, have been rhetorically constructed, treated under the law, and subsequently written about by historians. As Judith Butler has argued, bodies do matter; the materiality of the body has an intimate connection to the performativity of gender and hence the treatment of those bodies by the law, in the public sphere and in our conceptions of masculinity, femininity and otherness.[2]

While *Sexual Politics in Modern Ireland* develops themes in the history of sexuality, political protest, legislation and women's treatment under the law that have been part of previous collections, it also expands our knowledge in these areas and enters new terrain. It examines these aspects in new lights and with the benefit of new source material, building upon some of the pioneering, foundational work by scholars in the field over the last four decades. Current trends in historical research have been emphasising personal experiences that were marginalised, suppressed, or ignored in the major historical works on modern Irish history and this volume contributes both individual and collective experiences that will add to our knowledge of the cultural and social milieu of Ireland in the last two centuries. Women's relationship to cultural change has been interrogated in the recent book by Gerardine Meaney, Mary O'Dowd and Bernadette Whelan, *Reading The Irish Woman*, in which the authors argue for the centrality of culture, and more specifically, cultural encounters, as a lens through which to view processes of change in society and how Irish women engaged with it.[3] Similarly, in *Sexual Politics in Modern Ireland* the chapters weave a narrative that sees gender and encounters with the political sphere, or the politicisation of gender in the public sphere, as an important paradigm for understanding how people were shaped by and sought to shape their society.

While it is no longer the case that women's history is ignored in undergraduate and school curricula as was observed in the collection by Mary O'Dowd and Sabine Wichert in the 1990s, there still remains the 'more complex and more difficult to resolve [issue of] the relationship between women's history and 'mainstream' interpretations of 'general history'.'[4] This collection offers new insights into modern Irish history that are not incidental to 'mainstream' histories but are in fact crucial to a wider, more inclusive understanding of our shared past. As Mary Cullen has observed, this does not simply affect women's understandings of history: 'The absence of gender analysis in the writing of history deprives men and boys, as well as women and girls, of an important part of their group and individual memory.'[5] Yet while modern Irish gender history has moved beyond the simple process of recovery of women in the past, there are many groups that remain marginal to history as it is taught and written in many contexts, making it necessary to continue to revisit the past and our understanding of men and women's roles.

The editors of this collection are or have been members of the executive of the Women's History Association of Ireland (WHAI), (as are some of its contributors), a group committed to raising the profile of women's history and engaging the public in new research in regular colloquia. The diverse membership of the Women's History Association of Ireland and the interesting cross-section of people that attend its events attests to the appetite for insights from women's history on 'mainstream' or 'alternate' narratives of the past. It is hoped that this book will extend our collective forays into the past lives of women in Ireland, holding true as we do the belief that 'the history of half the human race is a worthwhile endeavour and integral to our continuing quests to understand the past' as Alan Hayes has asserted.[6]

This collection stems from the 2011 WHAI conference on Sexual Politics in Ireland, held at University College Cork, and the publication of these chapters follows that of many other important collections in modern Irish history that have sprung from this annual gathering. Bernadette Whelan's edited collection *Women and Paid Work in Ireland, 1500–1930* drew together a diverse range of scholars on women's employment in Ireland, resulting from the 1998 WHAI conference at the University of Limerick and highlighted the international context of Irish women's paid work, arguing that societal attitudes towards women working for wages were similar across Europe in the modern period.[7] Maryann Valiulis' edited collection *Gender and Power in Irish History* emanated from the 2006 WHAI conference and asked questions about how power operated in and flowed through Irish society in the modern period, with essays on witchcraft, crime, republicanism and nationalism, migration and urbanism.[8] Elaine Farrell's edited collection, *She Said She was in the Family Way,* examined pregnancy and infancy in Ireland from the seventeenth to the twentieth century and drew on the WHAI conference presentations at Queen's

University Belfast in 2010.[9] The collection explored these topics in their widest sense in Irish women's history, but with a focus on reproduction and the ways in which this process shaped social conventions and women's interactions with the state. Thus previous collections have in one way or another continued to examine issues related to women's traditional roles and deviations from these in the modern period.

The chapters in this book explore the elision between the categories of sexual identity and gender, whereby women have been reduced to their physicality in a variety of historical settings, or conversely, where a penalty has been exacted for not having a clearly defined gendered identity. While not wishing to conflate the categories of gender, sexual identity and sexuality, in many ways in history these ontological classifications have been collapsed, so that to be an Irish woman was to be a cis female, heterosexual, married and a mother. The heteronormative, conservative social and political environment of modern Ireland was shaped by contemporary attitudes to sexuality, gender and sexual norms, a legacy we continue to grapple with in the twenty-first century as we examine and question the relationship between the state and the Catholic Church, religion and nationhood in areas of women's self-determination. Like the collections investigating sexuality and lesbian experience by Sonja Tiernan and Mary McAuliffe, chapters in this volume interrogate narratives of lesbian experience, usually difficult to source in historical records but worthy of analysis in presenting a work that seeks to explore the full complexity of sexuality and sexual behaviour over the last two centuries.[10] In Nolan's chapter, she questions whether lesbian activity among a prisoner population can be viewed not simply as an expression of desire but also one of protest and dissent, an interesting angle on women's history that is in need of further exploration, but perhaps can be viewed as a feminist reaction to patriarchal bonds of control. Many of the chapters resonate with the wider project of Irish feminist studies in their examination of 'identity, subjectivity and women's engagement in public life' in Ireland and abroad, as part of the Irish diaspora.[11]

The individual's relationship to the law is a recurrent theme in this collection, from female convicts, to the laws regarding reproductive rights and to the ambivalence of the law in its treatment of intersex persons in Ireland. Women feature in many aspects of the legal treatment of citizens by the state, as victims, agitators, criminals and police women. Gender is a connecting point – persons are marked by their gender and their sexual identity within legal and national discourses, often resulting in discriminatory treatment. This is a history that continues to emerge and will likely fascinate historians for some time to come.

In assessing the contribution this makes to the field of women's history, we must look at our subjects in context. Senia Paseta has asserted that the 'women who were active in nationalist circles in the early twentieth century did not expect to be forgotten'.[12] These women were very consciously in the public sphere, making their demands within the context of a national struggle for independence on platforms, in the newspapers and in public meetings. While some of the groups discussed in this collection led public lives and protests, conversely, many of the women in this volume never expected to be remembered. While women's history has made enormous strides in exploring new territory and bringing to light previously untold stories, it seems that there is still further work to be done and this volume seeks to make a contribution to the narratives we have created of women in the past, whilst extending our gendered lens to include intersex persons, a heretofore neglected group and one that does not fall easily into our conceptions of gender identities presently or in the past.

Karen Offen has argued that feminist activity in the past can be seen as radical by definition given that it went against the gender norms of contemporary society, whether or not we view the aims of such women as radical now.[13] In this volume, it can be seen that the activities of women campaigners, whether they were identified as feminist or not, were often transgressive of the social norms of their day, from women's attempts to gain access to the police force, to the pro-choice activism of women in the late twentieth century who set themselves against the predominant conservatism of Irish society.

The social mores of nineteenth and twentieth-century Ireland reveal that sexuality and sexual behaviour became public and political issues as they interacted with the law, not simply through legal statutes but also with regard to land ownership and inheritance. Societal mores found expression in legislation, which in turn impacted on the limits of behaviours and defined the boundaries of transgression. Yet these mores were not simply confined to Ireland. To engage in a thorough examination of Irish gender history, researchers often look beyond the confines of the island in order to assess conditions for Irish women after they left their country of birth and to examine the circumstances which led them to depart. This is particularly evident in Bláthnaid Nolan's research on the transportation of female convicts, which identifies an increase in the numbers of Irish women transported to penal colonies after 1820. Nolan's contribution to this volume, stemming from her wider research, focuses on same-sex sub-culture in the prisons, known as female factories, on Van Diemen's Land (now Tasmania). The strict regime of the control and punishment of both male and female convicts in penal colonies was reflective of the attitude towards criminals in the early nineteenth century. British authorities viewed transportation as a solution to remove unsavoury characters from the general population and unburden overcrowded prisons in Britain. The control of female convicts included harsher punishments relating to considered sexual transgressions, such as engaging in prostitution or becoming pregnant outside of wedlock. Despite high levels of surveillance and the threat of often severe punishment, there is evidence of explicit sexual behaviour within the female factories on Van Diemen's Land. Utilising an abundance of primary source criminal records and the work of historians in this field, Nolan offers an enlightening discussion questioning whether women engaged in same-sex relationships as a form of dissent.

Sexual activity and sexual identity have also been addressed by Maeve O'Riordan in her chapter examining the intimate correspondence between members of the Anglo-Irish class at the turn of the twentieth century. Her exploration of the romance and engagement of Dermod O'Brien and Mabel Smyly offers an alternate perspective on sexuality and the bounds of propriety among their class and provides a rare glimpse of the personal and sexual desires of young men and women in this era through a series of letters they exchanged prior to their marriage. Contrary to representations of Irish women as pure and asexual, the moral ballast in romantic relationships, O'Riordan highlights the passion, both physical and emotional, that emanated from Smyly and was returned by O'Brien. Focusing on a minority population whose power and influence was in decline in this period, O'Riordan's chapter both conforms to the conclusions of previous historiography on such intimate relationships and expands our understanding of them.[14] The desires and feelings expressed by Smyly run contrary to the Victorian stereotype of the 'angel in the house' at times, but at others we see that she was still constrained by societal expectations of women of her age, status and class, and that her Protestant faith was a strong force in her life. The gendered double standards that cast women as passive recipients and controllers of men's sexual desires were paradoxically embraced

6

and rejected by Smyly, at times rhetorically playing the temptress yet at others wishing to be consumed and controlled by O'Brien. The microcosmic world offered in these letters shows there is no simple narrative of sexuality in the past; individuals have navigated the politics of sexual behaviour and identity in different ways at different times.

Conor Reidy's contribution also demonstrates how gendered double standards influenced attitudes to drunkenness in the late nineteenth and early twentieth-centuries, with alcoholism more tolerated in men than in women. High moral standards and self-control were expected of women as mothers, potential mothers and nurturers, with those perceived as deviant severely punished. Alcoholism was associated with moral danger but, as Reidy points out, it was also considered a hazard of prostitution because it was thought that prostitutes drank to obliterate the immoral world into which they had fallen. Reidy's chapter presents case studies of women labelled as 'prostitutes' on their entry to the State Inebriate Reformatory of Ireland, in Ennis, Co. Clare. A place of punishment and reform, run by the penal services, it continued the surveillance of detainees after their release. Reidy draws on the institution's records to provide insights into the lives of these women before they entered the reformatory, during their period in Ennis, and after completion of their sentences, as well as into the attitudes of those charged with reforming them in a society that judged them harshly and provided few effective social supports. Reidy's chapter thus interrogates the interaction between the individual and the law, highlighting the contested terrain of bodily integrity and society's attempts to regulate those whose behaviour falls outside accepted norms.

In Chapter 4, Jennifer Redmond examines the rhetoric surrounding female emigrant bodies in post-Independence Ireland, which focused almost exclusively on Irish women's sexuality and behaviour. In these discourses, which played out in religious and secular journals, national and local newspapers, Lenten pastorals and religious pamphlets from both the Catholic and Protestant Churches, and in government debates, we see the 'madonna/whore' dichotomy of womanhood is a latent presence, although such rhetoric is riven with contradictions and hyperbole. There was a continued questioning of women's sexual behaviour as a motivator for emigration, either to hide pregnancy or to embrace 'modern' sexual mores which was in complete contrast to the resounding silence on Irish men's behaviour, as emigrants or not. Women were problematised as emigrants according to sexual double standards that saw them either as temptresses or victims, but either way paying the ultimate price through illegitimate pregnancies. Women's bodies were central to this thinking: they were the site of sin, the literal embodiment of transgressive sexual behaviour through pregnancy, and thus control of them was essential in many people's eyes in order to diminish what was seen as a significant moral problem. As many historians have posited, post-independent Ireland observed a national obsession with sexuality and sexual practice, and this extended to those citizens who left its shores. Opinions on women's sexual practices as emigrants was also based on partial evidence of the phenomenon of unmarried mothers, and the opinions of religious charitable institutions in Britain which found themselves assisting in 'hiding Ireland's shame'. Women emigrating were often castigated, in contrast to the women of the home idealised in the 1937 Constitution, as sexually profligate, immoral or excessively naïve and susceptible to sin, and accused of bringing shame on the nation. They had no champions in political circles, and as this chapter outlines, the flawed conceptions about female emigrants had a long history that denied the reality of women's lives, which ironically conformed more closely to traditional, familist ideals promoted by the state.

Sexual Politics in Modern Ireland explores themes of sexuality, morality and the law, and while female emigrants broke no legislation, the moral condemnation of their actions had compelling force. In contrast, though women have also been on the 'other side' of the law, however, and were not simply victims or perpetrators of crime. Johnston-Kehoe's contribution on women in policing demonstrates how women's sexual and gender identity was used as a plinth to elevate their roles in the public sphere and conversely as the reason to diminish their contributions. Emerging from nineteenth-century notions of women's philanthropic contributions as having a special place in the world of social work, women's policing in Ireland began in the form of chaperoning female prisoners, a task thought innately suited to women based on a very physical understanding of the appropriateness of women dealing with women in intimate ways. Handling women during trials, conducting physical searches, controlling women as they navigated the courthouses, prisons and institutions of the state legal apparatus all required close contact, and hence women were seen as appropriate 'handlers'. Furthermore, there are particular class considerations emerging from this analysis, with police women being drawn from the lower middle classes, handling women for the most part from the lower working classes, and thus, within contemporary rhetoric, able to offer appropriate moral guidance and influence in their dealing with women. Despite these advantages, women in policing were not exempt from gendered discourses that saw them as acting outside the norms of their sex. Their presence on the streets and at stations, their patrol work and their public profile were outside the norms of the social and cultural milieu of early twentieth-century Ireland and critiques of their actions became politicised at the highest level.

Elizabeth Kiely provides a welcome analysis of the lively and, oftentimes contentious, public debates on sex education in contemporary Irish schools, and more specifically, on the introduction of the Relationships and Sexuality Education (RSE) between 1996 and 2002. Prior to this period few schools provided sex education; after 1994 the introduction of a national, compulsory, programme of sex education in schools was specified in government reports. However, the introduction of RSE was not without its problems and controversies. In researching the large archive of newspaper letters in response to the introduction of RSE, Kiely demonstrates the competing discourses on childhood innocence, youthful sexuality, the centrality of the family and its 'natural' protection of children as well as protection of the purity of the Irish nation used by the proponents and opponents of RSE. As she writes the idea that sex education shouldn't be given to children because it destroys their innocence has a long-standing history in Irish society; this idea along with the argument of the inviolability of the family and parental rights on moral and sexual matters dominated the arguments of those who opposed RSE. Those who supported the programme tended to have less faith in parents as sex educators, and argued for school as the most appropriate setting for sex education where children would be taught in peer groups. Despite the wide engagement of letter writers on the issue of RSE, Kiely has also shown that both proponents and opponents consistently used hetronormative discourses of sexuality when talking about the sexually responsible – always heterosexual – citizens which sex education, whether in the home or in school, would produce. The politics of young people's sexuality took the national stage, not for the first or last time.

In her chapter on abortion and activism in Ireland since the 1980s, Mary Muldowney considers the change in attitude of the Irish public, from the perspective of pro-choice activists. Using oral histories gathered from activists in three main campaigns, the 1983, 1992 and 2002 referenda, Muldowney charts the incremental changes in public attitudes to abortion and the change in the tactics of the pro-life organisations during these decades. The 1983 referendum was marked by a stark division between the forces who supported pro-life positions and were represented as defenders of traditional Irish society and Catholicism, and those who were seen as the pro-choice supporters of a more open, liberal, secular society. Success in 1983 went to the forces of traditional values when the 8th Amendment of the Constitution was passed and ratified. The pro-choice activists interviewed speak of a multi-faceted complex journey from battling the dogmatic forces of reaction in 1983 to a situation, by 2002, where most pro-choice activists believed that the Irish public was more open to repealing the 8th Amendment. Also demonstrated by their recollections is that the Irish public has journeyed on the road to the belief 'that abortion as a solution to a crisis pregnancy should be available to women who want to make that choice' with much more speed and clarity than Irish politicians.[15] Recent cases, most particularly the death of Savita Halappanavar, have revealed this topic to be one that can be considered a 'living' history, rather than ones that exists solely in the depths of the archives.

Legal controls stretch beyond issues of sex, sexuality and fertility, intruding into even the categorisation of gender. This position is highlighted by Tanya Ní Mhuirthile in her chapter detailing the legal history of intersex people in Ireland. Historically many societies acknowledged that outside the boundaries of what designated a body as either male or female, there naturally existed bodies which did not fit the standard definition, due to their sexual or reproductive anatomy. Tracing the legal position of intersex in Ireland reveals that rather than advancing legal recognition, in line with medical understanding, the modern Irish legal system effectively removed 'intersex' from legal awareness. Public awareness of the term intersex has increased in Ireland over the last ten years, due mainly to decisions surrounding the incompatibility of Ireland's laws in this regard under the European Convention on Human Rights. However, as Ní Mhuirthile shows, there remains a general misunderstanding in Ireland about what constitutes an intersex body. Through an assessment of the legal history, sometimes impacted by individual cases, this research offers a long overdue insight into Ireland's ineffective laws surrounding gender recognition.

CONCLUSION

It is almost twenty-five years since MacCurtain, O'Dowd and Luddy issued their agenda for modern Irish women's history, calling attention to the issue of sexuality as a need of further exploration:

> Having briefly surveyed the situation of Irish women in regard to religion and politics, we should not ignore the other branch of the triptych: sex. We know very little about the sexual activity of Irish women in the last century. How did women of the various classes view sexuality?[16]

While important work has been produced by scholars in recent times, including Earner-Byrne, McCormick, McAvoy and Ferriter, it seems we do not yet know enough to answer the questions posed by MacCurtain, O'Dowd and Luddy, thus it seems timely to revisit these questions through the varied approaches the chapters in this collection take.[17]

Sexual Politics in Modern Ireland explores issues related to sexuality, sexual practice, sexual identity and gender politics from the mid-nineteenth to the late twentieth century, a time that saw large-scale social, economic, political and demographic changes in Ireland. In these chapters gender is the primary lens through which to view these changes, mainly with regard to ways in which we can understand the political nature of sexuality in Ireland. Referring to scholarly understandings of work as gendered, Luddy has argued that 'women's history can raise new questions about the past and redefine our common understanding of fundamental historical issues'.[18] In the current volume, we argue that insights gained from scholars in gender and women's history in Ireland today can offer reappraisals of our understanding of the state, how it constructed gendered bodies, and how it treated its citizens on the basis of gender.

Despite it being a private matter in many people's analysis, sexuality and sexual practices in Ireland have frequently come to the fore: in the pastorals of bishops, in political speeches, in letters to local and national newspapers, in the courts, in private homes, in families, in schools. Although the topics vary and the time periods differ, the continuities throughout this volume remain: gender has been used in the public sphere to delineate the treatment of individuals under the law, in social and cultural practices and in intimate relations.

These historical episodes have resonances today, for although there have been decades of protests for the rights of women to determine what happens to their own bodies, Ireland is still embroiled in bitter political divisions on this topic. The treatment of those who do not conform to gender and sexual identity norms have been marginalised and remain liminal to broader narratives. This book hopes to contribute to a richer understanding of our past and to the contemporary debates on how Ireland developed its social and cultural mores on gender and sexuality.

The book offers many conclusions, most of which query the state's role in the regulation of bodies over the past two centuries. Reidy has questioned the effectiveness of the law and the state's institutions in their mission to reform women identified as prostitutes on their entry to the Ennis institution. In his analysis, the system offered little chance of the desired redemption for women with a narrow range of options and few resources. Most importantly, Reidy points to the silence that hangs over the women themselves as their voices were not recorded and their perspectives on their treatment are absent from the historical record. This is the case for the subjects of many of the chapters, and yet many have also managed to include direct evidence from women themselves, articulating their own thoughts and desires about marriage and intimacy in O'Riordan's chapter, to voicing their concerns about the state's approach to sex education in Kiely's analysis to the oral history approach in Muldowney's chapter. Historical research is a complex negotiation of perspective, subjectivity and evidence, and personal testimony is often lost in the bid to produce a rational, objective account of the past. Many historians now realise this is a fallacy and that a complex, nuanced narrative of past historical encounters cannot be created without regard to a multiplicity of sources; there is no value-free history.

Conceptualising the politics of the body in history allows us to widen our analytical lens from the gender binary of male/female interaction, although this continues to be important to analyse given the gendered power hierarchies that have prevailed in modern Irish history. However, as with much gender and women's history in recent decades, this volume also draws attention to the liminal, marginalised and interstitial narratives that have been ignored in historical analyses of social and cultural change. Ní Mhuirthile's examination of the impact the law's changing conception of corporeality has had on people with intersex bodies reveals their complete absence from public discourse prior to 2009, yet intersex persons had legal status since medieval times. It seems that in Ireland, such persons so transgressed the normative bounds of public and legal discourse that they could not be conceived of, and yet of course we know that persons categorised as intersex have always been a part of Irish society.

The chapters in this volume have all engaged with the lively debates and themes in Irish women's and gender history, in an attempt to create, as Mary Cullen has argued for, 'a more inclusive human history that approximates more closely to the reality it aims to uncover'.[19] *Sexual Politics in Modern Ireland* demonstrates that sexuality, sexual identity and sexual practice are complex and contested categories in Irish history and society, and it is likely they will remain so.

NOTES

1. M. MacCurtain and D. O Corrain (eds), *Women in Irish Society: The Historical Dimension* (Dublin: Arlen House, 1978).

2. J. Butler, *Bodies That Matter: On the Discursive Limits of 'Sex'* (New York and London: Routledge, 1993).

3. G. Meaney, M. O'Dowd and B. Whelan, *Reading the Irish Woman: Studies in Cultural Encounters and Exchange, 1714–1960* (Liverpool: Liverpool University Press, 2013).

4. M. O'Dowd and S. Wichert (eds), *Chattel, Servant or Citizen: Women's Status in Church, State and Society* (Belfast: Institute of Irish Studies, Queen's University of Belfast, 1995).

5. M. Cullen, *Telling It Our Way: Essays in Gender History* (Dublin: Arlen House, 2013), p.21.

6. A. Hayes, 'Afterword: A Feminine Occupation for a Female Audience?: A Future for Irish Women's History', in A. Hayes and D. Urquhart (eds), *Irish Women's History* (Dublin: Irish Academic Press, 2004), pp.199–202.

7. B. Whelan, *Women and Paid Work in Ireland, 1500–1930* (Dublin: Four Courts Press, 2000).

8. M. Valiulis (ed.), *Gender and Power in Irish History* (Dublin: Irish Academic Press, 2008).

9. E. Farrell (ed.), *She Said She was in the Family Way: Pregnancy and Infancy in Modern Ireland* (London: Institute of Historical Research, 2012).

10. See S. Tiernan and M. McAuliffe (eds), *Sapphists and Sexologists: Histories of Sexualities Volume II* (Newcastle: Cambridge Scholars Publishing, 2009) and S. Tiernan and M. McAuliffe (eds), *Tribades, Tommies and Transgressives: Histories of Sexualities Volume I* (Newcastle: Cambridge Scholars Publishing, 2008).

11. D.A.J. MacPherson and M. Hickman (eds), *Women and Irish Diaspora Identities: Theories, Concepts and New Perspectives* (Manchester: Manchester University Press, 2014).

12. S. Paseta, *Irish Nationalist Women 1900–1918* (Cambridge: Cambridge University Press, 2013), p.1.

13. K. Offen (ed.), *Globalizing Feminisms, 1789–1945*, (London: Routledge, 2010), p.xxxiii.

14. See, for example, M. Luddy, *Matters of Deceit: Breach of Promise to Marry cases in Nineteenth- and Twentieth-Century Limerick* (Dublin: Four Courts Press, 2011).

15. See page 142.

16. M. MacCurtain, M. O'Dowd and M. Luddy, 'An Agenda for Women's History in Ireland, 1500–1900', *Irish Historical Studies*, 28, 109 (1992), pp.1–37.

17. See Select Bibliography for details of scholarship mentioned.

18. M. Luddy, 'Women and work in nineteenth and early twentieth-century Ireland: an overview', in B. Whelan (ed.),*Women and Paid Work in Ireland, 1500–1930* (Dublin: Four Courts Press, 2000), pp.44–56.

19. Cullen, *Telling It Our Way*, p.409.

1

KNOWING DISSENT: LESBIAN SUB-CULTURE IN THE FEMALE FACTORIES OF VAN DIEMEN'S LAND

Bláthnaid Nolan

Almost 25,000 women were transported to New South Wales and Van Diemen's Land between 1787 and 1853. The LINC Tasmania network combines the resources of the State Library of Tasmania, the Tasmanian Archive and Heritage Office (TAHO), Adult Education and online access centres and provides information online illustrating different methods of calculation of transported convicts. LINC Tasmania suggests the most accurate number for the convicts transported to Van Diemen's Land between 1803 and 1853 was 73,566.[1] Relatively few women were transported from Britain and Ireland to Van Diemen's Land prior to the 1820s, however, from that date to the cessation of transportation to the area in 1853, approximately 13,400 women were sent there from Ireland, Britain and New South Wales.[2]

Most incarcerated women spent time in a female factory which was a women's prison constructed in Australia and Van Diemen's Land for transported convicts. It was called a female factory as its corrective nature involved labour. The atmosphere or culture in these institutions was often chaotic and intimidating and it could be argued that this was symbolic of the attitudes of colonial society towards convict women. In Van Diemen's Land, despite the methods of surveillance, control, and punishment exercised over convict women through a colonial authoritative gaze and discipline regime designed to produce submissive malleable female convicts, there is evidence of overt sexuality both heterosexual and homosexual within the female factories. The factories were gaols within the larger gaol of New South Wales or Van Diemen's Land. Each section of every factory was designed to conduct its punitive function. There were six main female factories on the island of Van Diemen's Land. Hobart Town Female Factory (1821–9), George Town (1822–34), Cascades outside Hobart (1829–79), Launceston (1834–1915), Ross (1848–54) and Brickfields Hiring Depot (1842–52).[3] Cascades was the largest factory and Brickfields the smallest one.

Gary Simes stated that convict women's sexuality cannot be read as the clearly defined 'sexual identities' or exclusive 'persuasions' that a twenty-first-century audience might be more familiar or comfortable with.[4] Eleanor Conlin Casella has claimed that demarcations of sexuality into categories of straight or lesbian only emerged with the development of a late nineteenth-century discourse on sexology, almost fifty years after the cessation of transportation to Australia.[5] According to Michel Foucault it was not until the late nineteenth century that the 'homosexual became a species'.[6] Foucault argued that prior to the advent of sexology and the definition of the homosexual as medically pathological, there were homosexual acts but not homosexual identities. However this may simply be a question of terminology. David Robinson makes the point that the discourse of literature used to define sex, gender and sexuality 'is only one of many clues to meaning and experience, and not necessarily the most important'.[7]

Of course sexologists did not 'invent' homosexuality. The debate around when and where the term lesbian was first used is a complex one. Whether the word is attributed to a poetess in the Classical Age of Greece in 600 BC, or used to insult a duchess in William King's mock-epic poem *The Toast* in 1736, there are supporters of the idea that the sexologists theorised about the 'third sex' or the 'invert' in the early part of the twentieth century.[8] Describing women in the past as lesbians can be dismissed as anachronistic, however; the more important question is whether some convict women of the female factories self-consciously identified as lesbian.

Within the female factories, the management of convict women was through order, daily routine, gauged tasks and regulated penalties.[9] Upon arrival to Van Diemen's Land, the women were classified into three levels in the factories. All classes of convict women had to wear coarse and plain clothes. There were advantages to being in the First Class. The women in this class received the best food and engaged in little or no work. They were there because they were waiting to be assigned into service. Some may have recently arrived in transport ships, some may have been returned to the factories by masters through no fault of their own, for example, if their master or mistress had died. Some had simply served their time and were waiting to receive tickets-of-leave and be sent into private employment where they could earn wages.[10]

The Second/Probation Class women had served part of their entire sentence in the Third/Crime Class for a minimum of three months. Second Class women also received better food. Their uniform betrayed their class by a large yellow C sewn onto their sleeves.[11] There was no significant difference between the discipline in the First and Second Classes and the biggest advantage over the Third Class was that they were entitled to small luxuries, such as 'coffee made from roasted wheat'.[12] Those that found themselves in the lowest class comprised of two types of women; free women who had broken the law through theft, prostitution or being drunk and disorderly; and female convicts who had broken a rule of assignment or the law, usually minor, and who were sent to the factory by their master for punishment. The most common infractions of the rules of assignment were; obstinacy, neglect of duty, absence without leave and being drunk and disorderly and probably in that order.

The other type or woman who was in the Third/Crime Class was unmarried and pregnant. Because of this, they were unable to perform their duties. Tony Rayner explains that 'perhaps the worst crime committed against women in history has been to degrade those who became pregnant whilst unmarried, or who through poverty asked a living by prostitution, whilst ignoring the most basic fact that procreation requires both a man and a woman'.[13] Men did not receive such punishment, nor were they legally obliged to provide financially for their offspring. Following the birth of their child and after whatever amount of time was deemed allowable by the authorities, these women were required to serve a six-month sentence of hard labour, a penalty for becoming pregnant. In the Third/Crime class, from 1826 and in the years that followed, the women's heads were shaved, a punishment said to be more upsetting to them than any other.[14] Their diet was poorer than the other classes and they also endured a large yellow letter C sewn on the back of their jacket, sleeves and shifts of their uniform.[15]

The Report on the Inquiry into Female Convict Discipline 1841–1843 (Inquiry FCD) presents a wealth of evidence of what were described as unnatural acts within the female factories of Van Diemen's Land but the query remains as to whether the women of the factory acknowledge this as being a specific identity that could be called lesbian. Did they celebrate their 'madness', embrace their 'badness' and engage in a 'reverse discourse' consciously?[16] Witness statements in the Inquiry FCD of dissenting sexual behaviour suggest that this was in fact the case. Higher standards were expected of women as clearly evidenced in the findings of the Committee assembled for the Inquiry FCD who found that a 'higher degree of reformation is required in the case of a female, before society will concede to her that she has reformed at all'.[17] The perceived wickedness of convict women arose from transgressions such as glaring sexual awareness and outspokenness, intemperance, smoking and crucially, their refusal to capitulate to the restrictions they faced within the convict system. Identifying these behaviours as transgressions may be more indicative, however, of the repressive nature of upper-middle-class principles between the early Victorian ages than of the supposed depravity or abandonment of the convict women. Where the women did reoffend it was against public order and the convict discipline system in which they were confined.

In this context it is the most incorrigible female convicts who warrant discussion. The women of the Third or Crime Class in the female factories were described as such because they had transgressed boundaries and instilled fear in the authorities who perceived their behaviour as symbolic of anarchy. In particular, convict women were considered to have committed the greatest offence when they traversed the feminine into the terrain of the masculine.[18] This could be done by adopting what was considered masculine behaviour such as abusive language and fighting. They refused to be submissive, they refused to work and absconded, they drank, they smoked or they were overtly sexually aware. Worst of all, they performed same sex acts.[19] In spite of incarceration, the women in the female factories persistently conducted themselves badly in what Kay Daniels refers to as 'a robust rough culture'.[20] This behaviour was shocking to a more upper-class observer with no experience of lower-class social interactions.

There was a stigma attached to this rough sub-culture. Indeed Casella adds to the documentary evidence and the works of historians such as Daniels and Joy Damousi, when she provides archaeological evidence supporting the trafficking of contraband, such as olive glass bottles and clay pipes, between the women in the crime class or solitary cells from other women in the factory that they were sexually involved with.[21] The evidence suggests that these women shared a group identity and it is precisely because lesbian acts were committed in the female factories that they were recorded in the Inquiry FCD. Unlike historians of sexuality who bemoan the tedious requirements made by traditional historians and biographers of proof that same-sex desire existed or acts occurred, the Inquiry FCD relating to the female factories in Van Diemen's Land gives clearly stated official sworn statements, outlining sexual relationships and using explicit language.

Recorded in this Report FCD are examples of when female convicts transgressed the boundaries of moral/immoral, order/disorder and male/female, as understood by the colonial authorities. The Superintendent at Launceston Female Factory, Robert Pearson, testified that although the women might have come into the factory with their virtue and innocence intact, so prevalent was the depravity and unnaturalness of the activities of the general population of the inmates that inevitably under the present system they became corrupted.[22] Common and recurring phrases in discussions of depravity or unnatural activities are used in relation to one group of women, as opposed to the other women or the well-disposed of women. In this context, the other women are the unspoken norm, described as the good, the proper, the moral women. These women were in the majority and they were offended by immorality and unnatural connexions. This is supported by the account of one inmate Mary Kirk. Kirk maintains 'that "unnatural conduct" was common … the "well-disposed" women were unable to avoid being corrupted as none could avoid associating with the others'. Kirk maintains that this is because 'the flash characters compel the others to follow their example.'[23]

At variance with this is the evidence given by Eliza Churchill, a turnkey in the factory who described how, 'there are many women who will not stay out of the factory when others with whom they carry on an unnatural connexion are in the building.'[24] Catherine Owens and Ellen Scott are amongst the women she names. She continued to note, that 'these women are quite jealous of each other. The other women are afraid to interfere although they dislike such practices, they are never carried on openly but at night, they are never associated with by the other women, [and] they generally sit together on one side of the yard'.[25] Kirk maintains that the 'well-disposed' women could not avoid this group of women, whereas Churchill claims that they were 'never associated with by the other women'. Mary Haigh, in her sworn statement, describes a group of women in the factory known as the 'Flash Mob'. They 'always have money, wear worked caps, silk handkerchiefs, earrings and other rings'. She refers to them as 'the greatest blackguards' in the factory, who lead younger women away by 'ill advice'.[26]

It should be noted that Haigh was granted a Conditional Pardon for the evidence she gave. Those who gave evidence to the Inquiry FCD were termed by the inmates as 'jacketters'. This presumably meant a turncoat. There may have been a myriad of potential reasons for the jacketter to speak, including jealousy or revenge for a former disagreement. Other reasons might have been the desire to distance themselves from unnatural practices, or the jacketters may simply have been trying to curry favour with the factory officials and manoeuvre into a more advantageous position in the factory, whether that was better sleeping accommodation, less labour intensive tasks, better food rations or other indulgences.[27] Churchill, for example, was sentenced to fourteen years in 1840 for larceny. As in the case of Kirk, in exchange for her testimony to the Inquiry FCD, Churchill received a Conditional Pardon on 1 April 1842, twelve years before her sentence should have expired.[28]

A riot that occurred in the Launceston Female Factory in 1842 is an example of when the boundaries of order and disorder were subverted. The relationship between two women was central to this incident. Catherine Owens was 19 years old when she was convicted in 1829 for receiving stolen goods and sentenced to fourteen years.[29] She was described as 'an extremely bad character, and one who has always ranked as a leader upon all occasions of misconduct'.[30] That same year Ellen Scott was transported for life at the age of 16 for assault. A life sentence of transportation could suggest that this was not her first conviction or her crime may have been a particularly aggravated assault.[31] Scott and Owens had 'accumulated so many reportable offences that' these were recorded in two Supplementary Conduct Registers.[32] Most notably, Scott was charged with 'violently assaulting Mr Hutchinson [Superintendent of Cascades] with intent to kill or do him some bodily harm' and was also charged with 'indecent behaviour during the performance of divine service'.[33]

It is generally accepted that Owens and Scott had a long-term sexual affair. Scott angered by the prolonged solitary confinement of her sexual partner Owens, seized control of the prison with the assistance of fellow inmates. The police were 'beaten off by the women who had ar ned themselves with the spindles and legs from the spinning wheels, bricks taken from the floors and walls of the building, knives forks &c and also Quart bottles in which some of them had received medicine'.[34]

The women were eventually subdued when the authorities 'ordered about fifty men from the Prisoners Barracks to proceed to the female House of Correction, and having been sworn in [as] special Constables and furnished with sledge hammers and crow bars, with the assistance of some constables the Crime Class ward was [suppressed]'.[35] The most violent of the reprobates were held in cells in the men's gaol. Owens and Scott were named as the ringleaders and regularly confined in separate cells due to their involvement in the black-market networks within the female factories, particularly for trafficking luxury goods, such as tobacco, pipes, sugar, alcohol and being in the possession of alcohol.[36] Stipulating that a woman be separated from her fellow inmates was code for separating those women who engaged in same-sex acts, from those who did not. Clearly, the sub-cultural group that was the Flash Mob challenged the convict administration system and the male authorities who sought to control it. Considered depraved, profligate, hardened and without remorse, it was hoped separate treatment would confine their licentious passions and protect the other women lest they become contaminated. Scott's last entry on her conduct page reads, 'this woman is to be kept separate at the Gaol... she is to be sent over to Hobart for that purpose'.[37]

Movement in the penal establishments at night-time was a punishable offence. Ann Nevin of the Australasia received four months hard labour in February 1850 for 'not sleeping in her authorised berth' at Brickfields, which was a hiring depot, not a female factory.[38] Moreover, not telling the factory authorities was also a punishable offence. Bystanders could be punished too. Ellen Heffernan, who also arrived on the Australasia, received one month hard labour in August 1850 for 'not giving notice of women shifting [from] their proper berths at night'.[39] The fear of being sent to solitary confinement persuaded some women to spy and may explain why women became jacketters.

Another investigation was ordered into transportation and its management, this time into the Probation System and provides further glimpses of concerns about female sexual behaviour. Probation was a new and supposedly improved official policy where upon arrival, convicts stayed in probation gangs in designated stations for a certain amount of time, usually six months, for moral and skills training. They were then hired out to emigrants or officials or the government for a wage. Depending on good behaviour they gained a probation pass, or a ticket of leave which allowed them to change employer, move area and demand higher wages.

In 1846, the Superintendent of Port Phillip in the Melbourne area, Charles La Trobe, was appointed to the role of Administrator of Van Diemen's Land where he was to conduct an official inquiry into the efficiency and workings of the Probation System. In W.E. Gladstone's dispatch, La Trobe had been warned in particular, 'to avoid any measure and indeed any debate respecting the financial and political questions controverted in the colony'.[40] The dispatch from Gladstone to La Trobe was a set of clear instructions for the job that he had been commissioned to undertake. Gladstone insisted that, 'he was to give his attention "to other and yet more urgent matters. I, [Gladstone], of course, refer to the state of the convicts whether in the probation gangs, in the Mines, or at the hiring depots."'[41] The primary purpose of his appointment was to carry out an investigation into the probation system and unnatural crime. Visits of probation stations and penal establishments were conducted 'with medical officers examining clothing and bedding for semen, researching medical records for symptoms that might indicate "habitual perpetration" and conducting cross-examinations'.[42] La Trobe was to question staff or persons who were happy to aid in his investigation. He was also tasked with producing a report for the Colonial Secretary in London, who was by the time of its completion Earl Henry Grey.

Cascades Female Factory acted as the chief laundry for the city of Hobart. La Trobe refers specifically to Brickfields hiring depot for women and Cascades Female Factory in his report.

> This conclusion has been arrived at not so much from what has been divulged by the women themselves, as from observations made in many instances of the women. One absconds the other follows immediately; one receives punishment for misconduct the other commits some offence with the hope of rejoining her companion... With regard to the Cascades Female Factory Hobart Town, whatever may have been the

case formerly and there can be no doubt but unnatural practices have prevailed, there exists at present no reason to suspect the existence of this vice within the walls of the Establishment...[43]

La Trobe even refers to the Orphan School in New Town on the outskirts of Hobart, expressing his wonder that 'the introduction of the most abominable practices ... by the acquaintance which all of the lower classes in the Colony, young and old, possess with the ... crime in question' and declares that only 'the most unwearied vigilance can secure the institution'.[44] Despite La Trobe's condemnation of Probation as a system and warning of the existence of vice and depravity among the convicts, further incidences were recorded in 1848 by the Superintendent of the Ross Female Factory. Disgust felt by the authorities emerged when the boundary between masculine and feminine was traversed by convict women and was discussed using language of disorder and disturbance. This account was given by the Superintendent of the remote Ross Female Factory, W.J. Irvine. In the report Irvine refers to arguments related to 'some of the women deserting the beds of those to whom they acted in the capacity of men, and [betook] themselves elsewhere'.[45] He continued by describing how 'there are some of the women who, by a preternatural formature, or sometimes by artificial means, are enabled to fill the vile part above mentioned, & who are known amongst their fellow prisoners by a peculiarly significant soubriquet'.[46]

Irvine alludes to elongated clitorises and artificial substitutions 'to play the male part' as well as mentioning code names used by the inmates. This is further evidence of a group identity which could be named as lesbian. There was an insistence on curbing what were termed as abominable habits. Irvine's discomfort with this type of mannish-woman, this pseudo-man is another example of the women traversing the boundaries of femininity and masculinity. He seems to have been equally alarmed by 'those young girls [who are in] the habit of decorating themselves, cleaning themselves scrupulously, and making themselves as attractive as they can, before resorting to the "man-woman" ... on whom they have bestowed their affections.'[47] Irvine also identified a 'large size masculine looking woman' Margaret Elliot. He accused her of 'approaching the very young and inexperienced and of seducing them and it appears the scenes that take place from depraved habits of such creatures as this woman are to the last degree disgusting and offensive to the better disposed ... [because of] nocturnal orgies and offending their sense of common decency by their licentious and unnatural practices.'[48]

One of the principle means of resistance the female convict utilised, which horrified officials, was to express an enthusiastic desire to return to the female factory, to re-join their friends, or that they preferred the camaraderie of the bad girls of the factory rather than being reassigned into service. Eliza Churchill reported that 'I have heard many of the women say that they do not care about being in the factory that they would as soon be there as serve the settlers.'[49] Also the women smuggled contraband goods back in with them.[50] Lucy Frost wrote of a feud between Pearson the Superintendent of Launceston Female Factory and Mr and Mrs Littler, the Gate-keeper and Sub-Matron. Churchill's evidence against the Littlers' aiding and abetting in trafficking goods, such as tobacco in and out of the factory, is called into question in light of the Conditional Pardon she knew she would receive.[51]

Casella's archaeological exploration of the Ross Female Factory uncovered 'a substantial amount of olive glass bottle fragments and kaolin clay tobacco pipes' in the Criminal Class dormitory of Ross and even more 'elicit materials' were discovered in the Solitary Cells.[52] Olive glass bottles were used to consume alcohol, a luxury item that convict women smuggled in. The instances of unnatural crime were recorded in the Conduct Register along with the punishment. This meant it was on their permanent convict record and could work against them for any future indulgence applied for.[53] These acts of resistance vary in strategy but provide examples of defiance and survival skills exercised by the convict women within the structured society of a colony that sought to control their every waking and sleeping moment. The Flash characters commanded elements of fear, admiration and support from the female prison population. Such acts of resistance demonstrate that the convict women could 'actively work the system to minimise their disadvantage'.[54]

Due to overcrowding issues, women in Cascades had to sleep two to a hammock. The following evidence was given to the Inquiry FCD.[55] Josiah Spode, Principle Superintendent of Prisoners, wrote to the Inquiry in 1843 that:

> [Another] case … is of a much more vicious and depraved character, and which there is reason to believe has been carried on to some considerable extent since the congregation of females in the Establishment has been

so great. I am compelled to request His Excellency's attention to the evidence of Ann Fisher, however unpleasant in its perusal, because it will clearly shew that without separate confinement in all instances be adopted, those dreadful occurrences can never be thoroughly put a stop to.[56]

The ward's woman was Ann Fisher and her hammock fellow was Jane Owen.[57] She recounted how Eliza Taylor came to their hammock and got in between them: 'In language which no one could misunderstand ... to be indecent with her ... Owen said she [was] unwell. They lay talking until near daylight. They supposed I was asleep.'[58] Fisher relayed that the following night, she and her hammock fellow Owen went to bed together but shortly afterwards:

[Taylor] came into bed to us and went and lay alongside of Owen, they conversed together in a very indecent way ... Owen said to Taylor that she never had been nailed and never would be .... The expression they mean by nailing is indecently using their hands with each other's persons. Taylor and Owen did behave on that night in the way I have above described. Owen made use of her hands on the person of Taylor indecently ... they behaved in this indecent manner for four or five minutes when I got out of bed and called Taylor a nasty beast.[59]

Taylor and Owen pleaded separately with Fisher, not to say anything to anyone. Speaking of Taylor, Fisher told the Inquiry 'she begged me not to say anything to anyone about it'.[60] Owen said that 'she did not mind me talking to her about it but if any of her own sort spoke to her about it she would wallow in her own blood for it'.[61] Both women displayed a sense of shame. When Owen spoke of 'her own sort' it is not clear if she is referring to her country women who would injure her for such transgressions or to the Flash Mob who because of jealousy, might attack her, as 'some of them [were] quite desperate and would not hesitate to use a knife to any one'.[62] It is worthy to note that, as Daniels and Murnane maintain, 'the account of the above is highly significant for both its explicit record of the exchange and its documentation of contemporary colloquial homosexual language'.[63]

A further example of same-sex practices took place in April 1851 in the Ross Female Factory. Agnes Kane was accused of sexually assaulting fellow prisoner Margaret Knaggs. Despite claiming her innocence, sufficient proof was presented and she received 18 months hard labour. Her accusers were Bridget Grady and Margaret Knaggs who maintained that she was persistent in her pursuit of Knaggs. 'Bridget Grady claimed to have seen Margaret Knaggs "in the act of letting down her clothes, she was crying, the Prisoner [Agnes Kane] told her to hold her tongue, when I [Bridget Grady] entered Kane's hand was under Knaggs' clothes having connexion with her."[64] Kane's determined amorous attentions towards Knaggs were displayed on many occasions: 'Kane had asked her … to do something – that Kane would show her – if she would let Kane go to Knaggs' berth at night. Knaggs insisted that she would not let Kane "destroy her" and that Kane had six or seven girls who liked her. "I told her I would not have that sin upon me", Knaggs claimed, to which Kane replied "it was no sin."'[65]

The authorities however, disagreed and punished Kane with solitary confinement for the specific unnatural practice as opposed to their treatment of bullying or persecution. It was also believed that by separating individuals such as Kane, a cure was possible. The presiding judge postulated that this conduct was symptomatic of 'the filthy sexuality so prevalent among the female convicts'.[66] Kane was an 'active, mischievous and debasing character' and for this reason had to be separated from other female prisoners lest she might 'approach [them] only to indoctrinate into the habits and practices of … filthiness'.[67] The judge was concerned that she would spread her 'mischief among many young girls'.[68] It should also be noted that once again in the account of Kane and Knaggs, the evidence was not only given by Knaggs, but also a third-party witness, Bridget Grady.

Undoubtedly, there was no misunderstanding amongst the women as to what nailing meant. Therefore, it can be concluded that there was a parlance amongst the women that was used to refer to sexual acts, including lesbian acts. That certain women were 'known amongst their fellow prisoners by a peculiarly significant soubriquet [nickname]' further indicates that there was a sub-group who had a distinctive identity within the factory. Lesbian acts further challenged efforts to discipline and punish. La Trobe's description of all the lower classes, are indicative of how his Victorian upper-middle class sensibilities created a level of discomfort with the 'Other' who has the ability to disrupt the normalised world. In his immense report he refers to 'a vicious and obnoxious system [and] unhesitatingly assert[s] the demoralising influence

... [adding that] its existence is a stigma upon the Colony.[69] La Trobe was concerned that because 'the public mind has become familiarised to the idea and mention of it, and [was] consequently tainted'.[70] The Probation System seemed to encourage the unmentionable crime rather than stamp it out. From La Trobe's report, the revulsion and discomfort of the colonists with regards to even an awareness of unnatural acts in the general population was a cause for panic. The contaminating influence of convicts, both male and female, was cited by those opposed to transportation, particularly those who had an interest in creating a respectable identity in a new country. It is difficult to separate the damning nature of La Trobe's report with regards to the existence of unnatural crimes and practices, as well as the general awareness of these crimes, from an indelible stain that reflected badly on the entire colony.

A fundamental lack of understanding existed between upper-middle-class values and working-class behaviour. Michael Sturma refers to judgements about female convict morality as, '[a]n almost obsessional interest in "feminine sin," more than a devised policy of social control, influenced perceptions of the women transported'.[71] Due to an 'ignorance of working-class habits ... within the period of transportation there was a strong tendency to place all unchaste women in one category,' hence all female convicts were termed as prostitutes or abandoned.[72] Intemperance and unchastity were the features found most disconcerting in women. On top of this, there was 'a preoccupation with sex which was the concomitant of an emerging cult of respectability' and which internalised conceptions of contamination, filth and cleanliness generated in the early years of the colony. Marriage was conceptualised as cleanser, as a state of wholesomeness and decency, capable of confining and conforming female sexuality.[73] Historians of transportation have, until recently, uncritically adopted contemporary accounts of the dichotomous Victorian asexual middle-class woman, juxtaposed by the depraved convict woman. The implication is not only of class differences in 'sexual behaviour but in sexual appetite – with the effect of making the sexual behaviour of convict women appear more anomalous than it in fact is, so that female sexual desire itself appears to be "deviant"'.[74]

Daniels poses a similar hypothesis to Sturma when she suggests that the roughness of the women 'so shocked upper-class observers, unaccustomed as they were to observing so closely intimate and convivial aspects of lower-class life'.[75] The attitudes of disgust towards unnameable crimes that pervaded colonial society reflected Victorian moral conservatism directly from and within Britain. Colonial middle-class society prided itself on its Britishness and specifically the Englishness of social respectability. Like immorality or prostitution, playing on the words of Sturma's title, 'homosexuality could be in the eye, or the suspicious mind, of the beholder, but there is no doubt it existed'.[76]

The new colonists sought respect from Britain and therefore, that the Victorian ideal of female chastity was perceived as the norm/as dominant/to dominate/within the colony, as opposed to 'the 18th century preoccupation with rampant and voracious female sexuality', was essential and any deviation from these high moralistic overtones spelled disaster for the colony's reputation.[77] It is, perhaps, the shamed identities of convicts as constructed through various Victorian Inquiries into the behaviour of the convicts and specifically the depraved homosexual behaviour, same-sex, or lesbian acts that have contributed in some part at least to a disavowal of Australian convict heritage and history.[78]

It is striking that despite its ostensibly punishing regime many female convicts wilfully returned to the factory. Eliza Churchill gave evidence to this effect. The contention is not that all female convicts who re-entered the gates of the female factory did so because of a woman she had what was termed as an unnatural connexion with, however, some certainly did. Evidence given to the Inquiry FCD suggests that a number of women in the female factories perceived themselves as not conforming to the majority of the other women. They may not have used the word lesbian as it was not part of the vernacular of the time but there was a parlance as evidenced by the use of the word nailing. The evidence would point to a conscious decision to form a sub-cultural group, based on a sexual preference for women. Robinson has stated that remaining open to similarity rather than differences through the ages is more productive in exploring 'the longstanding Western awareness that people often selectively conceal and disclose same-sex love and desire'.[79] When Rayner, Smith and Gilchrist use the term unnatural acts, they are referring to male convict sexuality. Damousi states her case more clearly. For her, lesbian acts were a strategy of defiance and disturbance to undermine power relations within the female factories. Daniels calls it rough culture as opposed to lesbian behaviour but affirms that same-sex relationships between convict women formed the basis of the rough culture and institutional politics of the female factory, causing many problems for the officials in charge of the institutions.[80]

That some convict women intentionally used their lesbian relationships as a form of dissent is patent. That some convict women were in lesbian relationships because they wanted to be regardless of dissident sexual behaviour can be assumed. Whether these same women went on to get married to men after they were granted freedom is irrelevant to this argument. Perhaps paradoxically, the lesbian identities of the convict women who were part of the female factory lesbian sub-culture were not always or necessarily stable or fixed identities that were held in place after factory life. In modern parlance, these women might be termed situational lesbians, that is lesbian while confined in a same-sex segregated environment but who would choose a male partner if that choice was available to them. It might also be argued that the society of Van Diemen's Land at that time was one of compulsory heterosexuality and so perhaps the women who had seemed to enjoy lesbian sub-culture within the factory had no such alternative outside that factory space.[81] These questions can neither be answered nor reconciled and they are beside the point of acknowledging that rough culture of the mid-nineteenth-century Van Diemen's Land female factory was a lesbian sub-culture.

NOTES

1. LINC, Tasmania. 'Guide to the Public Records of Tasmania Section Three: Convict Department: Archives Office of Tasmania.' (Hereafter referred to as AOT.) http://www.linc.tas.gov.au/tasmaniasheritage/popular/convicts/convictdept/appendix-d (accessed 12 February 2012.)

2. Ibid.

3. T. Rayner, 'Historical Survey of the Female Factory Historic Site Cascades Hobart', in *National Parks and Wildlife Service, Tasmania Occasional Paper*, 3 (1981), pp.38–40. Some of these institutions were in use as recently as a century ago as invalid depots or asylums.

4. G. Simes, 'The Language of Homosexuality in Australia', in R. Aldrich & G. Wotherspoon (eds), *Gay Perspectives: Essays in Australian Gay Culture* (Sydney: University of Sydney, 1992), pp.31–58.

5. E. Conlin Casella, '"Doing Trade": A Sexual Economy of Nineteenth-Century Australian Female Convict Prisons', *World Archaeology*, 32, 2 (Autumn 2000), p.215.

6. M. Foucault, *The History of Sexuality: Volume One. An Introduction* (London: Penguin Books, 1978), p.43.

7. D. Robinson, *Closeted Writing and Lesbian and Gay Literature: Classical, Early Modern, Eighteenth-Century* (Burlington: Ashgate, 2006), p.xx.

8. K. O'Donnell, 'Irish Lesbian History: Searching for Sapphists', in B. Lalor (ed.), *Irish Lesbian History Encyclopaedia* (Dublin: Gill and Macmillan, 2003).

9. K. Daniels, *Convict Women* (St Leonard's NSW: Allen & Unwin, 1998), p.71.

10. L. Frost, 'Introduction', in Female Factory Research Group (ed.), *Convict Lives: Women at Cascades Female Factory* (Hobart: Research Tasmania, 2009), p.10. See Daniels, *Convict Women*, p.107.

11. Daniels, *Convict Women*, p.116.

12. Ibid.

13. Rayner, 'Historical Survey', p.25.

14. Head shaving as a punishment began in 1826. When it ended is unclear, it was either 1836 or 1837. Josiah Spode (1790–1858) worked in the Principle Superintendent's

Department between 1829 and 1843 and in his evidence to the CSO 22/50 AOT *Inquiry into Female Convict Discipline* (1841–3), he described the act of head shaving as being abandoned 'about five years since', p.162.

15. Daniels, *Convict Women*, p.116.

16. Foucault, *The History of Sexuality*, p.101.

17. AOT, CSO 22/50, p.332.

18. J. Damousi, *Depraved and Disorderly: Female Convicts, Sexuality and Gender in Colonial Australia* (Cambridge: Cambridge University Press, 1997), p.80.

19. Ibid., p.92.

20. K. Daniels, 'The Flash Mob: Rebellion, Rough Culture and Sexuality in the Female Factories of Van Diemen's Land', *Australian Feminist Studies*, 8, 18 (Summer 1993), p.137.

21. E. Conlin Casella, 'Bulldagers and Gentle Ladies: Archaeological Approaches to Female Homosexuality in Convict-Era Australia', in R.A. Schmidt & B.L. Voss (eds), *Archaeologies of Sexuality* (London: Routledge, 2000), p.144. See also Casella, '"Doing Trade"', p.215.

22. Robert Pearson, AOT, CSO 22/50, p.284.

23. Mary Kirk, AOT, CSO 22/50, p.290.

24. Eliza Churchill, AOT, CSO 22/50, p.292.

25. Ibid., p.293.

26. Haigh, AOT, CSO 22/50, p.315.

27. This is similar among accounts of male prisoners' and 'unnatural' crimes. See also I. Brand, *The Convict Probation System: Van Diemen's Land 1839–1854* (Hobart: Blubber Head Press, 1990), p.149.

28. L. Frost, 'Eliza Churchill Tells…' in L. Frost & H. Maxwell-Stewart (eds), *Chain Letters: Narrating Convict Lives* (Melbourne: Melbourne University Press, 2001), pp.79–80.

29. AOT, CON40/1/7, p.152. See Frost, 'Eliza Churchill Tells…' p.88.

30. A. Gardiner, AOT, CSO 22/50, p.380.

31. AOT, CON40/1/9, image 82.

32. Ellen Scott's substantial record of re-offences can be found in AOT, CON32/1/1, image 333 & CON32/1/4, image 106. Catherine Owens' litany of re-offences is also recorded in AOT, CON32/1/1, image 122, although this page is very badly damaged & CON32/1/4, image 18.

33. Frost, 'Eliza Churchill Tells', p.88. See also Damousi, *Depraved and Disorderly*, pp.69–70.

34. Gardiner, AOT, CSO 22/50, p.382.

35. Ibid., p.384.

36. K. Daniels & M. Murnane, *Uphill All The Way: A Documentary History of Women in Australia*. (St Lucia: University of Queensland Press, 1980), p.20. Other publications by Daniels, Damousi, Casella and T. Rayner, *Female Factory Female Convicts* (Tasmania: Esperance, 2005), p.106, include accounts of the riot citing AOT, CSO 22/50.

37. AOT, CON32/1/4, image 106.

38. AOT, CON41/1/24, image 165.

39. Ibid., image 95.

40. Brand, *The Convict Probation System*, p.63.

41. Ibid.

42. J. Boyce, *Van Diemen's Land* (Melbourne: Black Inc, 2009), p.238.

43. Brand, *The Convict Probation System*, p.156.

44. Ibid., p.157.

45. Damousi, *Depraved and Disorderly*, cites W.J. Irvine to Comptroller-General, pp.70–1.

46. Ibid.

47. Ibid.

48. Ibid.

49. Churchill, AOT, CSO 22/50, p.292.

50. Daniels & Murnane, *Uphill All The Way*, p.74, Pearson, AOT, CSO 22/50, p.281.

51. Frost, 'Eliza Churchill Tells...' pp.86–7.

52. Casella 'Bulldagers and Gentle Ladies', pp.149, 153.

53. Ibid., p.154.

54. Ibid., p.157.

55. In Daniels' and Murnane's account the second name is not printed, for example Ann F----- was entered for Ann Fisher. In 1997 and 2000, accounts of the same incident are given by Damousi and Casella respectively, providing both first and second names. This is indicative of recent changing attitudes to the shame produced by the 'convict stain' and homosexual acts.

56. Josiah Spode, AOT, CSO 22/50. pp.377–8. Original text underlined.

57. A ward's woman was given the responsibility of ensuring that the rules were followed on her ward/area. She too was a prisoner. She may have been in the female factory for a particular amount of time, or perhaps because she was favoured by the factory authorities.

58. Fisher, AOT, CSO 22/50, p.423. See also Casella, '"Doing Trade"', p.216 and Damousi, *Depraved and Disorderly,* p.70.

59. Fisher, AOT, CSO 22/50, p.424. Daniels & Murnane, *Uphill All The Way*, p.23.

60. Fisher, AOT, CSO 22/50, p.425.

61. Ibid.

62. Churchill, AOT, CSO 22/50, p.284.

63. Daniels & Murnane, *Uphill All The Way*, p.217.

64. Damousi, *Depraved and Disorderly*, citing 'Transcript of Evidence before R.P. Stuart and Benjamin Horne, 10 April 1851', p.49.

65. Ibid.

66. Ibid, citing Stuart to Comptroller-General, 14 April 1851, in Transcript of Evidence, Tasmanian Papers, p.70.

67. Ibid.

68. Ibid, citing Stuart to Comptroller-General, 14 April 1851, in Transcript of Evidence, Tasmanian Papers, p.70.

69. Brand, *The Convict Probation System*, pp.159–60.

70. Ibid.

71. M. Sturma, 'Eye of the Beholder: The Stereotype of Women Convicts, 1788–1852', *Labour History*, 34 (May 1978), p.4.

72. Ibid.

73. Ibid.

74. Daniels, *Convict Women*, p.163.

75. Daniels, 'The Flash Mob', p.137.

76. B. Smith, *Australia's Birthstain: The Startling Legacy of the Convict Era* (Crow's Nest, NSW: Allen & Unwin, 2008), p.241.

77. Daniels, *Convict Women*, p.157.

78. Smith also suggests a link between this and the relatively late decriminalisation of homosexuality in Tasmania which was not enacted until 1997; perhaps convict history had defined the area for many years.

79. Robinson, *Closeted Writing*, p.9.

80. Daniels, *Convict Women*, p.165.

81. A. Rich, 'Compulsory Heterosexuality and Lesbian Existence', in A. Rich, *Blood, Bread and Poetry: Selected Prose, 1979–1985* (London: Virago, 1987).

2

ELITE COURTSHIP: THE CASE OF MABEL SMYLY AND DERMOD O'BRIEN, 1901–2

Maeve O'Riordan

Marriage was an essential feature of upper-class life in Ireland in the twentieth century; it ensured the safe passage of property from father to legitimate son, and tied socially and politically compatible families together, at a time when land and property were still reliable indicators of social position. It was common for intermarriages to occur between the children of the landed gentry, and the sons and daughters of the professional classes.[1] These predominately Anglican elite members of society valued their shared sense of identity, status and ideals, and were unwilling to contract marriage partnerships with those whom they considered to be of a lower social background, or indeed, with those of a different religion.[2] Despite such strong social and economic incentives to marry within a circumscribed sphere of eligible singletons, within this small pool, marriage partnerships could be based on attraction and love.[3]

When the heir to a country estate, Dermod O'Brien[4], proposed to a society doctor's daughter, Mabel Smyly[5], in 1901, he received universal praise from his friends and family. The benefits of gaining a wife were seen to be so strong, that his best friend wrote: 'I am very glad, I was beginning to fear that you would not marry at all ... I think I should have been glad, whoever you were marrying.'[6] His father echoed this view, and was 'heartily glad' that Dermod was forsaking the life of 'old bachelordom', believing that it was 'no small point' to the success of the marriage that he was 'to marry into so very nice a family'.[7] Dermod's step-mother, who went 'off her head' with joy at the news, believed that a wife, and 'this wife' in particular, would provide him with 'not only the happiness ... but the added power, confidence in yourself, freedom of will and action ... for your aims will be hers, she will stand between you & hindrances and make you have your own life more abundantly.'[8] Still, Dermod's father also stressed the importance of love and attraction, and was 'delighted' to see that 'in spite of all the women you have met & (if I may say so) flirted with you are just as much in love as if you were 21'.[9] He reassured his son that there was little 'danger that the flame will burn itself out'.[10]

The perceived benefits of marriage for Dermod's fiancée, Mabel, were even stronger. She would enter a state of more complete existence. As an unmarried woman she could never achieve full adulthood. Greater respect was shown to married women within families, even when they were younger than their single relatives.[11] Unmarried women were to remain biddable girls, no matter their age. Mabel could still be 'sent' to bed, and her activities and acquaintances were vetted by her family. At the age of twenty-six, she might still be reprimanded for not observing the Sabbath in a suitably sombre way.[12] She consistently wrote, and most likely believed, that she was becoming more of a complete personality by marrying, and especially by marrying a man she loved:

> Somehow I feel as of then [marriage] I shall be more of an identity, more myself from being part of you ... I have all my life submitted more or less, rather more than less, to other people's stronger wills and views, partly from a sense of duty, partly from policy, partly because it seemed too much trouble to resist, and partly I think because I find it very difficult to put my feelings into words. With you I think it will be different because I feel you don't only want to make me a shadow of yourself but to bring out what is in me, good or bad, and make the best of it. My tendency is towards repression and shrinking into a shell, but I always feel as if you were drawing me out and making me expand. I wonder what you will make of me in the end: but I have a great trust in you.[13]

This courtship was not the stereotypical match between a young debutante and her dashing young gallant. Dermod O'Brien was thirty-six before he proposed to Mabel, who was thirty-two. This was not out of the ordinary. It was common for elite women at the turn of the century to delay marriage for a number of years after declaring one's marriagability by coming out in society, and men were frequently in their thirties before their first marriage.[14] The couple were suited socially, politically and economically; neither was perceived to have much money, but both were of respectable families.[15] Their family backgrounds were not identical, and the two moved in slightly different social circles. The O'Briens, as landholding magnates were in decline, but they maintained a comfortable nomadic existence between Ireland, London and continental Europe, moving in artistic and creative circles. Dermod had been given considerable freedom as a young man, and developed the ambition to become an artist. Despite showing little early talent, he persuaded his father to support him through the relevant training in various European cities.[16] His decision to set up his studio in the smaller city of Dublin in 1901, and away from the heavier competition of London, may have been influenced by an awareness of his own artistic shortcomings.[17] This move to Dublin coincided with the escalation of his relationship with Mabel.

Mabel, aside from a couple of months in Rome, had lived her unmarried life in Dublin's Merrion Square with her parents and siblings. The Smylys were deeply concerned with philanthropic activities.[18] Mabel helped run schools, gave classes, and sat on committees. Both Mabel and Dermod were very religious, but she wore her Protestantism more outwardly, while he was more critical. Dermod was completely tolerant of Roman Catholicism, while she defended proselytising.[19] They shared a great love of music, though Dermod's more liberal upbringing meant that he had a wider knowledge of classical music. He lamented to his step-mother that Mabel had an 'upbringing among Hymns & the lowest church people', but insisted that she had 'any amount of the right stuff in her'.[20]

It may well be that Dermod approved of Mabel's sheltered and controlled life among hymns, as it categorized her as a conventional moral woman. This granted him greater power within the relationship as the more cultured and experienced partner, who could act as the moderator of her tastes once they were married. His ideal woman would remain quietly in the female domestic sphere, and his idolisation of her slight physical form and gentle manners was influenced by the still popular 'angel in the house' motif. He did not want a wife who would overtly defy social conventions. He was physically attracted to her small and neat frame, and compared her favourably to his clumsy aunt (the humanitarian campaigner Charlotte Grace O'Brien) for her ability to 'softly & silently vanish from a room'.[21] He consistently reprimanded her, sometimes severely, for taking on so much philanthropic activity, and presented her as a weak and sickly person in his letters. He constantly commented on her health, and feared that she might fall ill from the most innocuous activity. When she did get a cold, he could not but find her new weakness a further attraction, and liked to visualise her as an otherworldly figure:

> It is most terribly becoming all the same: terrible because it makes you look like some pure ethereal spirit; I stretch out my hands to feel if there is any substance ... the bracelet comes warm off your arm & even so I am only half convinced.[22]

Practical and organised Mabel did not always like to be idolised in this way, and wrote: 'Don't put me on a pedestal, the doormat position is much more in my line'.[23] Contemporary views on male domination and female submission were so ingrained in society, that she often reverted to a desire to be dominated and physically overpowered. She thought it was 'wonderful' to think of herself as 'little and weak', and Dermod as 'big and strong', with the ability to 'crumple [her] up into nothing' if he chose.[24] On the 10 January 1902, she wrote: 'I like to feel that you are my master and that there won't be any question about who is to command'.[25]

A certain amount of this submissive and dominant language did not reflect the reality of their relationship. In a long letter, written shortly after their engagement, Mabel essentially told Dermod that he could never induce her to do what she did not want to do:

> It is hard to argue about what cannot be. If you wanted me to do what I thought was wrong you would come upon the Puritan rock in me which cannot move, but as I know you never would and my trust in you is absolute, I cannot see how the question would arise.[26]

The physical domination did not always run in the same direction either, and Dermod liked to visualise Mabel in different guises as 'Dainty beguiler, Torment of [his] life, Heart's easer & smoother of cares; ... fond wife, foolish woman, little mother, All ... in the kiss of one girl.'[27]

Sometimes she acted the baby, sometimes the submissive maid, but occasionally the indulgent mother. She liked him to lie with his head on her lap while she rocked him to sleep, pretending he was the child 'little D'.[28] He readily submitted to this treatment and told her secrets of his childhood.[29]

Dermod and Mabel's relationship began properly when Mabel was a guest of Dermod's elder sister, Nelly, at a house party at his family seat of Cahirmoyle, Co. Limerick.[30] The party facilitated romance, as the guests consisted of married and unmarried members of their own generation. Chaperonage was light. The couple were able to spend time alone together, and enjoyed talking while leaning together against a secluded gate.[31] When the party broke up, Dermod went to London, and Mabel returned to her family home. It was then that the courtship of letters began. The correspondence surrounding Dermod O'Brien's proposal and engagement to Mabel Smyly survives almost completely intact. He proposed on 3 December 1901 and they married just over three months later on the 8 March 1902. Rarely did he allow a day to pass without writing a letter, or two. By the eve of their wedding day, he had written 165 surviving letters, totalling 600 pages. Mabel was less prolific, and only managed eighty-seven letters, totalling 300 pages, between 1 October, and her wedding day less than six months later. These 900 pages of correspondence can be divided into three stages. The first, and shortest, took place between September and October when Dermod was in London, and still addressed Mabel as 'Miss Smyly'. In mid-October, he dropped the 'Miss Smyly', and his letters became more flirtatious, while she continued to uphold polite social conventions. The last, and longest, phase began on 2 December 1901 when his proposal was accepted, and both parties perceived themselves to be married in spirit.[32] From this time, the letters became more explicit, longer, and more frequent, on both sides. Throughout this written relationship, there is a sense that the couple perceived themselves a modern couple, enjoying a passionate love that was not experienced by everyone. Their letters reveal that they believed that they were stretching, rather than breaking with, existing sexual practices and gender roles.

Before their engagement, physical contact was minimal. On visits to Mabel's family home, Dermod was tantalised by the proximity of her body but limited himself to touching the lace of her sleeve 'when no one was looking', holding her bracelets while she played the piano, presenting her with flowers to wear in her lace blouse, turning the pages of music while she played the piano in order to look at her neck, and holding her arm briefly when he was permitted to lead her into supper.[33] Mabel did not express whether she felt a similar sense of frustration, and wrote of her surprise at the depth of her own sexual arousal during the engagement period. She subscribed, or at least felt it more proper to appear to subscribe, to the contemporary notion that respectable women were incapable of the same levels of sexual desire and fulfilment as men. Expert opinion believed that men were supposed to crave sex, while good respectable women submitted to their husband's desires within marriage, without any real pleasure for themselves.[34]

This relationship, however, demonstrates that there were many differences between the image of the arranged and cold courtships of the elite classes, and the reality of lived experiences. Members of the social elite believed firmly in romantic love for their own class by the turn of the twentieth century. Elite couples were expected to marry a socially acceptable partner for love. Judith Schneid Lewis has argued that the degree of emotional attachment required for a successful elite marriage altered during the mid-nineteenth century, and by 1860, it was necessary to be 'perfectly in love' with one's partner.[35] It is probable that many, if not most, elite courtships were conducted with considerable freedom while the couple were in the sheltered privacy of the woman's family home. *Manners and Rules*, an extremely successful etiquette manual, condemned the 'strict ideas' held by some parents who would allow their daughters no private time with their beaux.[36] Elite engagements should be short, but the couple should enjoy relative freedom. When Dermod's parents were courting in 1863, they would sit alone together in the woods while the chaperone went for a walk.[37] M. Jeanne Peterson has convincingly argued that broken engagements were so shocking to the elite during the Victorian period because extensive sexual experimentation during this time was the norm.[38] Her account of the experiences of a middle-class couple in England, Charles and Fanny Kingsley, who were engaged during the 1840s, demonstrates that Mabel and Dermod's explorations of each other's bodies were in no way unique.[39] Peter Gay has also come to this conclusion through his analysis of the diary of the American bourgeois Mabel Loomis Todd, who went to her marriage only 'technically a virgin'.[40]

Mabel and Dermod were permitted to spend increasing amounts of time together as their relationship progressed. Dermod had feared that 'conventions' (like those damned by *Manners and Rules*) which would prevent them from seeing each other privately, might be imposed by her conservative family, but his fears were unfounded. They spent many hours with Mabel sitting on his lap, kissing and caressing each other. At first, he was surprised at how far Mabel would allow him to go, and was nervous to put his arm around her when they first shared a chair.[41] Mabel found that she hungered for physical contact, and enjoyed seeing him get into 'heat'. She liked to hug and kiss Dermod while he wrapped them both in his coat, or to 'ram [her] chin into [his] neck', and to see 'illuminations' light up in his eyes. Dermod often disturbed her hair pins in his fervour, and occasionally partially opened her dress to kiss her throat.[42] On one walk home, Dermod was forced to go to his club 'to cool down' after the state she had brought him into. He wrote enigmatically: 'you have me fair bewildered with your arts called in from improper French novels. To think of your doing such a thing & I who looked on you as an innocent guileless creature'.[43] This behaviour was implicitly permitted by Mabel's conservative family who left the couple alone together, which suggests that it was perceived as normal for even the most respectable engaged couples to engage in sexualised behaviour in the privacy of their own homes. Private sexualised activity was permitted by outward shows of severe respectability.[44]

Still it is unlikely that they ever explored deep underneath each other's clothes, and they both appeared to be in agreement that the step of marriage, from virginal state to married state, 'should be a big step, that it is not quite right to make the transition gradual'.[45] Mabel Smyly was technically, and completely, a virgin when she married. This was assumed, and desired, by her fiancé. He repeatedly addressed her as a 'maid' and expected that if he died before the wedding, she would be a 'virgin widow'.[46] It was deemed correct that women would only ever be sexually active with one man.[47]

Their attitudes towards their previous relationships reflected normal sexual practices and expectations among unmarried members of elite society. Men and women had very different opportunities. Mabel's most significant previous relationship had been a one-sided longing where she 'did truly care for some one [sic] else for a long time ... There was never any explanation or point to the whole affair but [she] went through a very bleak time.'[48] Despite the apparently trivial nature of this relationship, Mabel felt compelled to confess it to Dermod as she felt 'rather ashamed'. However, Dermod, who would never need to protect his reputation in the same way as an unmarried woman, believed that 'to care for a person or love them is a fine thing', and magnanimously wrote: 'I see no difference in that between a man & a woman ... all of us make mistakes, but ... it is better to do so than never risk anything.'[49] Dermod, had made more considerable mistakes in his past loves, and told his fiancée about 'Stella' who he had had some form of relationship with in the past.[50] He felt no shame in his past experiences and once blithely remarked that he had been in love with another woman, before she married his friend, for whom he was best man.[51] He even revealed an early infatuation with his step-mother, whom his father had married when Dermod was fifteen, and likened the first time he saw his fiancée's bedroom to a time when

> Aunt Julie [step-mother] first came to us & we three [he and his sisters] used to visit them in the morning while they were in bed, Nelly or Mary told me to feel how smooth & soft Aunty's skin was on her chest & how shy I felt about putting the tip of a tentative finger as if I might get burnt. That was the self-consciousness of a boy.[52]

Dermod even wrote that, though he did not want anyone else, he 'might feel tempted by a strange shoulder or nape in a kind of speculative way'. He took a light-hearted view of such 'casual kisses' which 'are mostly impersonal and mean only a conjunction of opportunity & desire'.[53] Such a casual approach to relations with the opposite sex certainly implies that he had, at some time, enjoyed relatively free relationships with women.

With such differing expectations of male and female sexual desires, the role of moral watchdog fell heavily on the female partner. Mabel was very careful to protect her reputation, especially in the days before their official engagement. She was cautious not to write him more letters than propriety might allow, and passed on invitations from her mother, rather than offering them herself. In the month before their engagement, Dermod consistently tried to spend time alone with her, away from her house, at art galleries, shopping, concerts, or at his home. Mabel would not countenance such plans. When he attempted to arrange a trip to town to buy tools for one of her classes for ragged children, she firmly reprimanded him: 'Dear Mr O' Brien, We are strong on propriety in Our Village and I neither could nor did invite you to come and buy tools for the Carving Class in company.'[54]

To be seen walking alone with him would be a public statement that they were engaged,[55] and was as strong a declaration of intent as anything that might occur within her home. Mabel, and her family, were already stretching propriety by accepting Dermod's almost daily correspondence for two months before he proposed. These letters caused her mother to go into 'a state of fizzle', and were only permitted because Mabel had 'attained to years of discretion'.[56]

As Mabel's movements were so tightly curtailed by her family, and by her own qualms, letters were an essential aspect of their relationship: the letter travelled where the author could not, and allowed for many fantastical sexual encounters to occur. Dermod wrote most of his letters late at night when he imagined Mabel was asleep. Before they were engaged, he repeatedly enquired into the location of her bedroom. When she was sick, he used the medium of the letter to picture her 'sitting up in bed'.[57] By 6 January he had grown braver, and wrote that he had 'no sense of decorum' and imagined himself invading her little room to look at her and kiss her while she slept.[58] Two weeks later he allowed himself to imagine that she was awake:

> I find you thinking of me & welcoming me with your eyes & I kneel by your bed & put my arms about you despite all conventionalities & draw your small night clad person 'sweet as boughs of May' close up against me; oh I make you blush too, for I insist on undoing a top button that I may kiss your throat & play at drawing the cough out of it.[59]

While he luxuriated in these images, he had no intention of performing such activities in reality, for he believed that a 'girl's room at all times is a sacred temple'. When he finally stepped inside her bedroom he became shy 'to see the place where you have spent so many hours of your life ... dressing & undressing'.[60]

While Mabel initially deflected his enquiries as to the location of her bedroom, after the engagement she was happy to imagine that he had 'crept up quite quietly last night and kissed the cough out of [her] throat'.[61] Like Dermod, she preferred to keep such night-time encounters in her imagination, as she 'should not have thought it correct' for him to visit her in her room.

After some initial qualms on her (and especially her mother's) part, Mabel took on Dermod's view that there would be nothing improper in her visiting his sick room, as a man's room was 'just a room'. She was permitted to visit – provided his sister acted as chaperone.[62]

Letters also facilitated the couple in saying things that they were too embarrassed to say aloud. In one of his early letters from London, Dermod first introduced the topic of sexualised behaviour by describing a couple he had seen at the theatre who were 'holding each other's hands and rub[bing] their shoulders together like two cats'.[63] He would not get the opportunity to discuss such subjects in person for some time, as he was confined to general group conversations on his early visits to her home.[64] He once wrote to her while she sat 'close pressed' against him, and used it to tell her that he was 'longing all the time to fling down the pen & just enfold [her] body & soul'.[65] As the wedding day drew nearer, and marriage settlements were drawn up,[66] both Mabel and Dermod's thoughts, and letters, turned increasingly towards the subject of sex. Marriage, sex, and conception were intrinsically bound up in both of their minds, as they were in Irish society generally at the time. Despite her attraction to Dermod, Mabel occasionally felt a sense of panic at her impending marriage.[67] When she thought of their longed-for future 'shadow children', she admitted that with the 'mystery and happiness', she felt 'a little thread of fear' at how they might be produced.[68] She found it difficult to discuss their future children face-to-face in Dermod's house, where such children would likely be conceived, and preferred to put her thoughts in writing while sitting in her girlhood home.[69]

Such ignorance and fear of sex was not unique among middle- and upper-class women of the era. Margaret Cousins (née Gillespie), the middle-class suffragist, was married in 1903 to James Cousins. The marriage did not promise the same sexual attraction as that of the O'Briens, but ignorance also contributed to the utter repugnance Margaret felt on her wedding night. Their memoir demonstrated just how uneducated a woman might be on consummating her marriage:

> My new knowledge, though I was lovingly safe-guarded from it, made me ashamed of humanity and ashamed for it. I found myself looking on men and women as degraded by this demand of nature. Something in me revolted then, and has ever since protested against, certain of the techniques of nature connected with sex.[70]

Margaret and her husband would make no attempt to produce children 'until the evolution of form has substituted some more artistic way of continuance of the race'. Luckily for Mabel, she was attracted to her husband, and preliminary sexual activity suggested that her marital experience would not be so shocking.

Dermod was not fearful for himself when he thought of sex, but he was very conscious that his fiancée felt '[a] little more shyness about looking into the future & its possibilities'.[71] He assumed that she, as a woman, would have a lower sexual appetite, and knowledge. In the month preceding the wedding, he tried to calm her nervousness, and to prepare her for 'what it may be like to be married in very fact ... to walk & sleep & live' beside each other.[72] He hoped she would not be shocked when he argued that sex was natural, and that love was not 'entirely made up of that fine essence of the unity of soul with soul, but it is indefinably mixed up with desire of one body for the other, only the finer elements make it permissible'.[73] He looked forward to going to bed with her kisses on his lips and 'the pulse of [her] being trilling [him] through body & soul'.[74]

Dermod leaned on Mabel's strong religiosity, rather than lust, to present sex within marriage as an elevated, and essential, religious duty. He prayed that they 'may have courage to dare & strength to perform such acts as [they] may be impelled to by His Holy Spirit'.[75] It is quite likely that Dermod and Mabel, with their strong faith, believed that sex, within marriage for the purpose of conceiving children, was an act of God. M. Jeanne Peterson, who noted the same tendency in the middle-class clerical couple in her study, argued that such a linkage 'was the natural outcome of their deep religiosity'.[76] Dermod accepted that however pleasurable sex might be, it would ultimately cause Mabel the pain of childbirth, but reverted to gender stereotypes to reassure himself that she would feel it worth the suffering:

> I would that you might be spared the Pains [*sic*] & the anxiety of maternity did I not know that every woman would joyfully undertake them for the subsequent blessings. It seems most unfair that you the woman should have all the trouble & care while the man goes about his daily business. It is not a thing that I the man can face in a light spirit.[77]

Mabel Smyly and Dermod O'Brien got to know each other's personalities, and bodies, better during the engagement period. Both freely admitted that they knew much more about each other even a month after they had agreed to

46

marry. Still, they were happy to make a commitment with some knowledge of the others' suitable personality and family background. Letters allowed them to explore each others' views. It was through letters that Dermod tried to mould Mabel's opinions, and take her away from her 'low church' past by discussing Darwin and the theatre; and it was through letters that Mabel defended her philanthropic and proselytising activities. Dermod used his letters to describe his opinions on how women should behave, and Mabel took great care to demonstrate her beliefs on the perfect marriage, where a wife was not an ornament, but a full partner.[78] Like, Dermod's step-mother, Mabel believed that a wife could contribute positively to the success of her husband's career by being his confidant and helper. In this regard, as with their sexualised activity, Mabel felt that they were moving the relationship between the sexes forward, in a non-reactionary way. As the wedding day drew nearer, Mabel reflected on the social conventions which restricted her activity more than Dermod's, without any sense of injustice:

> Of course times change but I suppose it is the individual actions of people like ourselves that make them change. I am very glad that our lot is cast in a generation where it matters more to be true and honest than to be orthodox and conventional. Not that I want to break away from either orthodoxy or conventions but to use them instead of bowing down to them.[79]

These letters demonstrate that despite the sexual double standard prevalent at the time, individual couples were able to conduct themselves in a manner which approached equality. The parameters of sexual gender roles were fluid, and dependent on space. Dermod was surprised and delighted that his outwardly puritan fiancée was capable of the arts found in improper French novels, and he was determined to provide her with a positive sexual experience. Mabel was careful to keep a certain distance from Dermod before he proposed, but then trusted him enough to display the depth of her sexual desire. There was an accepted contradiction between their respect for propriety, and their private activities and words. Despite the fears Mabel expressed at the unknown mysteries of married life, and for all the lip service she paid to the ideal of the submissive wife, she viewed this marriage as an opportunity, and it was. She would have more independence and freedom of expression and action by marrying. She would gain a sense of partnership, households to manage, as well as sexual fulfilment. Both Mabel and Dermod appear to have been happy with this socially and personally compatible match. They married on 8 March 1902 and conceived a son almost immediately. During their first separation of married life, when he took a business trip, Dermod addressed Mabel as the 'Best of Wives', while she missed tousling his hair.[80] It would appear that despite some nerves, the narrow opportunities for unmarried women meant that Mabel gained personal and sexual fulfilment by her decision to become 'a little bit of [his] empire,' rather than to remain 'a small independent province of [her] own'.[81]

NOTES

1. M. O'Riordan, 'Home, family and society, women of the Irish landed class, 1860–1914: a Munster case-study', unpublished PhD thesis, University College Cork, 2014, Table 5: 'Daughters' destination on marriage by husbands' occupation, 1858–1914', and Table 6: 'Munster landlord's wives origin on marriage by fathers' occupation, 1858–1914', pp.144–5.

2. Ibid., p.145.

3. Ibid., p.152.

4. His family were a junior branch of the Inchiquin baronetcy of Dromoland, with an estate at Cahermoyle, Co. Limerick. The family estate was sold in 1919, as it was no longer economically viable.

5. Mabel was the daughter of a leading physician, Sir Philip Crampton Smyly, and the niece of William, 4th Baron Plunket, Anglican Archbishop of Dublin. See Sir Philip Crampton Smyly, M.D., DUH, Obituary Notices, *Journal of Larynology, Rhinology and Otology*, Vol. XIX, No. 6, June 1904, pp.286–7.

6. Arthur Cane to Dermod O'Brien, 4 December 2014, NLI MS 36,797 (3).

7. Edward O'Brien to Dermod O'Brien, 7 December 1901, NLI MS 36,773 (7).

8. Julia O'Brien to Dermod O'Brien, 7 December 1901, NLI MS 36,777 (2), emphasis original.

9. Edward O'Brien to Dermod O'Brien, 7 December 1901, NLI MS 36,773 (7).

10. Ibid., 15 December 1901.

11. Anon., *Manners and Rules of Good Society: Or Solecisms to be Avoided*, 33rd edn ([1911], London, 2004). See also J. Gerard, *Country House Life: Family and Servants, 1815–1914* (Oxford: Blackwell, 1994), p.32.

12. Ellen Smyly to Mabel Smyly, 5 December 1896, NLI MS 36,784.

13. Mabel Smyly to Dermod O'Brien, 22 December 1901, NLI MS 36 699 (1).

14. O'Riordan, 'Home, family and society', p.268, and Gerard, *Country House Life*, p.24.

15. Edward O'Brien to Dermod O'Brien, 22 December 1901, NLI MS 36 773 (7).

16. L. Robinson, *Palette and Plough: A Pen-and-Ink Drawing of Dermod O'Brien* (Dublin: Brown and Nolan, 1948), p.54.

17. Ibid., p.71.

18. O. Walsh, *Anglican Women in Dublin: Philanthropy and Education in the Early Twentieth Century* (Dublin: UCD Press, 2005), p.53.

19. Dermod O'Brien to Mabel Smyly, 16 November 1901, NLI MS 36 694 (2).

20. Dermod O'Brien to Julia O'Brien, 14 October 1901, NLI MS 36, 778 (10).

21. Dermod O'Brien to Mabel Smyly, 2 November 1901, NLI MS 36 694 (2).

22. Ibid., 11 December 1901, NLI MS 36 694 (4).

23. Mabel Smyly to Dermod O'Brien, 5 November 1901, NLI MS 36 699 (1).

24. Ibid., 14 December 1901, for example.

25. Ibid., Mabel Smyly to Dermod O'Brien, 10 January 1901, NLI MS 36 699 (2).

26. Ibid., 16 December 1901.

27. Dermod O'Brien to Mabel Smyly, 28 January 1902, NLI MS 36 694 (7).

28. Mabel Smyly to Dermod O'Brien, 2 January 1902, NLI MS 36 699 (2).

29. Dermod O'Brien to Mabel Smyly, 2 November 1901, NLI MS 36 694 (2), and Mabel Smyly to Dermod O'Brien, 10 December 1901.

30. Dermod O'Brien to Mabel Smyly, n.d., NLI MS 36 694 (2).

31. Mabel Smyly to Dermod O'Brien, 16 January 1902, NLI MS 36 699 (2).

32. Dermod O'Brien to Mabel Smyly, NLI MS 36 694 (4-8), and Mabel Smyly to Dermod O'Brien, NLI MS 36 699 (2-3).

33. Ibid., 9 December 1901, NLI MS 36 694 (4).

34. C. Quinlan, *Genteel Revolutionaries: Anna and Thomas Haslam and the Irish Women's Movement* (Cork: Cork University Press, 2002), pp.76-7, 79-80.

35. J. Schneid Lewis, *In the Family Way: Childbearing in the British Aristocracy, 1760-1860* (New Brunswick, N.J., 1986), pp.31, 30, 36.

36. Anon., *Manners and Rules* p.250.

37. O'Riordan, 'Home, Family and Society', p.157.

38. M.J. Peterson, *Family, Love and Work in the Lives of Victorian Gentlewomen* (Indiana: Indiana University Press, 1989), pp.75-7.

39. Ibid.

40. P. Gay, *The Bourgeois Experience: Victoria to Freud* (Oxford: OUP, 1984), pp.80–1.

41. Dermod O'Brien to Mabel Smyly, 8 January 1902, NLI MS 36 694 (6).

42. Ibid., 30 January 1902, NLI MS 36 694 (7), Mabel Smyly to Dermod O'Brien, 10 January 1902, NLI MS 36 699 (2).

43. Ibid., 6 February 1901, NLI MS 36 694 (8).

44. *Manners and Rules* advised newly engaged couples to spend little time in public together, and not to dance together.

45. Dermod O'Brien to Mabel Smyly, 27 February 1901, NLI MS 36 694 (8).

46. Ibid., 27 January 1901, NLI MS 36 694 (7).

47. For discussion on this in the wider community, see M. Luddy, *Matters of Deceit: Breach of Promise to Marry Cases in Nineteenth and Twentieth-Century Limerick* (Dublin, 2011), p.35.

48. Mabel Smyly to Dermod O'Brien, 5 December 1901, NLI MS 36 699 (2).

49. Dermod O'Brien to Mabel Smyly, 5 December 1901, NLI MS 36 694 (4).

50. Mabel Smyly to Dermod O'Brien, 5 December 1901; see also Robinson, *Palette & Plough*, p.84. The Stella referred to is Stella Duckworth, half-sister of Virginia Woolf.

51. Dermod O'Brien to Mabel Smyly, 19 February 1901, NLI MS 36 694 (7).

52. Ibid., 18 February 1901.

53. Dermod O'Brien to Mabel Smyly, 26 January, NLI MS 36 694 (6).

54. Mabel Smyly to Dermod O'Brien, 5 November 1901, NLI MS 36 699 (1).

55. Luddy, *Matters of Deceit*, p.25.

56. Dermod O'Brien to Mabel Smyly, 25 January 1902, NLI MS 36 694 (7), and Ibid., 25 January 1902, NLI MS 36 699 (2).

57. Dermod O'Brien to Mabel Smyly, 13 November 1901, NLI MS 36 694 (2).

58. Ibid., 6 January 1902, NLI MS 36 694 (6).

59. Ibid., 20 January 1902, second letter.

60. Ibid., 25 January 1902, second letter.

61. Mabel Smyly to Dermod O'Brien, 1 January 1902, NLI MS 36 699 (2).

62. Ibid., 25 January 1902.

63. Dermod O'Brien to Mabel Smyly, 7 October 1901, NLI MS 36 694 (1).

64. Ibid., 22 October 1901, NLI MS 36 694 (1).

65. Ibid., 11 December 1901, NLI MS 36 694 (4).

66. Marriage settlements were legal documents drawn up in advance of elite marriages which arranged for the control of the couple's property and inheritance. Settlements prepared contingencies for the numbers of children born.

67. Mabel Smyly to Dermod O'Brien, 24 December 1901, NLI MS 36 699 (1).

68. Ibid.

69. Ibid., 26 February1902, NLI MS 36 699 (3).

70. J. Cousins and M. Cousins, *We Two Together* (Madras: Ganesh 1950), p.108.

71. Ibid., 27 February 1902, NLI MS 36 694 (8).

72. Dermod O'Brien to Mabel Smyly, 20 January 1902 (second letter), NLI MS 36 694 (7).

73. Ibid., 4 February 1902.

74. Ibid., 3 February 1902.

75. Ibid., 16 February 1902.

76. Peterson, *Family, Love and Work*, p.76.

77. Dermod O'Brien to Mabel Smyly, 16 February 1902, NLI MS 36 694 (8).

78. Mabel Smyly to Dermod O'Brien, 1 January 1902, NLI MS 36 699 (2).

79. Ibid.

80. Dermod O'Brien to Mabel Smyly, 28 October 1902, NLI MS 36 694 (9), and Mabel Smyly to Dermod O'Brien, 14 September 1902, NLI MS 36 699 (3).

81. Mabel O'Brien to Dermod O'Brien, 16 December 1901, NLI/MS/36,699/1.

3

'LOOSE AND IMMORAL LIVES': PROSTITUTION AND THE FEMALE CRIMINAL INEBRIATE IN IRELAND, 1900–18

Conor Reidy

During the second half of the nineteenth century there was a new focus on the drunkard, as an abandoned psychiatric patient rather than as an individual marked largely for their boisterous and disruptive nature.[1] Two parallel movements sought to resolve the problem of alcohol and its social effects during the century. Temperance associations required full abstinence from drink, while the reformatory movement prescribed an institutional solution based on forms of medical and psychological intervention. One remedy that emerged by the final years of that century was the state inebriate reformatory. This was a reincarnation of previous institutional concepts, the difference being that this one would combine detention as a form of treatment and punishment. Treatment was intended for habitual addiction to alcohol and punishment was for any one of a long list of drink-related criminal offences. Citing studies on the inebriate reformatory system in Scotland, Warsh describes how it 'became an institution for women convicted of prostitution and child cruelty'.[2] There is considerable merit to this statement. This chapter will examine case histories of women registered as prostitutes on entry to the State Inebriate Reformatory for Ireland, located in Ennis, county Clare. While it will show that there was only limited disquiet about the sexual behaviour of these women, there was a greater concern with the threat they posed to their children, their immediate community and to society as a whole. The courts and agencies of intervention showed little sympathy for the women or for the circumstances that led them to their 'immoral lifestyle'.

The State Inebriate Reformatory for Ireland was unique among institutions operated by the General Prisons Board (GPB) for several reasons. It was the first that was overtly mandated to 'reform' as well as punish its inmates. Secondly, it was the only institution during the board's fifty-one-year tenure for which comprehensive before and after 'histories' of inmates were collated. This allowed reformatory administrators and, by extension, historians, to understand the lives of these troubled individuals in ways that were not otherwise possible. This understanding is heightened by newspaper court reports which exposed their flaws of character and behaviour, thereby fuelling a public loathing and greater than ever isolation of the inebriate. Using these sources the chapter will examine a number of case studies to reveal a dual challenge of treating and reforming a class of women whose allegedly broken morals could not be repaired.

The inebriate reformatory system should not be confused with the temperance movement that also gained momentum during the nineteenth century. The reformatory system emerged from a movement to create new legislation and practical provisions that would address the problem of habitual drunkards. Radzinowicz and Hood point out that supporters of such steps did not necessarily favour outright prohibition.[3] From the early nineteenth-century, however, alcohol was recognised as an enormous societal challenge with unquestioned links between drink, poverty and escalating crime. Barton underlines a view, held by many in the so-called 'respectable classes', that women were particularly susceptible to the debasing influences of alcohol.[4]

Following decades of legal and scientific discussion that saw the establishment of committees, homes for drunkards and increasing attempts at medical understandings of their problems, the first major legislative breakthrough came in Britain in 1879 with the passing of an *Act to facilitate and control the cure of Habitual Drunkards*. This defined an habitual drunkard

– male or female – as one who 'not being amenable to any jurisdiction in lunacy, is notwithstanding, by reason of habitual intemperant drinking of intoxicating liquor, at times dangerous to himself or herself, and his or her affairs'.[5] This definition was adopted in Britain and Ireland for the remainder of the nineteenth-century and underpinned the 1898 legislation that established a long called for institutional response to the problem of the criminal inebriate drunkard.

The Inebriates Act 1898, was the final and most significant step in a century-long quest to understand and address some of the social consequences of excessive drinking. Initially designed only to establish a system in England, Scotland and Wales, on its second reading it was extended to Ireland.[6] It provided for the establishment of three new institutions for the reform and/ or punishment of habitual drunkards, the majority of whom committed criminal acts associated with their addiction. The first, the inebriate retreat, was the only institution of voluntary admission; in other words, one did not have to have committed a criminal act to be treated there. Bretherton explains that a degree of 'less-than-legal coercion' was used in many cases in order to get individuals to commit themselves to these retreats. Once admitted, the managers had powers to detain them for a fixed time in order to try and exact some level of reform.[7] The only inebriate retreat in Ireland opened in Belfast in 1902 under the management of the Irish Women's Temperance Union. It accepted only Protestant women 'of the better working classes'.[8] The second institution under the 1898 Act was the certified reformatory. Established privately, it was licensed, supervised and part-funded by government.[9] There were two certified reformatories in Ireland. One, opened in Waterford in 1906, catered for men, while a women's reformatory was established in Wexford in 1908.[10] The third and, from the point-of-view of inmates, the most undesirable of the institutions was the state inebriate reformatory. This was operated by the prison system and was seen as the place of ultimate sanction. While less hardened criminal drunkards might be sentenced to the somewhat less severe certified reformatory, the regime at the state institution was more in line with that of a local prison, albeit with some adjustments. The Irish state inebriate reformatory opened in the old county gaol at Ennis, county Clare, where it began receiving inmates in 1900. This institution was set up and managed by the GPB which controlled the penal system in Ireland following its centralisation in 1877.

In examining a regionally-based institution such as Ennis inebriate reformatory it is necessary to remember the wide extent of its catchment area. When it began receiving inmates, Ireland was served by a network of local prisons, bridewells and convict prisons. Local prisons met the needs of the geographical region directly surrounding each institution and that could be one county or a number of counties depending on the next closest prison. Trends in criminality represented in a given institution were reflective of that locality rather than any other part of the country. Ennis inebriate reformatory, on the other hand, was not at all parochial and did not solely represent trends in drunkenness and criminality in Clare and its surrounding counties. A national institution, in its lifetime it housed only eight inmates from the county in which it was located.[11] To place the drunkenness problem in Ireland in context, it is notable that in 1900, the year that Ennis received its first inmate, half of those imprisoned in Mountjoy prison, Dublin, were deemed to be drunkards.[12]

LOCATING THE INEBRIATE PROSTITUTE

Almost all we know about those detained within Ennis inebriate reformatory comes from its register of inmates and the unique casebook of before and after 'histories'. Some miscellaneous individual inmate files and records have also survived. The casebook was generated because the GPB ordered the governor at Ennis to record anything that was known about an inmate's life prior to their detention and to monitor their progress for an unspecified period following discharge. The post-release record is hugely significant as it gives the best possible account of the success or otherwise of the reform process applied to each inmate of the state reformatory. No other such recording process was used for the inmates of any institution of the GPB during its life-span from 1877 to 1928.[13]

The gender composition of inmates in state inebriate reformatories has been well debated among historians. The higher numbers of females in detention was as much a trend in Ireland as it was in Britain. Between 1900 and the beginning of 1918 there were 126 male and 204 female inmates detained at Ennis.[14] In Britain, at least 80 per cent of inmates of the broader inebriate reformatory system were female indicating, according to Hunt, Mellor and Turner, that significant and powerful elites perceived women as reproducers who were in danger of passing on their own 'unfortunate' characteristics to their children.[15] This concern for a generation perhaps yet unborn was matched by a reluctance to send men to inebriate reformatories where they would be detained for longer than they might be at a local prison. Morrison points out that, as men were primary breadwinners, a long period of detention would leave families dependent on local rates and might damage future employment prospects. Additionally, institutional treatment was not considered necessary for male drunkards as alcoholism among men was often considered a 'disease of the will'. As men were believed to have greater willpower than women, it followed they would be able to cure themselves.[16] There appears to have been little outward concern for the well-being of women as individuals or the physical and physiological dangers posed to them by a drunken lifestyle. Another factor in historical debates surrounding the higher female inebriate detention rates is contemporary attitudes to the contrasting mental states and abilities of men and women. Though as many as three quarters of those apprehended for drunkenness were men and more likely to qualify as habitual drunkards, late-Victorian society conceptualised the problem as a gendered one, associated mainly with women.[17] Nineteenth-century social reformers and penal authorities considered it essential to control young, sexually active women. By the end of the century many non-statutory bodies cared for, rehabilitated and controlled women, focussing firstly on sexual activity but expanding to female criminality and drunkenness.[18] C.F. Marshall, a surgeon at the British Skin Hospital stated in 1910 that many prostitutes turned to alcohol 'to attain temporary oblivion from the misery of their deplorable existence' and that alcohol was not a cause but result of prostitution.[19] In somewhat of a contradiction, women were seen as dangerous *and* vulnerable, corrupting *and* corruptible: capable of asserting influence over others, but susceptible to external influence themselves and therefore in need of care and protection.[20]

Contemporary opinion during the late-nineteenth century complained of the on-going economic burden regular imprisonment of drunken women imposed. It cited maintenance in police cells, cost of police surgeons, accommodation in prisons, policing costs, property damage and repeated cost of transportation between court and prison.[21] Most of this expenditure would also have applied to male drunkards but with deviant and drunken behaviour perceived as more acceptable among men, greater offence was taken at the economic burden caused by women. Zedner points out that women were assumed to be 'morally superior to men', with expectations of higher standards of behaviour. They were thought less inclined to dishonesty, perjury, stealing or cheating and less in danger of committing sexual crimes because they were, by nature, more chaste.[22] Such expectation of higher standards of behaviour fed into greater levels of outrage when women deviated from these societal norms.

McCormick points out that the word 'prostitute' was probably employed in many cases where women were not working in the profession but may have had some fringe involvement or gave that appearance.[23] Nineteen women whose occupations were registered as 'prostitute' were detained at Ennis reformatory between 1900 and 1918. They ranged in age from nineteen to sixty-five years old; nine women were in their thirties, five in their forties, three in their twenties, one in her sixties and one in her teens. Twelve were married or widowed while seven were single. Four were convicted of attempting suicide, a crime common across the institution. Four were convicted of malicious damage, three of child neglect, three of assault, two each of drunk and disorderly behaviour and being drunk on a public highway. Just one was convicted of larceny. It should be remembered that all the inmates in the state inebriate reformatories of Ireland and Britain were convicted of being habitual drunkards – this was a condition of entry. Eighteen of the women were registered as Roman Catholic and one as Methodist. Seven gave Dublin as their last place of residence, by and large reflecting the overall population-composition of the institution and the reality that urban settings provided the best opportunity for prostitution. Five were from the city of Derry or Londonderry as it was variously described on the register of inmates. Two were listed as having 'no fixed' address while Galway, Sligo, Antrim, Kildare and Belfast provided one inmate each listed as a 'prostitute'.[24] The following case studies of inebriate prostitutes have been selected at random but largely on the basis of the best, most complete, primary sources.

When sentenced to two years at Ennis, in October 1903, Annie A. had a lengthy list of convictions dating back to 1887. A forty-year-old single woman from Derry, her next-of-kin was her mother whose address was a workhouse in the city. Almost all her convictions were for vagrancy but recent charges included attempted suicide and indecent exposure. Her prison record indicated that she was a prostitute.[25] In the early twentieth century, women named as prostitutes or prosecuted for that offence were often convicted for a range of other crimes such as larceny and theft, indicating, perhaps, that prostitution did not provide a sufficient living for these women.[26] Annie had a further twenty-nine convictions for 'minor' offences such as drunkenness. In total she had accrued 152 short prison sentences.[27] The annual reports of the GPB show that it was inmates such as Annie that penal administrators and prison staff most despaired of because they had become so familiar with the system that it ceased to be a threat or, by extension, a deterrent.

By comparison with other female inmates at Ennis, Annie was at the higher end of the scale both in terms of prior detentions and character description. A 'woman of the unfortunate class', she reportedly spent the greater part of her life in prison often becoming suicidal when drunk. She once attempted to strangle herself while detained in a police cell. Apart from her mother, described as a drunkard and a prostitute, she had no other known relatives. Physically, Annie was a malnourished snuff-addict and prone to headaches when 'deprived of it'. All her bodily organs were healthy and she menstruated regularly. This latter medical detail appears only in notes relating to prostitutes. Mentally she was violent, possessed a 'vile' temper while drunk and also often displayed it in prison. In a telling summation, Annie's institutional case history described her as having been 'a prostitute from childhood'.[28]

Annie was discharged from Ennis in October 1905 having served her full sentence. A March 1906 first progress report came from one J. Heatley, an unknown supporter who clearly had some influence over her post-release well-being. Heatley declared that Annie was 'doing wonderfully well' and gave more hope every day. While 'uncertain in her moods', he believed she was trying her best, that she was 'just a little cracked' and that her most promising feature was that when her temper rose she did not succumb to alcohol. Since the money earned in the institution ran out, she had become 'self-supporting', although Heatley does not spell out in what way. Every Monday night, unprompted, she brought her earnings to Heatley to hold and pay her rent. An April 1908 report, however, shows that there was some inaccuracy in this first account of Annie's post-discharge life. A local RIC sergeant reported that between November 1905 – one month after her release – and January 1908, Annie had appeared in court thirty-four times on charges including drunkenness, being drunk and disorderly and vagrancy.[29] Clearly, between October 1905 and March 1906, J. Heatley was either unaware of Annie's conduct or lying to protect her from further prosecution. By April 1910 she had accrued a further nineteen drunk and disorderly convictions and eight more by February 1911. This final report described her as 'doing very badly'.[30] Nothing was recorded in the after-history of her 'moral conduct' and so it cannot be ascertained whether the authorities continued to deem her a prostitute.

Little has been recorded about the 'professional' activity of women labelled as inebriate prostitutes and so, as McCormick points out, like many prostitutes, 'they have left little trace for the historical record'.[31] While we do have some traces of the life and lifestyle of Margaret M., we do not know much about her alleged profession. Margaret was 37 years old when she appeared before Derry Quarter Sessions in January 1903 and was convicted of neglecting her child and being an habitual drunkard. Her occupation was listed as 'prostitute' but as with all of the nineteen women, this was not the charge set against her in court. Her last known residence was Derry city and her next-of-kin was her mother. She was sentenced to seven days imprisonment followed by two years detention at Ennis inebriate reformatory.[32] Though not arrested in Dublin, Margaret typified the category of inebriate who was apprehended by the police for drunk and disorderly behaviour, child neglect or even cruelty. As Luddy points out, such women were often prosecuted by the National Society for the Prevention of Cruelty to Children.[33] According to her institutional casebook record, Margaret had been married for twenty-five years when committed to Ennis, suggesting she wed when 12 years old, the lowest legal marriage age for girls. She began drinking soon after her marriage and for twenty years her life was one of 'drunkenness, vice and crime'. She had thirty-seven convictions for offences including neglecting or ill-treating her children, larceny, being drunk and disorderly or drunkenness. These convictions might be described as associated with her lifestyle but there were none relating to her alleged occupation of prostitution. Margaret's marriage ended some years prior to her conviction and she spent the intervening period either in prison or travelling through counties Derry and Donegal. She was the mother of 'quite a number of children, both legitimate and illegitimate'.[34] Her eldest child was 19 years old and the youngest was 12 months.[35]

Margaret's upbringing was described as good, her father as a 'respectable man and in average circumstances', but her mother was reportedly 'of extremely drunken habits'.[36] Physically she was considered 'below average' though with no disease and a 'normal' menstrual cycle.[37] Mentally, Margaret was deemed 'weak-minded and hysterical', a result no doubt of a twenty-year addiction to alcohol. In the institution she was apparently a good worker, her only problem being that she complained about the 'most trivial matters'. On completing her sentence, Margaret was released from the reformatory on 18 January 1905.[38] It is unclear why she was not discharged on licence from Ennis because there is nothing to suggest that her behaviour precluded her early release.

Margaret was unique among discharged inmates in that she remained in Ennis, intending to settle there following her release. Governor John King of the reformatory reported that she found employment as a charwoman. For a month after leaving, she worked as a general servant for the station-master's wife 'and touched intoxicating drink in no shape or form'. On leaving this job she was established in a small house, likely provided by philanthropic groups associated with the reformatory. The governor indicated that a number of individuals and organisations paid a keen interest in Margaret, including local clergy and the Sisters of Mercy. For about a fortnight after moving to this house she performed well at work and visited the institution every evening to report on her progress. Then an individual described as 'a tramp from Londonderry whom she had known previously' entered Margaret's life. The result was that she got drunk in his company, was arrested for disorder, returned to Londonderry and was given a one-month prison sentence.[39] This outcome must have been particularly difficult for the reformatory because it was rare that staff had such a level of post-discharge access to an inmate, particularly one who willingly returned each day to report on her progress.

Having returned to Londonderry it seemed that Margaret resumed her old ways and revolving-door prison sentences. By April 1909 she had accrued five further convictions for drunkenness, being drunk and disorderly and vagrancy. During the following year she visited the city on only two occasions and both times was arrested for drunkenness. Otherwise, she was 'tramping through the North of Ireland', seldom venturing into the city of Derry. In 1910 she was arrested for drunkenness and vagrancy but by February 1911 nothing further was known of her whereabouts.[40] There is no reference in her 'after-history' to the moral conduct that so occupied the minds of officialdom at the time of Margaret's conviction. Nor is there any reference to the fate of the 12-month-old infant who would have been around three years old when she was discharged.

The label of living a moral or immoral life was attached to many inmates of the inebriate reformatory, particularly to women. Galway-woman Bridget P. was 22 years old, single, and living in Dublin when convicted of assault and being an habitual drunkard at the Dublin City Sessions on 20 March 1911. Her occupation was recorded as 'prostitute' but she was not convicted of prostitution on this occasion. She was sentenced to eighteen months in Ennis.[41] Bridget's father was described as a 'labouring man' from Laurencetown in Galway, where she grew up. At fifteen she was employed as a domestic servant and began 'keeping company' with a former soldier. It was alleged that at this time she began leading an 'immoral life' and became addicted to alcohol. She and her sister Mary were 'denounced' by the local parish priest and both left Galway for Dublin.[42] This to some extent reflects a pattern postulated by Walkowitz in her study of British prostitutes in Victorian society that saw the women drawn to the nearest big city where they would 'eke out a precarious living' in the job market.[43] Two years later Bridget returned to Galway, to Ballinasloe, where her employment in domestic service was terminated due to her alcoholism. She moved in with a woman 'suspected of keeping an immoral house', was arrested for the larceny of a watch in 1908 and was sentenced to three months in prison. For two years prior to March 1911 she lived in Dublin, working as a prostitute and accumulating twenty convictions for assault and drunkenness. Bridget's parents were described as 'respectable, industrious and sober' but she, her sister Mary and her brother were apparently 'fond of having their own way'.[44] Every aspect of her physical and mental health suggested that Bridget was in a good state, perhaps reflecting her youth. She was discharged from Ennis on 19 September 1912 having served her full sentence.[45]

Prior to her release, there was clearly some apprehension about her return to Galway. An individual described as her parents' employer, J.E. Kenny, wrote to the reformatory governor on their behalf asking that some employment could be found for Bridget away from Galway, possibly in Ennis. The enquiry questioned whether a home existed for such discharged girls or if, perhaps, she could be employed in a laundry. Kenny, having obviously received a negative response to the query, wrote again four days later to state that it was unfortunate no such solution could be devised as Bridget would 'be no credit to her family in this part of the country'. Her parents did agree to take Bridget into their home as they felt it was most important that she have somebody to look after her upon release.[46] Representations such as the one made by J.E. Kenny were not uncommon in these situations where those from the so-called 'labouring classes' did not have the confidence to address or lobby the authorities themselves.

The first formal report on Bridget's post-discharge progress came from a local police constable in Galway and it was not positive. On 9 November 1912, two months after her release, Constable Mollaghan reported that, though not coming to police attention in *his* district, she had been 'canny' and carried on her social activities, namely her drinking, in the sub-district of Eyrecourt where she was convicted of being drunk and incapable on 1 October 1912. Constable Mollaghan believed that Bridget consumed alcohol 'on the quiet' to conceal her behaviour from police.

An 18 January 1913 report recorded that she had departed Galway, apparently for Dublin. It appeared that she was drinking 'all the intoxicating drink she could get' and the police claimed that her 'moral conduct' was again questionable. This is borne out by at least two appearances by Bridget in Mountjoy prison registers in August 1914. Listed as having 'no fixed' address, she was convicted of soliciting and sentenced to seven days imprisonment and a fine on each occasion. In September 1914 she was sentenced to a month in Mountjoy for threatening behaviour and, within days of release, she served a further week for soliciting. In November 1914, at the Dublin Metropolitan Police Court, she was sentenced to a month in prison for being drunk and disorderly. January 1915 saw her receive a one-week sentence for soliciting, with Meath Place, Dublin, listed as her most recent address.[47] By 6 March 1915 Bridget came to the attention of John Bolton of the Dublin Discharged Prisoners' Aid Society (DDPAS) who described her as 'a questionable character'. She had no fixed residence and ten convictions during the previous two years, mainly related to drunkenness. A February 1916 report recorded charges including soliciting for the purpose of prostitution and in a final report, one year later, Bolton revealed that Bridget had not since come to his attention mainly because he could not trace her whereabouts.[48] It clearly caused no difficulty for an individual of the age, good health and acumen of Bridget to disappear in a city such as early twentieth-century Dublin. A month after this final 1917 report, however, Bridget appeared at the Dublin City Police Court and was given two weeks in Mountjoy for soliciting. In June of the same year she received two different seven-day sentences for the same offence and another fourteen days in July.[49] This was the final time Bridget appeared on the Mountjoy prison register and her ultimate fate is unknown. Evidence of her activity as a prostitute is clear and the failure of her reform at Ennis is without question.

Detention at Ennis was not necessarily the first time in an inebriate reformatory for any inmate and there is evidence of its use as the 'institution of last resort'.[50] Immediately prior to her detention there, Bridget M. was sentenced to three months' hard labour in Waterford prison for what appears to have been a violent outburst at Wexford inebriate reformatory. In May 1915, she was convicted of causing malicious damage after breaking two mirrors, six vases and two panes of glass. Bridget was 25 years old and a prostitute who provided the name of her soldier brother as next-of-kin.[51] On release from Waterford, Bridget was returned to the Wexford reformatory but subsequently transferred to Ennis. This suggests that her behaviour was beyond what could be managed in Wexford and that management viewed her reform there as hopeless. She arrived at Ennis on 2 August 1915 on a direct transfer from Wexford. She had been charged with being drunk and disorderly on a highway and sentenced to eighteen months in Wexford and was simply transferred to Ennis to complete the sentence. She now listed her sister Mary as next-of-kin.[52]

Ennis inebriate reformatory was Bridget's third place of detention in as many months. She was 25 years old, single and held twenty-six previous convictions. Her record at Ennis describes her as 'a rather bad class of prostitute' and many of her convictions were for offences such as drunkenness, disorderly conduct, assaults and soliciting. Her last known address was at a house in Ash Street in Dublin which was 'much frequented by women of the unfortunate class who lodge there'. Indeed the area was believed to be 'a very bad quarter'.[53] The use of particular terminology to describe such houses in official documents should not cause confusion. The house in which Bridget resided in Ash Street was effectively a brothel. In 1916 there were reportedly fourteen brothels operating in Dublin and two years later this had decreased to eight. Luddy claims that from time-to-time, the police were attentive to the problem of brothels but this was most often in response to public pressure. Into the early years of the twentieth century, many prostitutes in Dublin plied their trade without obstruction from the police.[54] The terms 'lodging house' or 'low lodging-house' were often used to describe brothels. According to Walkowitz lodging-house keepers did not necessarily explicitly operate brothels but it was in their best interest that the women living there sought out male clients. The relationship between the older woman and these girls was 'more ambivalent' as she might provide assistance when they were down on their luck. The lodgings may also have housed men and children, members of the brothel-keeper's family, who might have lived in a separate residence within the same building.[55] Most of Bridget's family were believed to be alcoholics but there was no known insanity or other mental problems. Apart from a 'constant hacking cough', her physical health was described as fair. Mentally she was defined as 'good' with no illusions but a bad disposition. It was noted that kind treatment had no effect on her and that she was deceitful. Bridget spent 409 days in Ennis and was discharged on the expiration of her sentence on 16 September 1916.[56] Not permitting early release on licence suggests poor behaviour while in detention, something in keeping with the inmate's past history.

Bridget was discharged into her sister Mary's company in Dublin. She assured the governor at Ennis of her best efforts in keeping Bridget sober and out of trouble. She promised to work hard to ensure her sister did not fall back in with the same company 'who taught her to drink' and indeed would strive to prevent those individuals from finding out about her release. Along with the agent for the DDPAS, John Bolton, Mary met her sister at a Dublin train station on the day of her release from Ennis. Both Bolton and Mary gave further assurances to the reformatory that they would work to protect Bridget from herself and others.[57] These assurances were standard between all the parties to a release process; the institution was thanked for all its hard work, the Discharged Prisoners' Agent took control of allocating the inmate's remittances and the family promised to give every support. Five days after her release, on 21 September 1916, Bridget was convicted of soliciting at the Dublin Metropolitan Police Court and sentenced to one month in Mountjoy. In November of that year she was again convicted of soliciting and sentenced to fourteen days in Mountjoy. This occurred again in December 1916 and in February 1917. In March 1917 she was convicted of drunkenness and given seven days in Mountjoy.[58] In January 1918, John Bolton who was still monitoring Bridget declared that she was 'a night walker' with no fixed address who continued to build up convictions for soliciting and drunkenness.[59] She was unquestionably one of the spectacular failures of Ennis reformatory; whether that was because of her own unwillingness to reform or the reality of a system that was ill-equipped to help her is open to debate.

Around one-third of detainees at the Irish state inebriate reformatory were women convicted of a child-related offence such as neglect, ill-treatment or cruelty. Ferriter identifies the reports of the Dublin Aid Committee of the NSPCC as offering an important perspective on the reality of child life under the care of such parents. He cites words used such as 'neglect', 'starvation', 'ill-treatment' and 'abandonment'.[60] This same language was used in cases involving inebriate mothers at Ennis. Mary D. was the first woman sent to the reformatory at Ennis in July 1900. Aged 31, she was listed as a prostitute who was married with one living child and one deceased. Mary had 172 previous convictions and on this occasion she was found guilty of neglecting her son Christopher and being an habitual drunkard.[61] Her case history described Mary as 'an all-round bad character' who slept in 'low lodging houses, open halls and lobbies'. Further to this she consorted with the 'lowest prostitutes and is looked upon as being about one of the most depraved of that class'. Just one sentence made up her 'after history' file – Mary was transferred out of the reformatory to the local lunatic asylum in Ennis.[62] Tough, uncompromising descriptions of Mary were indicative of the disdain with which not only prostitutes, but prostitutes who were condemned as bad mothers, appear to have been held by the authorities. According to NSPCC reports, immoderate drinking was the principal cause of child neglect and women in particular were singled out for their alcoholism with many labelled 'confirmed drunkards'.[63] This phrase was used time and again to describe the status of new inmates at Ennis.

Edith C., 30, posed a threat to the middle-class sensibilities of her husband's family when she was detained in Ennis in August 1900. Sentenced to eighteen months for malicious damage and being an habitual drunkard, Edith held seventy-six prior convictions for various offences including assault and soliciting.[64] Like many of the prostitutes detained at Ennis, concerns around Edith did not focus on that aspect of her life but on her being a disruptive and potentially violent force in the lives of those around her. Once a children's governess, in the ten years since a divorce from her medical student husband, she had lived a 'loose and immoral life'. Her marriage ended because of her adultery and she had allegedly succumbed to a 'desperate and dissipated' existence and became a continual source of aggravation for her husband's family.[65] In advance of her release from Ennis on 31 January 1902, the authorities frequently repeated that Edith had conducted herself badly while in detention, with Governor King declaring that 'there is no prospect of reformation in the case of inmate Edith [C]'.[66]

Extraordinarily, it emerged that in the months prior to her release, Edith's former father-in-law, George O'C, of Landsdowne Road, Dublin, travelled to Ennis in an attempt to persuade Governor King to prevent her return to Dublin. He believed that she would prove a 'continual source of annoyance to him and his family, although he had assisted her in every way'. In a follow-up letter to Governor King shortly before her release, George revealed his family's heightened anxiety at her possible reappearance in Dublin. The family had moved house but he was worried that she would return to their previous residence and attempt to do damage. In a pointed reference to his family's connections with officialdom, George revealed that David Harrel, the Under Secretary for Ireland, had assured him that every 'precaution possible will be taken to have the woman watched'.[67] By early 1903 and the first post-release report to Ennis, Edith was in a lunatic asylum where she died in 1910.[68] This case probably raises more questions than others, not merely because of the involvement of the official apparatus of state at higher levels than would normally be appropriate. Her estranged husband's family demonstrated no concern for her career as a prostitute and were instead concerned with her propensity for violence. The question arises as to whether this latter concern masked a fear that her 'immoral' lifestyle might pose some hazard to their standing in society. Significantly, there must be a question over the family's role in Edith's committal to a lunatic asylum within a year of her release from Ennis. With no record of *her* voice, it is difficult to ascertain the extent to which she was a victim or a perpetrator.

CONCLUSION

None of the cases described in this chapter had what might be described as a 'happy ending'. Efforts to reform these women clearly failed. The question is whether that failure rested with the women or with the institution. Evidence suggests that absence of aftercare was among the most important shortcomings of the process in Ireland. In Britain, organisations such as The Inebriates' Reformation and After-care Association were mandated to support discharged inmates. That body, for example, was charged with promoting the reformation and restoration of inebriates, providing for their after-care, assisting county and borough councils as well as magistrates and acting as a central information hub in relation to the Inebriate Act and its provisions.[69] No such supports existed for inebriates in Ireland, let alone for women from the so-called 'unfortunate classes' whose lives were played out in the complex world of 'low lodging-houses', courts, pubs and streets. There are two significant unanswered questions about the Ennis inebriate women pertaining to the accuracy of the numbers declared as prostitutes. Firstly, what portion of their lives did the low number of women who self-reported their occupation as such actually devote to the 'profession'? If for example, a women declared herself to be a nurse or a governess then we could assume that she worked full-time at this occupation. Yet, none of the women in Ennis appear to have been engaged in the full-time practice of prostitution. Secondly, to what extent might women have under-reported their activity in the sale of sexual favours? A mere nineteen women, 5.75 per cent of the inmate population, were formally listed as prostitutes. This appears low when the strong association between alcoholism and prostitution is considered. The accuracy of this figure has to be questioned, however, when the number of women in the state reformatory, including prostitutes, noted as having poor moral habits, rises to forty-nine.[70] In all forty-nine cases there is overt reference to the sexual behaviour of the women. Without the necessary post-release support such women had little chance of escaping what was often described as their 'depraved' lifestyles, yet the principal formal intervention following discharge from the Irish state reformatory was monitoring. Despite the richness of the historical traces for the Ennis inebriates, their own voices remain largely unheard amidst a chorus of condemnation, accusation and suspicion.

NOTES

1. C.K. Warsh, "'John Barleycorn must die": An Introduction to the Social History of Alcohol', in C.K. Warsh, *Drink in Canada: Historical Essays* (Quebec: McGill-Queen's University Press, 1993), pp.3–26.

2. Ibid.

3. L. Radzinowicz and R. Hood, *A History of English Criminal Law, Vol. 5: The Emergence of Penal Policy* (London: Stevens, 1986), p.288.

4. A. Barton, 'Wayward Girls and Wicked Women: Two Centuries of "semi-penal" Control', *Liverpool Law Review*, 22 (2000), pp.157–71, 165.

5. Cited in Radzinowicz and Hood, *A History of English Criminal Law*, p.299.

6. B.A. Smith, 'Ireland's Ennis Inebriates' Reformatory: A Nineteenth-Century Example of Failed Institutional Reform', *Federal Probation*, 53 (1989), pp.316–49, 58.

7. G. Bretherton, 'Irish Inebriate Reformatories, 1899–1920: A Small Experiment in Coercion', *Contemporary Drug Problems*, 13 (1986), pp.473–502.

8. Ibid., p.479.

9. Smith, 'Ireland's Ennis Inebriates' Reformatory', p.58.

10. Bretherton, 'Irish Inebriate Reformatories', p.484.

11. GPB, Ennis Inebriate Reformatory, *Register of Inmates*, 1900–18. Clonmel borstal in county Tipperary experienced similar trends during the first phase of its existence between 1906 and 1921 with just 18 out of 660 inmates originating from within that county. See C. Reidy, *Ireland's Moral Hospital: The Irish Borstal System 1906–1956* (Dublin: Irish Academic Press, 2009).

12. T. Carey, *Mountjoy: The Story of a Prison* (Cork: Collins Press, 2000), p.136.

13. The inmates of the borstal institution at Clonmel were subjected to post-discharge monitoring under the terms of the Prevention of Crime Act 1908 but this progress was not recorded on a case-by-case basis or preserved in the same way as it was for the inmates of Ennis inebriate reformatory.

14. GPB, Ennis Inebriate Reformatory, *Register of Inmates*, 1900–18.

15. G. Hunt, J. Mellor and J. Turner, 'Women and the inebriate reformatories', in L. Jamieson and H. Corr, *State, Private Life and Political Change* (London: Macmillan, 1990), pp.163–82.

16. B. Morrison, 'Controlling the Hopeless: Re-visioning the History of Female Inebriate Institutions c. 1870–1920' in H. Johnston (ed.), *Punishment and Control in Historical Perspective* (London: Palgrave Macmillan, 2008), pp.135–58.

17. Morrison, 'Controlling the Hopeless', p.138.

18. R.P. Dobash and P. McLaughlin, 'The Punishment of Women in Nineteenth-Century Scotland: Prisons and Inebriate Institutions' in E. Breitenbach and E. Gordon, *Out of Bounds: Women in Scottish Society 1800–1945* (Edinburgh: Edinburgh University Press, 1992), pp.65–88.

19. C.F. Marshall, 'Alcoholism and Prostitution', in *The British Journal of Inebriety*, 8, 1 (1910), pp.29–31.

20. A. Barton, 'Wayward Girls and Wicked Women: Two Centuries of "semi-penal" Control' in *Liverpool Law Review*, 22 (2000), pp.157–71.

21. Morrison, 'Controlling the Hopeless', p.143.

22. L. Zedner, *Women, Crime, and Custody in Victorian England* (London: Clarendon Press, 1991), p.23.

23. L. McCormick, *Regulating Sexuality: Women in Twentieth-Century Northern Ireland* (Manchester: Manchester University Press, 2009), p.16.

24. GPB, Ennis Inebriate Reformatory, *Register of Inmates*, 1900–18.

25. Ibid.

26. McCormick, *Regulating Sexuality*, p.29.

27. GPB, Ennis Inebriate Reformatory, *Casebook*, 1900–18.

28. Ibid.

29. Ibid.

30. Ibid.

31. McCormick, *Regulating Sexuality*, p.13.

32. GPB, Ennis Inebriate Reformatory, *Register of Inmates*, 1900–18.

33. M. Luddy, *Prostitution and Irish Society, 1800–1940* (Cambridge: Cambridge University Press, 2007), p.179.

34. GPB, Ennis Inebriate Reformatory, *Casebook*, 1900–18.

35. GPB, Ennis Inebriate Reformatory, *Register of Inmates*, 1900–18.

36. GPB, Ennis Inebriate Reformatory, *Casebook*, 1900-18.

37. Ibid.

38. Ibid.

39. Ibid.

40. Ibid.

41. GPB, *Register of Inmates*, 1900–17.

42. GPB, State Inebriate Reformatory, Ennis, *Casebook*.

43. J. Walkowitz, *Prostitution and Victorian Society: Women, Class and the State* (Cambridge: Cambridge University Press, 1982), p.15.

44. GPB, State Inebriate Reformatory, Ennis, *Casebook*.

45. Ibid.

46. Ibid.

47. GPB, Mountjoy Prison, *Register of Inmates*, 1914–15.

48. GPB, State Inebriate Reformatory, Ennis, *Casebook*.

49. GPB, Mountjoy Prison, *Register of Inmates*, 1917.

50. Smith, 'Ireland's Ennis Inebriates' Reformatory', p.58.

51. GPB, Waterford Prison, *Register of Inmates*, 1915.

52. GPB, *Register of Inmates*, 1900–17.

53. GPB, State Inebriate Reformatory, Ennis, *Casebook*.

54. Luddy, *Prostitution and Irish Society*, pp.22–3.

55. Walkowitz, *Prostitution and Victorian Society*, p.28.

56. GPB, State Inebriate Reformatory, Ennis, *Casebook*.

57. Ibid.

58. GPB, Mountjoy Prison, *Register of Inmates*, 1916–17.

59. GPB, State Inebriate Reformatory, Ennis, *Casebook*.

60. D. Ferriter, *Occasions of Sin: Sex and Society in Modern Ireland* (London: Profile Books, 2009), p.46.

61. GPB, *Register of Inmates*, 1900–17.

62. GPB, State Inebriate Reformatory, Ennis, *Casebook*.

63. Ferriter, *Occasions of Sin*, p.46.

64. GPB, *Register of Inmates*, 1900–17.

65. GPB, State Inebriate Reformatory, Ennis, *Casebook*.

66. GPB, Correspondence Register (CR), Governor's memorandum, 17 January 1902, GPB/780/1902.

67. GPB, CR, George O'C to King, 21 January 1902, GPB/780/1902.

68. GPB, State Inebriate Reformatory, Ennis, *Casebook*.

69. A.J.S. Maddison, 'The Aftercare of Inebriates' in *The British Journal of Inebriety*, 3, 2 (July 1905), pp.40–4.

70. GPB, State Inebriate Reformatory, Ennis, *Casebook*.

4

THE POLITICS OF EMIGRANT BODIES: IRISH WOMEN'S SEXUAL PRACTICE IN QUESTION

Jennifer Redmond

> In a nation seeking to define and assert its own unique voice, sexuality was an unmentionable subject that lurked beneath every conversation. In a society preoccupied with establishing and maintaining order, sexuality constituted a principle of chaos.[1]

Historians of modern Ireland have argued that sexual behaviour and its regulation became a national obsession in the post-independence era in an effort to prove decency, respectability and capability in governing Ireland as an independent nation.

In Howes' analysis quoted above, sexual matters were 'lurking' within discourses ostensibly outside sexual matters. What was lurking, however, was proscribed according to the mores of the time and rooted in a Catholic analysis of the situation in Ireland, one that conceived only of heterosexual relations; there was little public commentary or censure of lesbian relationships, for example, so far were they outside the norms of post-independence Ireland. Hill has pointed to the difficulty in identifying same-sex relationships in the past, given the public censure on openly discussing 'female sexual identity in even a general way', and our evidence from literature and the archives suggests those in homosexual relationships may have felt 'that they could not publicly acknowledge them'.[2]

Although this may seem like an obvious point, it is important to acknowledge so as not to simply replicate the discourses in which same-sex relationships have been silenced. The point is to highlight the limits of contemporary discourses – moral concern was directed at 'illicit' sexual behaviour by cis males and females in a strictly heterosexual context for, as Tanya Ní Mhuirthile has outlined in this collection, those who did not fit clearly defined gender binaries were not considered by successive stakeholders in modern Ireland.

While moral concerns also preoccupied the Church of Ireland community at this time, there does not seem to be the same volubility and panic over a perceived decline in moral standards as existed in the Catholic Church and expressed in Lenten pastorals and newspaper articles. In the context of this chapter, the migration of young Catholic women appeared to heighten fears about modern sexual behaviour; emigrants, no longer under the watchful eye of family and community, were at risk of sexual transgression once the bonds of propriety exercised so strongly on them at home were gone.

Lest we forget the consensual, religious nature of the state and Catholicism, this was not a case of the Catholic Church imposing its values on an unwilling, bohemian population ready to embrace modern values and free love after the revolution. As Kennedy has posited, 'the Irish desired and received from their clergy a very strong emphasis on the dangers and sinfulness of sex among single persons.'[3] Elsewhere I have emphasised the single status of female emigrants as being at the heart of the concern for their behaviour, particularly of a sexual kind.[4] Extending this analysis, this chapter seeks to build upon the scholarly contributions on Ireland's past sexual mores, including Luddy, Ferriter, McAvoy, Ryan and Valiulis, in highlighting the ways in which the body was conceptualised as particularly problematic. Emigrant bodies, what they did or had done to them, concern over the dangers and perils of taking them out of their normal environments, was at the heart of much of the negative discourses about women emigrants. This was, in short, the reason they were consistently posited as needing guidance of a moral nature.

J.H. Whyte argued that the preoccupation of the Catholic Church with issues of sexual behaviour arose from 'objective signs of a decline in moral standards' such as a rise in illegitimacy rates.[5] What can be added to this observation is that it was in women's bodies that these 'objective signs' could be read and hence why women were continually imbued with a 'deviant' sexuality in religious discourses. As Luddy has highlighted, concerns over moral welfare were intimately linked to concerns for the morality of the new state, and the 'rise in illegitimacy levels was attributed to a loss of parental control and responsibility during the period of the war of independence and civil war. That parental control, it was argued, had never been restored'.[6] Examining the evidence for this phenomenon reveals a small minority of births in Ireland registered as illegitimate: in the period 1921–23, illegitimate births accounted for 2.6 per cent of all births; this rose to 3.5 per cent in 1933–34 and to 3.9 per cent in the years 1944–46.[7] Even allowing for the fact that reported figures are probably lower than the actual rates, they do not suggest an 'epidemic of immorality in modern Ireland'.[8] Thus, as Whyte suggested, some 'have suspected that the Irish Catholic preoccupation with sexual morality is subjective rather than objective in origin: that it is motivated not by evidence that this [illegitimacy] is a serious problem in Ireland, but by some kind of inner necessity that obliges Irish people to harp on the subject'.[9]

Concern regarding promiscuity and illegitimacy was not confined to Éire or to Catholics. Bishop John Hind's pamphlet, *Welfare Work in the Church of Ireland* detailed the endeavours of the Moral Welfare Committee in the six Northern Ireland dioceses to combat promiscuity, extra-marital relations, unmarried motherhood and the increased use of contraceptives which prevented married couples from fulfilling their duty of producing a family.[10] The Moral Welfare Committee employed a full-time moral welfare worker and supported a number of homes for unmarried mothers in the Belfast area. It is interesting to note again that those dealing with unmarried mothers tended to perceive the problem in crisis terms. Reactions to sexual immorality thus could be broadly similar across the confessional divide and the political border, the perception being that standards were slipping and a religious response was required. Given the influence and power of the Catholic Church in southern Ireland, it is unsurprising that moral concerns received prominent attention and legislative responses on Catholic principles. The term 'moral welfare' is never defined in literature of this kind, which assumes the readership will understand both the definition and the necessity of this kind of work. Moral welfare work, in both Catholic and Protestant contexts, appears to have been focused on sexual propriety above all else; while having a 'good character' encompassed religiosity, manners, decorum and appropriate behaviour, much of this hinged on sexual activity.

Sandra McAvoy has identified three broad areas of concern in the Free State: access to contraceptives and information on sexuality; the 'problem' of unmarried mothers; and sexual crime and public morality, including prostitution.[11] All of these matters are inherently concerned with women's bodies and the ways in which they could become problematic for the state. Concerns resulted not only in a discursive preoccupation with these topics, but also the official investigation of sexual behaviour and the enactment of specific legislation. Hence the convening of the investigative committees such as the Committee on Evil Literature (which included the examination of birth control literature) and the Carrigan Commission to investigate matters related to sexual behaviour.[12] Both enquiries led to the adoption of legislation that limited access to information about sexual reproduction in 1929 and banned the use of contraception in 1935. This environment led to an intense focus on women rather than men, illustrating the sexual double standards of the time. As Spivak has argued, there are value codings of the body in society that make them become gendered, and in the Irish context, it appears that values in modern Ireland that were rooted in women's bodies codified them as pure but vulnerable to sexual sin.[13] Indeed there is a connection between women's bodies and the nation that is not replicated for men. Nations being codified in rhetoric as female has a long history, and in Ireland this can be seen through two lenses. As Ryan among others have highlighted, women being used as emblems of the nation, while not unique to Ireland, was certainly a feature of nationalist rhetoric: 'The female gendering of Ireland has led to a plethora of womanly representations – Erin, Hibernia, Cathleen, Roisin Dubh. In the blurring of boundaries between representations of the people and the country, these allegorical women stood for both Ireland and Irishness.'[14] In the pre-independence era, 'feminine' Ireland was often under the threat of the physical and political power of 'John Bull' or Britain, as was often represented in publications such as *Punch* magazine, much like the masculine/feminine dichotomy played out during the First World War of depictions of an aggressive German Fatherland in the 'rape' of Belgium.

In a rhetorical sense, women as resonant of a pure Ireland followed the image of Mary in being both maternal and chaste. In Werner-Leggett's analysis, the Virgin Mary was used as a role model to prepare women for motherhood, particularly due to her role in healing and promoting the welfare of children.[15] This discourse therefore was problematic for women who did not fit this mould, in particular single women. There was a 'connection in the minds of many in Catholic Ireland of the 1920s, 30s and 40s between the state of singleness and the state of sin'.[16] Women who crossed the boundaries of sexual propriety were offered a different, more problematic religious icon: Mary Magdalene. Institutions appropriating her name were established first within the Protestant faith and then more widely by the Catholic Church in Ireland, exemplifying local iterations of an international movement having its 'origins in the tradition of evangelical women's philanthropic endeavours throughout the nineteenth century' in America and elsewhere.[17]

If Ireland was worried about its depleting population, it certainly did not want the deficit to be made up by illegitimate births. Indeed as Ryan has argued, while women were national symbols of positive attributes, this also made them signify 'national weakness, vulnerability and susceptibility to corrupting foreign influences' or 'the threat of immorality or impurity'.[18] Thus great attention was paid in parish sermons and Lenten pastorals, published in detail in national and religious newspapers, to dissuade parents from allowing their sons, but most particularly their daughters, too much freedom in their personal lives lest immorality could occur.

Reports of the views of the Catholic hierarchy were published in full, without comment or critique from the newspaper editors. While this may imply fear of censure or a lack of open critique of the views of the Church, it may also imply an acceptance of such statements and values. As might be expected, the religious press published views of the hierarchy, and opinion pieces on the morality (or otherwise) of emigration, more frequently than the secular press. *The Irish Catholic* newspaper published frequent exhortations to girls to stay in Ireland to avoid temptations and the pitfalls of life in Britain, referring in 1936 to the 'disastrous consequences' that 'usually' befell the Irish who had not previously been away from home.[19] The euphemistic 'disastrous consequences' surely references sexual impurity, such coded language being easily understood by a readership accustomed to reading moralistic journalism of this kind. It also reported views of the hierarchy in Britain, such as an editorial on the warning from the Most Rev. Dr Downey of Liverpool that girls were in peril from answering 'innocent-looking advertisements' without using the services of moral welfare organisations to vet them first.[20] The issue being highlighted was the threat of 'a kind of mild slavery or even worse' that could lead a girl to suffer 'degradation and dishonour'.[21] This dramatic language is clearly synonymic for sexual danger, the propriety of the publication being too strict to spell it out in clearer language, although another article on the same theme referred to 'unmentionable purposes'.[22] This language is also evident in the prominent reporting of the Lenten pastorals of 1937 in the *Irish Independent* in which emigration featured as a conspicuous, and gendered, theme. Archbishop of Tuam, Dr Gilmartin railed against the 'terrible risks to soul and body' young girls going to England faced if they went without job or family to meet them, while Dr MacNamee of Ardagh and Clonmacnoise referred to jobs 'where modesty and virtue may be exposed to great dangers'.[23] The body is overtly and implicitly expressed in these statements as at risk, of endangering spiritual and moral purity, of being the site of sin committed against the girl. This idea of Irish women being targeted was a frequent theme in *The Irish Catholic*, often quoting Catholic welfare organisations such as the International Catholic Girls' Protection Society on the dangers of travel: 'We also solemnly warn all intending emigrants to be on their guard against the agents of the white slave traffic, who, we have good reason to believe, are always trying to carry on their nefarious work on most of the outgoing transatlantic liners.'[24] Although 'all emigrants' are referred to here, the Society only dealt with female emigrants, as did their counterparts in Britain, and the danger from such gangs was solely in terms of women's entry into prostitution.

At the same time as this rhetoric emerged in newspapers, the state enacted a series of laws that restricted knowledge about sexual matters and family planning, introduced compulsory retirement of women on marriage in the civil service and primary school sector, limited women's access to the higher echelons of the civil service and to serve on juries, banned contraceptives, regulated women's employment in factories and enshrined and valorised a maternal, domestic role for women in the 1937 Constitution. In this era, political parties, despite their bitter Civil War rivalries, appeared united and women found few allies in parliamentary circles or the public sphere in general.

Emigration provided a break from this community and parental censure, a feature that worried many and provoked much verbiage on the moral problems of leaving Ireland. As most Irish men and women migrated before the age of twenty-five for much of this period and were unmarried, the problem of confining sex within the marital state was one explicitly associated with migrants who could no longer be influenced by societal and community norms and might, it was feared, become reckless through life in English cities. Yet there are some distinct gender differences that must be borne in mind; an analysis of newspaper commentary reveals that while alcohol was thought to be the root of sin for men, for women it was sexual behaviour. Both practices are associated with the body and had, in contemporary discourses, deleterious effects on physical, moral and spiritual welfare. However, while reform could be hoped for men who fell into alcoholism and its attendant problems of homelessness and isolation, what hope was there for women who besmirched their and their family's name through sex outside marriage? Was this not a permanent stain on their soul? The newspapers, journals and pamphlets of the time might certainly suggest so, and the high rates of literacy, availability and accessibility of national and local newspapers at this time have been suggested by Ryan as reasons why we should take their messages seriously in analysing the formation of the new state, revealing the 'conflicting and competing discourses' they contained.[25] There was, as might be expected, less variation in Catholic newspapers of the period as their narratives were informed by church teachings and religious principles with a heavy emphasis on morality. These are not included in Ryan's impressive study of Irish journalism but are quoted here in order to broaden the analysis of discourses current in post-independence Ireland. The impact printed sermons or journalism had on women's sense of self, or even their decision to migrate, is impossible to know, and the point must be made that we cannot uncritically assume that the powerful hegemony attempted to be asserted by governments and the Catholic church was passively accepted. As Conway, Bourque and Scott argue:

> To complicate the picture, institutions do not always succeed in their task of inculcating culturally acceptable conduct or conventional behavior [sic]. Individuals do not seem to simply accept or reflect normative designations. Rather, their notions of their own gender identity and sexuality are manifested in their refusals, reinterpretations, or partial acceptances of the dominant themes.[26]

This may have been understood well at the time, and church and state leaders appear to have interpreted the large numbers of women leaving Ireland through the first decades of independence as rejecting the 'dominant themes' that were posited as ideal for women citizens.

Furthermore, continued questioning of women's sexual behaviour as a motivator for emigration, either to hide pregnancy or to embrace 'modern' sexual mores was in complete contrast to the resounding silence on Irish men's behaviour, as emigrants or otherwise. Women were problematised as emigrants according to sexual double standards that saw them either as temptresses or victims, but either way paying the ultimate price through illegitimate pregnancies. Women's bodies were central to this thinking: they were the site of sin, the literal embodiment of transgressive sexual behaviour through pregnancy, and thus control of them was essential in the eyes of many in order to diminish what was seen as a significant moral problem. Ferriter has cautioned as to the complexity of the sexual history of Ireland and questioned whether we can assume a national sexual morality or characteristics of sexual behaviour.[27] Inglis' work in examining the theories of Foucault and Bourdieu as they may apply to sexuality in Irish history has outlined discourses that were shaped by Catholicism as the church rose to power throughout the long nineteenth century.[28] Inglis draws attention to the reductionism in this paradigm, focusing on sexual morality, as opposed to pleasure, and resulting in 'a classification of who could do what to whom, when, where and how'.[29] Effectively this created conformists and non-conformists, the latter included 'the unmarried mother, the homosexual, the lesbian, the fornicating bachelor farmer' who were 'excluded from society and put into convents, homes and asylums', or, in my analysis, out of sight on the boat to England.[30] This 'policing' of bodies in a sexual context created a society that saw private sexual behaviours become in some ways an issue between government and citizen whilst being shrouded in silence and shame. Although Ferriter rightly points to 'dissent, different opinions, double standards and a more complex sexual identity and practice' than he feels Inglis' analysis allows for, in the early years of independence the evidence does suggest that suppression was more powerful than dissension.[31]

The discourses that constituted sex as an 'obsession' extended to those citizens who left its shores. Opinions on women's sexual practices as emigrants was often based on evidence of the phenomenon of unmarried mothers and the opinions of religious and charitable institutions in Britain which found themselves assisting in 'hiding Ireland's shame'. As the Commission on Emigration and Other Population problems noted, dealing continually with problem cases may have skewed the views of such groups in their reporting to the newspapers as they dealt with a problematic cohort of the emigrant population, rather than the population as a whole.[32]

One such example is evident in a 1923 letter from the National Vigilance Association (NVA) in Britain to the Irish High Commissioner, Mr James McNeill,[33] in which he was urged to address the problem of Irish women coming to Britain. Such women were stated to be often without money, luggage or a job, or, alternately completely unfit for jobs they were accepted for and which they quickly lost. Mr Sempkins, head of the NVA, pointed out that although many women were helped in their travel arrangements by the International Catholic Girls' Protection Society in Cork and Dublin[34], he:

> ... would suggest that the girls for whom special protection is most needed are <u>not</u> the girls who seek the help of these two Societies; but are rather those girls who either come over in entire ignorance of the dangers and difficulties awaiting them, or those who think they are quite capable of taking care of themselves.[35] (Emphasis in original)

Women thinking they were 'quite capable of taking care of themselves' is thus problematic in this analysis. This may not be unexpected given the emphasis of their work and the influence of dealing with problematic migrations leading perhaps to a tendency to see *all* women's migrations as problematic. The class, as well as the gender, aspects to this kind of rhetoric are latent but strong; moral philanthropic work was not aimed at female doctors, for example, but rather domestic servants and other unskilled workers.

Archival evidence suggests that the attitude expressed by the National Vigilance Association above infused many Catholic organisations that interacted with them. The Catholic Girls' Society ran a London hostel which provided cheap accommodation for Catholic girls in a spiritual environment. Their 1938 report also details their work with 365 girls not living in the hostel but having been brought to their attention (by whom and for what reason is not elaborated upon, although local priests are acknowledged as providing 'help and encouragement').[36] The report thanks the NVA for their cooperation (again unspecified), and highlights three examples of their work with young girls, two of which relate to Irish girls:

(1) An Irish girl of sixteen was found working in North London, in very undesirable surroundings, she was persuaded to leave and brought to the hostel, where she worked until her return to Ireland

(2) In answer to an appeal from the Lady Almoner of one of the big hospitals, our visitor befriended a young Irish girl of eighteen whose parents were abroad. She was escorted to various interviews with prospective employers till she found suitable work.[37]

In these examples, girls are specifically sought out in order to provide help and guidance they are thought to be lacking. While it may appear helpful and benevolent, it is also the case that this kind of activity was confined to women, and furthermore, the assumption is clear that as working-class women they should accept such offers of help unquestioningly. There is evidence also that the Westminster Diocese was particularly active in their moral welfare work, and given the high numbers of Irish who went to London, it is unsurprising that they interacted with Irish women.[38] However, the level of control displayed by the Moral Welfare Committee of the diocese again calls attention to the degree to which behaviour, or the suspicion of immoral influences without any immorality having taken place, was thought justification for interference in the lives of emigrant women.

The body was the site of success or failure for female emigrants, for as I've argued elsewhere: 'failed emigrants were to be found in maternity homes; successful emigrants sent money home to their mothers'.[39] The perception that emigrant behaviours were reflective of national traits was shared by the Irish government and the Catholic Church, thus immoral sexual activity cast an air of profligacy and licentiousness on the Irish 'character' as a whole. Although there is far less commentary in the Protestant *Church of Ireland Gazette* on emigrants' behaviour, newspapers in particular appear to have been fascinated by this topic and were largely responsible for creating the impression that emigrants lapsed in their moral standards in Britain. Whether or not the newspaper headlines can be believed as delivering an accurate picture of public opinion, or whether these stories had any impact on emigrants is not as important to consider as the fact that the persistence of stories related to morality and behaviour created the space for a version of 'truth' in describing emigrants in Britain.

A Department of External Affairs memorandum in 1947 constructed the migration of women, in contrast to that of men, as lonely, unsafe and unprotected in their workplace environments:

. . . there is a significant difference between male and female emigrants: the former usually proceed in groups to factory or building work where arrangements are made for their moral and religious welfare and often for the maintenance of an Irish atmosphere, whereas the bulk of the female emigrants who are engaged in domestic service or allied work take up employment individually and are scattered singly throughout Great Britain, the moral atmosphere of which young and inexperienced girls are only too often unfitted to withstand.[40]

This assessment denies the fact that while some women may have emigrated singly, they did so within a wider nexus of family and social support. As Lambert has noted, family links and support were crucial to the emigration process.[41] However even if this were the case, it is problematic to accept this analysis that the sole emigrant female body was as weak as posited here – did women, uniquely, require a certain 'moral atmosphere' in order that their bodies comply with social strictures? If Irish women were imbued with religion throughout their lives before emigration, why were they so vulnerable in Britain?

Irish female emigrants were, on the one hand, protected from sexual knowledge through censorship and a lack of open discourse about sexual matters, yet at the same time symbolically marked as sources of sexual knowledge and desires that would get them 'into trouble' upon leaving the country. In reality, it seems that the overriding experience of Irish women, at home and in Britain, in relation to sexual matters was a mixture of ignorance and dread.[42] These testimonies suggest that the moral panic over the sexual activities of single Irish girls was probably vastly overestimated. However, the very fact that this was an issue of major concern in this time period suggests that women in general, and single girls in particular, were a disturbing cohort, especially when they left Ireland.

Conclusion

Inglis has posited that the 'practices of postponed marriage and permanent celibacy became associated with a perception of the Irish being a sexually repressed, priest-ridden people who sublimated their libidinal drives in religion and alcohol'.[43] If this perception was shared by those in post-independence Ireland, is this perhaps a reason why emigrants were accused of seeking sexual pleasure through migration? If so, this still fails to explain why women were castigated as having this motive while men were not. It does, however, fit with Butler's theorisation of the body as appearing, enduring and living 'within the productive constraints of certain highly gendered regulatory schemas'.[44]

Theoretical insights can be helpful to the historian in trying to understand the complex and competing discourses about Irish sexuality and sexual behaviour in the past and how issues of sex were discussed in the public sphere. Bourdieu refers to the 'unquestioned social conceptions' which he 'refers to as *doxa*'[45] and this concept neatly encapsulates the attitude to female emigrants in many quarters during this period – it appears to have been an unquestioned belief that they were associated with sinful sexual behaviour, either being the instigator or victims of transgressions of this kind. In my analysis this was not simply dogma preached by the Catholic church and followed to the letter by a slavish population; attitudes to female sexuality were reflective of wider cultural and social mores in which the protection of family lines of inheritance were as much at stake as personal reputations and moral judgements on sexual behaviour, a conclusion that accords with Foucault's analysis of the 'deployment of sexuality' and with Inglis' analysis of the particular way this played out in Ireland.[46] Foucault's writings on power and the body have illuminated the ways in which the state regulates bodies as an expression of its power over them, individually and collectively as a society. This is achieved when 'their supervision was effected through an entire series of interventions and *regulatory controls: a bio-politics of the population*' (emphasis in original).[47] The collaboration between the Catholic Church and the government in regulating women's bodies was a feature of successive governments in the post-independence period. While this system may also have been restrictive to men in Ireland who did not fit with hegemonic norms of masculinity and sexuality, as emigrants they were discursively free of moral censure with regard to sexual behaviour, unlike their female counterparts.

Theoretical approaches, particularly psychoanalytic conceptions of identity, have led historians into explorations of

> ... the relationship between history and individual psyches, and into what might be called the politics of sexual identity. It suggests that sexual identities are not biologically rooted, but instead continually

84

pursued, and that this pursuit, whether heterosexual or homosexual, is made possible in contexts at once political and personal.[48]

An examination of archival material, public statements and newspaper articles reveals that female emigrants and their bodies were part of the sexual politics of the time.

The agency of young women in migrating to Britain in the twentieth century is perhaps also at the heart of the moralistic concerns over their behaviour, for their propensity to migrate alone or with other single women highlighted, for some, their sexual availability, unprotected by marital or family status: 'If more female emigrants to England or elsewhere had been married or had moved in family groups, it is doubtful whether there would have been such curiosity, vitriol or debate about them.'[49] This is perhaps attested to best by the *lack* of concern over female seasonal workers. Even when commentary on their conditions of work and accommodation became prominent after the Kirkintilloch tragedy in 1937 in which a number of young men died in a fire in their accommodation, moral concerns over sexual behaviour did not emerge in public rhetoric despite the close contact young men and women had with each other in this line of work.[50] It was because women were working within groups controlled by men and alongside relatives that concern for their moral welfare was not evinced in the same way it was for domestic servants, for example, who were framed in many analyses as wayward.

Ryan's work on newspapers in Ireland in the 1920s and 1930s importantly reveals that women's bodies were repeatedly referred to in the context of emigration in national and regional contexts.[51] In her analysis, it is women's *bodies* that are symbolically representative of population failure, economic stagnation, morality, Irishness, Catholicism and, most viscerally, the 'threat of rural depopulation, low marriage rates and falling birth rates'.[52] By reifying purity and morality in women's bodies in the new state, church and state leaders cast their hopes on the success of the new nation also in women's behaviours. When these women left, it may have seemed like hope for the future nation left with them.

NOTES

1. M. Howes, 'Public Discourse, Private Reflection, 1916–70', p.923, in Angela Bourke *et al.* (eds), *The Field Day Anthology of Irish Writing: Volume IV: Irish Women's Writing and Traditions* (Cork: Cork University Press in association with Field Day, 2002), pp.923–930.

2. M. Hill, *Women in Ireland: A Century of Change*, (Belfast: The Blackstaff Press, 2003), p.32.

3. R. E. Kennedy, *The Irish: Emigration, Marriage and Fertility* (Berkeley: University of California Press, 1973), pp.14–15.

4. J. Redmond, 'Sinful Singleness? Exploring the Discourses on Irish Single Women's Emigration to England, 1922–1948', *Women's History Review*, 17, 3 (2008), pp. 455–476.

5. J.H. Whyte, *Church and State in Modern Ireland, 1923–1970*, (Dublin: Gill and Macmillan, 1971), p.31.

6. M. Luddy, 'Sex and the Single Girl in 1920s and 1930s Ireland', p.82, *The Irish Review*, 35, (2007), pp.79–91.

7. Whyte, *Church and State*, p.31. Note that Whyte's figures are taken from the Annual Reports of the Registrar-General.

8. Ibid.

9. Ibid. Whyte suggests that, while the preoccupation with sexual morality in Ireland may have been extreme, it is also the case that this was a trend seen all over the world.

10. Bishop John Hind, *Welfare Work in the Church of Ireland*, pamphlet based on a paper read at the Clerical Society, A. Nelson, Belfast, [no date, c.1944].

11. S. McAvoy, 'The Regulation of Sexuality in the Irish Free State, 1929–1935', p. 253, in E. Malcolm and G. Jones (eds), *Medicine, Disease and the State in Ireland, 1650–1940*, (Cork: Cork University Press: 1999), pp.253–266.

12. The Carrigan Commission is the more commonly used name for the Committee on the Criminal Law Amendment Acts (1880–85) and Juvenile Prostitution which was set up in June 1930 to investigate whether changes were needed in the current Criminal Law Amendment Act.

13. G.C. Spivak, 'In a Word; Interview with Ellen Rooney' in *Outside in the Teaching Machine* (New York: Routledge, 1993), pp.1–24.

14. L. Ryan, *Gender, Identity and the Irish Press, 1922–1937: Embodying the Nation*, (Lewiston: Edwin Mellen Press, 2002), p.1.

15. A. Werner-Leggett, *Being Mary?: Irish Catholic Immigrant Women and Home and Community Building in Harold Hill Essex 1947–1970* (The Hague: Eleven International Publishing, 2012).

16. Redmond, 'Sinful Singleness', pp. 455–6.

17. J. Redmond, 'In the family way and away from the family: examining the evidence in Irish unmarried mothers in Britain, 1920s–40s', p165 in E. Farrell (ed.), *'She Said She was in the Family Way'. Pregnancy and Infancy in Modern Ireland* (London: Institute of Historical Research, 2012), pp. 163–185. For more on the US context of this movement, see R. G. Kunzel, *Fallen Women, Problem Girls: Unmarried Mothers and the Professionalization of Social Work, 1890–1945* (New Haven: Yale, 1993).

18. Ryan, *Gender, Identity and the Irish Press*, p.2. See also B. Gray and L. Ryan, '(Dis) locating "woman" and "women" in Representations of Irish nationality' in A. Byrne and M. Leonard (eds), *Women and Irish Society* (Belfast: Beyond the Pale, 1997).

19. 'Keep Your Daughters at Home', *The Irish Catholic*, 8 August 1936, p.8.

20. 'Notes and Comments' Editorial Column, 15 August 1936.

21. Ibid.

22. 'A Fearful Evil: Archbishop's Warning to Irish Girls', *The Irish Catholic*, 15 August 1936. The article is carried in the main body of the paper as well as in the editorial column.

23. Report on Dr. Gilmartin's Lenten Pastoral, *Irish Independent* 8 February 1937. For further analysis of the Lenten pastorals, see Ryan, *Gender, Identity and the Irish Press*, p.111.

24. 'Catholic Girls Emigrants: Fine Work of Protection Society', *The Irish Catholic*, 24 May 1930.

25. Ryan, *Gender, Identity and the Irish Press*, p.6.

26. J.K. Conway, S.C. Bourque and J.W. Scott, 'Introduction: The Concept of Gender', p.XXIII, *Daedalus*, Vol. 116, No. 4, Learning about Women: Gender, Politics, and Power (Fall,1987), pp.XXI-XXX.

27. D. Ferriter, *Occasions of Sin*, (London: Profile Books, 2009), p.2.

28. T. Inglis, 'Foucault, Bourdieu and the Field of Irish Sexuality', *Irish Journal of Sociology*, 7, (1997), pp.5–28.

29. Ibid., p.5.

30. Ibid.

31. Ferriter, *Occasions of Sin*, p.3.

32. Commission on Emigration and Other Population Problems, *Majority Report*, Chapter 7, Part 2, paragraph 319, p. 137, National Archives of Ireland, DT s14249/ Annexe.

33. James McNeill (Born 1869–Died 1938), was a brother of Eoin McNeill, co-founder of the Gaelic League and first Minister of Education for the first Free State government. James McNeill acted as High Commissioner from 1923 and acted later Governor General of the Irish Free State, replacing Timothy Healy in 1928.

34. For more on the International Catholic Girls' Protection Society and the network of emigrant philanthropy organisations in Ireland and Britain see J. Redmond, 'Safeguarding Irish Girls: Welfare Work, Female Emigrants and the Catholic Church, 1920s–1940s' in C. Delay and C. Brophy (eds), *Women, Reform, and Resistance in Ireland, 1850–1950: Ordinary and Outcast* (New York: Palgrave, 2015).

35. Letter from Mr Sempkins to Irish High Commissioner in London, dated 10 August 1923, 4NVA/04/02 BOX FL098, Women's Library.

36. Catholic Girls' Protection Society, *Annual Report 1938*, Westminster Diocesan Archives, Hi. 2.215 Miscellaneous Societies.

37. Ibid.

38. This is evident in the Westminster Diocese Moral Welfare Committee's involvement in setting up the Repatriation Scheme to return Irish emigrant women who had become pregnant in Ireland (as opposed to Britain). For more on this see L. Earner-Byrne, *Mother and Child: Maternity and Child Welfare in Dublin, 1922–60* (Manchester: Manchester University Press, 2007), Redmond, 'In the family way', and L. Earner Byrne, 'Moral Repatriation: The Response to Irish Unmarried Mothers in Britain, 1920s–1960s' in P. Duffy (ed.), *To and From Ireland: Planned Migration Schemes c. 1600–2000* (Dublin: Geography Publications, 2004).

39. Redmond, 'Sinful Singleness', p.467

40. Memorandum for the Government from the Department of External Affairs, p.4, 30 August 1947, Department of Foreign Affairs files, National Archives of Ireland, DFA 402/25, p. 6.

41. Redmond, 'Sinful Singleness', pp. 465–6.

42. For example, the testimony of Mary Walker (a pseudonym), who talked about fear as a contraceptive is typical of many oral history accounts in their explanations of sexual knowledge and behaviour in twentieth-century Ireland. In C. Dunne, *An Unconsidered People* (Dublin: New Island Books, 2003), p.104.

43. Inglis, 'Foucault, Bourdieu', p.7.

44. J. Butler, *Bodies That Matter: On the Discursive Limits of 'Sex'* (New York: Routledge, 1993), p.xi.

45. Ibid., p.8.

46. Ibid., p.13.

47. M. Foucault, *The History of Sexuality, Vol. 1: An Introduction* (New York: Vintage, 1990), p.139.

48. Conway et al., 'Introduction', p.XXVI.

49. Redmond, 'Sinful Singleness', p.458.

50. For more on the Kirkintilloch tragedy see B. Coghlan, *Achill Island, Tattie-hokers in Scotland and the Kirkintilloch Tragedy, 1937* (Maynooth: Maynooth Studies in Local History, 2006).

51. For a more recent analysis of newspaper journalism in Ireland, see M. O'Brien & F. Larkin (eds), *Periodicals and Journalism in Twentieth-Century Ireland*, (Dublin: Four Courts, 2014).

52. Ryan, *Gender, Identity and the Irish Press*, p.112.

5

'WHENEVER A WOMAN WAS NEEDED': GARDA WOMEN ASSISTANTS IN 1950s DUBLIN[1]

John Johnston-Kehoe

In the mid-1950s four middle-aged widows became 'Garda Woman Assistants': full-time, plainclothes, auxiliaries to the national police, An Garda Síochána.[2] 'Whenever a woman was needed, we were there,' recalled one of the women about the role they served.[3] This chapter examines the employment of these women during the four-year period in which they served as the female adjunct to the Garda establishment in Dublin, before female membership of the Garda was permitted under the Garda Act, 1958. This chapter illustrates how the exclusion of women from membership of the Garda belied the long-established employment of a few women on a full-time, but sub-formal footing. It details how a 'maternal' police role was fulfilled by a few, unofficial female police agents, while feminist lobbyists campaigned for an official female police function, which indirectly threatened the employment of the semi-formal Women Assistants.[4]

The employment of policewomen in Dublin was considered imperative to the continuation of a long-standing practice that young children and teenage girls in police custody be escorted by women. The conveyance of children to institutions under court order was a duty of the Garda.[5] Department of Justice policy, as stated in 1948, was that 'whenever possible, children and young persons are conveyed by women'.[6] This practice seems to have been based on the belief that the custodial care of young children would be more appropriately and effectively attended to by a woman than by a man. Where policemen did perform juvenile escort duty, they did so in plainclothes, and the performance of the work by women was in line with attempts to moderate legal formalities in the direct management of juveniles. Juvenile escort duty was more onerous in Dublin because the rate of committal of children to residential institutions was 'disproportionately high in Dublin', and because most of the schools that were not in Dublin were situated a significant distance away from the city.[7]

Since the First World War period, a small number of plainclothes unofficial policewomen were employed by the police in Dublin on police duties, including escort duty. These women were not technically members of the police, which was constituted as a 'body of officers and men', and they did not have technical police authority.[8] These women had been in full-time police employment since 1917–20, following their service as Women Patrols: volunteer feminist civic patrols organised by the National Union of Women Workers of Great Britain and Ireland (NUWW, later National Council of Women) during the First World War.[9] The NUWW's women patrol scheme was a platform for the entry of women to full-time police employment in Dublin and in several cities in Britain.[10] In addition to escort duty, the policewomen were deployed in 'the detection of begging, the suppression and detection of conduct of an indecent nature, the detection of prostitutes loitering and soliciting for purposes of prostitution, the rendering of assistance in cases such as fortune-telling, shebeening, brothel keeping, indecent exposure, indecent assaults on females and concealment of birth.'[11] In 'cases of indecency in which females were concerned', the policewomen 'accompanied females for examination by the Medical Officers, to and from Courts, and were present during Police investigations and court proceedings'.[12] The policewomen underwent a brief course of training and an exam under the Dublin Metropolitan Police, but it was their gender that was the basis of their employment and the basis on which selected police work was assigned to them.

The role and number of women in policing in the United Kingdom between the 1920s and the Second World War has been characterised as 'static' and 'latent'.[13] Stasis characterised the position of women in policing in independent Ireland during that period. No change to the position of the Dublin policewomen occurred between the transferral of the DMP to the independent government in 1922 and the Garda Act, 1958. The establishment of a small uniformed female police corps in the Garda was supported by Garda Commissioner Eoin O'Duffy in 1930.[14] The proposal was endorsed by a state committee of inquiry concerned with criminal justice reform in 1931, but it was rejected by Government.[15] Gerald Boland, Minister for Justice 1939–48 and 1951–54, told the Dáil in 1944 that he did 'not think women police are needed at all,' and that he had 'no use for them'.[16] The quasi-martial nature of aspects of Garda recruitment and training were affirmed during the 1940s.[17] Stout opposition to an official female police role was the background to the discreet maintenance of a cohort of sub-formal female police in Dublin. By the 1940s, policewomen were a feature of the official establishment of urban police forces in Britain, where, by 1950, there were over 1,300 policewomen.[18] In Northern Ireland, women began to be admitted as members of the Royal Ulster Constabulary (RUC) from 1943.

When an inter-departmental committee conducted a major organisational review of the Garda in 1950, it considered female policing.[19] The committee was established with a cost-saving purpose, but it interpreted its brief in a progressive, technocratic manner, and researched practice in British forces. The report of the committee constituted a blueprint for the reconfiguration of the Garda. It recommended the reduction of the force in the countryside, an increase to the force in Dublin, and the development of motor and communications technologies. It also recommended that a female Garda corps be formed in Dublin. Garda Commissioner Michael Kinnane dissented from important elements of the report, including its recommendation for policewomen, which he sought to relegate until existing (male) recruitment objectives had been met. Kinnane's death in 1952 led to the appointment of another senior civil servant, Daniel Costigan, as Garda Commissioner. Commissioner Costigan requested that the Department prepare legislation to permit the admission of a maximum of 100 women to the Garda.[20] In a publicly reported after-dinner speech, Costigan 'disclosed that "three aids which we have not got in this country – police horses, police dogs, and police women" were "under consideration".[21] However, Minister Boland was not dissuaded from his view that policing was 'a man's job', and the initiative was rejected.[22]

Irish feminist interest in a female police role was sustained during the middle-third of the century. The Joint Committee of Women's Societies and Social Workers (JCWSSW), an umbrella organisation formed in 1935, maintained a vigorous interest in an expanded, regularised police role for women.[23] The JCWSSW may be regarded as a lynch-pin of the 'network of organisations' identified as 'collectively aiming to improve the position of women across Irish society in this period'.[24] It was a consultative and coordinating hub for feminist and welfare interest in a broad range of social and legal issues, including probation, juvenile justice, adoption and succession laws.[25] The JCWSSW's independent, non-denominational identity was significant to its ability to offer critique and present alternative proposals in the sphere of juvenile justice practice, in which a Catholic-State axis predominated.[26]

Mrs Mary Kettle, the moving figure in the JCWSSW, had experience of local electoral politics as a member of Dublin Corporation.[27] Her interest in female police spurred the JCWSSW's activity on the issue.[28] The JCWSSW made representations to Government, generated newspaper correspondence, and advanced the proposal to the inter-departmental inquiry of 1950–51, mentioned above. The renewal of the Joint Committee campaign for policewomen in 1949 was prompted by its awareness of the advancing age and declining number of serving policewomen.[29] One policewoman retired in April 1947, another died in January 1949, and a third died in December 1954.[30] The JCWSSW was probably buoyed by the knowledge that a social welfare organisation, the Belfast Council of Social Welfare, had prompted the Government of Northern Ireland to canvass police opinion on the issue in 1942, which led to the admission of women to the RUC the following year.[31]

'From Mrs Kettle comes a cry for female policemen,' remarked *Irish Times* columnist 'Myles na Gopaleen', in November 1954; a proposal he regarded as 'most unromantic'.[32] The ambit of the JCWSSW campaign broadened to elicit support from local government assemblies in Dublin and elsewhere. Although local government did not directly fund policing in Ireland nor have any executive role in its administration, local government offered a mechanism for leverage in national politics, partly due to commonalities of personnel and political parties at local and national level. Around this time, government posture shifted from outright rejection of the proposal for female police to one of indeterminacy. A recurrent response to parliamentary questions on the subject was that it was 'under consideration'. Boland's successor as Minister for Justice, James Everett of the Labour Party, resisted an initiative by officials in the Department to circulate a memorandum to Government about female police in 1955. This memo catalogued seven parliamentary questions on the subject since 1953.[33] Maureen O'Carroll (Labour), a government backbencher, was a committed advocate of the proposal during her single term in parliament, 1954–57.[34] Notably, unlike other Dublin politicians, such as Colm Gallagher (Fianna Fáil), Celia Lynch (Fianna Fáil), and Maurice Dockerell (Labour), O'Carroll did not confer with the JCWSSW on this, or other issues of common concern, and O'Carroll's posture differed from the principled position of the JCWSSW, as shall be analysed below.[35]

The decline in the number of policewomen in Dublin to a single woman of advanced years by December 1954 impelled the authorities to act. The Garda argued that 'the practical requirements of the police service' demanded that 'the number of women police for this Division should not fall below four for any considerable period'.[36] Four appointments were made between April 1954 and May 1956 under the existing, temporary terms, and its auxiliary basis was emphasised by the title 'Woman Assistant to the Garda'. A Justice official observed that 'the fact that there would be four women available to assist the Garda might help to keep quiet some of the parties who are pressing for the appointment of women Police'.[37] As this suggested, the measure was calculated to diminish the basis for further female recruitment under broader terms. Departmental authorisation for the latter two appointments was conditional on the Garda stating that the four women would perform duties in addition to escort work.[38]

The appointments were made privately by the Garda: 'Only unmarried women or widows would be eligible for appointment'.[39] The recruitment did not occasion any publicity, and the successful applicants were notified of the opportunity to apply. Historians of policing in previous centuries have documented instances in which police wives served their husband's profession in circumstances where social propriety rendered male action fraught or unfeasible.[40] It had been suggested by Garda Commissioner O'Duffy in 1930 that 'the widows of Gardaí would, from their acquaintance with police matters, be particularly suitable' for employment as policewomen.[41] One of the first six RUC Women Constables was the widow of a deceased member of that force. Of the four Garda Woman Assistants, three were widows of deceased members of the force, and a fourth, who was also a widow, was the niece of a serving Detective Garda.

A disinclination to appoint single women as probation officers, station matrons, or policewomen, and a preference to appoint widows, is evident in a number of instances around this period.[42] In the police occupation, as in electoral politics, 'the identity of widows often remained closely linked with that of their deceased husbands'.[43] The adoption of the widows as candidates by political parties following the death of a politician is comparable to the preferment that was shown towards the women employed by the Garda as Women Assistants. Widowhood and motherhood were crucial to the women's occupational identity. The acceptance of the women by the police establishment was largely based on the perception of them as dutiful and trusted affiliates of policemen, as demonstrated in marriage. In the sad circumstances of widowhood, the direct marital affiliation of the three police widows was a basis for their entry to employment. The high degree to which marital affiliation acted as a vehicle for the employment of these women by the police suggest an unusual extension of how, in widowhood, 'her husband's position' and 'the total police structure of thought' would influence a woman's situation.[44] Employment among colleagues of their deceased husbands may have affirmed the women's identity as widows, since at least three of them never re-married or co-habited.[45]

The selection of the Women Assistants and the solidarity between them and their male colleagues, indicated the operation of occupational and political loyalties. The deceased husbands of two of the women had been members of the detective section, and the uncle of a third woman, a serving member of this section, advised her about applying. Those three men were among a group of approximately 390 who were admitted to the Garda between 1933 and 1935, despite their non-compliance with standard recruitment criterion.[46] This cohort, pejoratively referred to as 'Broy Harriers', owed their police careers to their 'republican pedigree' as former militant revolutionaries, recruited by the newly-elected Fianna Fáil Government for armed protective and investigative police duties.[47] Most of the 'Broy Harriers' were directly assigned to the detective section on their recruitment, contrary to Garda convention. The induction of the quartet of Garda Women Assistants in the mid-1950s bears relation to the recruitment of the 'Broy Harriers' in the 1930s, with whom three of the four women were affiliated. A notable difference was that membership of the Garda was not conferred on the irregularly recruited women as had been on the Broy Harrier recruits.

'Does Mrs Kettle intend that the post of policeman should be offered to a married woman?' Myles na Gopaleen teased. 'Is she to be allowed to bring her pram with her while on patrol?'[48] The joke played on the traditional sexual politics of policing but approximated the actual concerns of the Women Assistants. All four women had children of national school age when they entered police work. In three cases, the women were the mothers of 'garda orphans', the children of members of the Garda who died before the children reached maturity. The number of children dependent on a policeman's widow was a principal determinant of the level of the Garda pension paid to her. Maternal status was a qualifying requirement for the non-contributory statutory pension under the Widows' and Orphans' Pensions Act, 1935.[49] A concerted and consistent interest in the welfare and educational progress of 'garda orphans' was exhibited by policemen in home visits and in the conduct of recreational events to entertain and treat them. The notes of the Garda Superintendent who interviewed the women averred to their affection for children: 'Excellent candidate. Fond of children'; and 'Very good candidate. Very fond of children.'[50] But the women were required to demonstrate that they could defray their personal maternal obligations as the exigencies of *occupational* maternalism required. 'My brother and sister have both come to reside in the vicinity, and have undertaken to look after my children in my absence, should I be appointed to this position,' wrote an applicant.[51] The eldest child of one Woman Assistant lived with childless relatives in the west of Ireland from the time of his mother's police employment.[52]

In 1958, the Deputy Commissioner reported that 'the major portion' of policewomen's duty was 'taken up in escorting of juveniles to schools and convents in the city and to various centres in the country', and sometimes to England; work that had been performed 'with entire satisfaction'.[53] Three work notebooks of one of the Women Assistants and the logbook of another, trace their attendance at the Children's Court and their fulfilment of escort duties.[54] Some of the entries illustrate the young age of many of the children escorted, some of whom were infants. Among the schools referred to repeatedly were industrial schools for girls that were certified to receive very young boys: St Joseph's Kilkenny; Clifden, Co. Galway; Tralee, Co. Kerry; and Moate, Co. Westmeath.[55] A prison van transported children ordered to residential institutions from the Children's Court up to October 1951, when a large car began to be used for the purpose.[56] The logbook of one of the policewomen detailed that in the mid-1950s many of the escort journeys to remote schools were by train. Several entries indicate that more than one child of the same family was ordered to an institution. The notebooks suggest that in most of these cases the boys of the family were ordered to one institution, and the girls to another.[57] To the rear of three small notebooks of one of the policewomen are lyrics of stoicism ('Don't Quit'), hope ('Tomorrow's Opportunity'), and fellowship ('The Travellers'). The Women Assistants had a work bag of toys and equipment to care for and occupy the children during long journeys.[58]

No suspicion of the maltreatment of children in residential institutions was uncovered in the personal papers of the Women Assistants, nor were their children aware that their mothers held any such suspicions. Harsh and abusive treatment of children during the 1950s in residential institutions to which children were escorted by the policewomen, such as Tralee, Goldenbridge and Clifden, are documented in the Commission of Inquiry into Child Abuse Report (CICA Report).[59] A deficit of state inspection of the industrial schools is a major theme of the Report, which noted the propensity of school management to temporarily ameliorate conditions on advance knowledge of an inspection.[60] The attitude of Henry A. McCarthy, Judge of the Dublin Children's Court 1941–57, towards the schools has been characterised by the CICA Report as 'somewhat critical'.[61] It remarked that 'from the 1950s [...] the courts displayed a greater reluctance to send children away for long periods and when they did so it was only for shorter terms'.[62] It noted that 'after the high point of the 1940s, the population [of children in industrial schools] declined gradually in the 1950s and more steeply in the 1960s and 1970s'.[63] A social worker told the Commission that her view of the schools in the 1960s was that they were 'safe places where the child would be if not positively cherished at least protected from harm'.[64] But a district court clerk who served in the 1960s advised the Commission that some court officers 'knew about the sexual abuse in the schools because one of the Gardaí who drove the children to the schools told us about it'.[65]

97

The Women Assistants worked in two pairs from 1956, and the pair not on court or escort duty usually performed plainclothes patrol duty of city-centre shopping districts. The Women Assistants became known to the staff of the shops and to the street traders. One of the policewomen's children recalled that her mother sometimes attended street traders' prams to allow them a short break in the comfort that their pram of merchandise was secure.[66] A memoir of Dublin in the 1950s recalled that 'women ran the house and they went to the shops every day. No freezers, no fridges.'[67] 'Self-service' stores, where goods were within customers' reach, rather than behind a counter, became more prevalent in Dublin.[68] If shoplifting or some other offence was detected by the Women Assistants on street patrol, they usually enlisted a male colleague to effect an arrest. To achieve this, it was necessary to shadow the suspect and to draw the attention of a policeman, or use a public phone to call the station to despatch a policeman. Instances of such apprehensions were noted in one Woman Assistant's logbook:

> Patrolled Principle Streets in 'B' Division and visited Woolworths Stores Grafton Street where I observed three Girls taking Articles off the Counter. I kept them under observation for some time as they were coming out the door I asked them to come back with me I searched them and found goods total value £1.14.9 in a Paper Carrier bag which she purchased in the store they admitted taking all the articles and not paying for them they were taken by squad car to College Garda Station and Cautioned in the presence of their mothers by Inspector [named], College Garda Station.[69]

It is difficult to assess the extent to which the Women Assistants participated in the Garda response to sexual crime that involved women or children. Lists of the duties of Garda women referred to 'visiting of picture houses for the purpose of detecting acts of Indecency' and 'private house visits to detect indecency'.[70] The Garda Manual of Criminal Investigation (1946), a guide-book circulated to members, stated that it was 'desirable that another woman should be present' when statements related to sexual crime were to be taken.[71] Thomas O'Malley has written that during the middle-third of the twentieth century in Ireland, the law 'was often little more than an ancillary instrument to be used when other methods failed'.[72] The 'shadow' of unrecorded crime is acute in relation to statistics of sexual crime in Ireland as elsewhere.[73] Of the crime recorded by the Garda as having been reported, a high rate of prosecutions followed.[74] The dominant category of sexual offence, indecent assault, was an indictable offence, but most prosecutions for this offence were disposed of summarily at District Court level, rather than by indictment before a jury. In the period from 1947 to 1960, over 90 per cent of prosecutions for indecent assault recorded by the Garda were disposed of summarily.[75] The Minute Books of Dublin District Court cannot be located, with the exception of the minute books of the Children's Court, which are not open for academic research.[76] Extant court files related to this category of offence seldom refer to the role of policewomen, and even in an incest case referred to below, in which a Woman Assistant assisted in interviewing the victim, no reference to her involvement featured in the court records.

The logbook of one of the Women Assistants records her involvement in the Garda response in two sexual offence cases. In May 1956, 'accompanied by Det. Sgt. [named]' a Garda Woman Assistant 'travelled to St Kevin's Hospital where I assisted in taking a statement from [named girl] age 17 years of [listed south-city address] in relation to an indecent assault charge against her Father of [same address]'.[77] The victim's first report of the matter had been to her local priest. The accused man pleaded guilty at trial, and the sole witness at the trial was the Detective Sergeant.[78] In a second case, in July 1956, the same Woman Assistant 'assisted Sgt [surname] in taking statement from [named woman] age 22 years of [named rural town] whose having being [sic] charged on this day in concealing the birth of her unnamed female child, escorting her to Bridewell Garda Station where she was remanded in custody for 1 week'.[79] At trial in August, the charge was considered proven. The woman was placed on probation for three years. Under the terms of the court order, she spent a year residing in the home of the Woman Assistant that had been involved in the case, where she performed some childcare and domestic work.[80] This constituted a remarkable – and apparently exceptional – departure from the common practice of committal to reside in a convent and comply with convent authority, as an alternative to a term of imprisonment.

'The male police in the cities would prefer that preliminary investigation of sexual offences against females would be conducted by properly-trained women police,' Garda Deputy Commissioner Garrett Brennan wrote in 1950.[81] Brennan considered that 'in the cities, the existence of women police might result in the discovery of more cases than normally comes to light, particularly in the poorer areas where the proportion of undiscovered offences is stated to be high.'[82] Brennan noted that Commissioner Kinnane, did not 'believe that the employment of women police would make the parents of injured children any less reluctant to report these offences'. By mid-century, some officials of the Department of Justice were convinced of the utility of policewomen in this sphere. 'It cannot be denied that the investigation of sexual offences is much less embarrassing and likely to be much more effective when it involves the questioning of women and children if conducted by women police,' a memo of 1950 asserted.[83]

An explicit connection was drawn between the police response to sex crime and the lack of female police by a local politician and lawyer, Gerard B. MacCarthy (Fianna Fáil).[84] MacCarthy told Dún Laoghaire Borough Corporation 'that women police could do great work' as 'they could take depositions and statements from women and children, particularly in a case of an indecent offence when a young girl would naturally be reticent about giving details to a policeman'.[85] MacCarthy 'did not suggest that the Civic Guards were incompetent to deal with such offences, but some of them were just not suitable'.[86] An English newspaper reported that MacCarthy had 'found several cases in which girls who have been attacked have been too embarrassed to tell men police what happened'.[87] In March 1956, Dublin County Council supported MacCarthy's motion for the formation of 'a Women's Branch of the Garda Síochána to deal with certain routine duties and, in particular, with certain other duties which could be more appropriately carried out by women'.[88] JCWSSW records suggest that MacCarthy's interest was prompted by its lobbying of local political assemblies in 1955.[89]

As the admission of women to the Garda became a probability, the Women Assistants became concerned for their jobs. The papers of two of the women include notes of commendation from officers that mainly related to the period 1958–9, which coincided with the introduction of official female membership of the Garda.[90] 'Cases of the escort or removal of babies in arms often arise in the course of their duties, and it is felt that those women, being mothers and therefore experienced in the handling and care of babies, are better suited for this type of work than young girls,' suggested their commanding officer.[91] However, with the arrival of official uniformed policewomen, the Garda Commissioner intended that the Women Assistants be retained only for six months to 'assist the young women police in getting a knowledge of their duties after their allocation for duty in the city'.[92]

Notwithstanding the Commissioner's intention, the political-occupational nexus that had facilitated the selection of the Woman Assistants was mobilised to secure their retention. The 'republican pedigree' of deceased husbands was invoked to sustain the employment of their widows. 'Representations on behalf of the Women Police Assistants in the Dublin Metropolitan Division' were made by two Fianna Fáil Dáil Deputies, one of whom referred to one of the women as the 'widow of late Det. Officer [named], a great friend of mine and an old column man pre-truce & afterward'.[93] The Minister for Justice, their Fianna Fáil colleague Oscar Traynor, was reputed to have 'hand-picked' the first batch of those selected for appointment to the Garda as 'Broy Harriers' in 1933–5.[94] Traynor gave an assurance that 'the position of these Assistants will not be affected by the appointment of women as members of the Garda Síochána'.[95] The women continued to serve at the Dublin Children's Court and to perform escort duties arising from it. One Garda Woman Assistant passed away in 1970. One retired in 1972, and another retired in 1978. In 1983, the last serving Woman Assistant retired.[96]

Support for the employment of sub-formal policewomen such as the Women Assistants varied among those interested in female membership of the police. Maureen O'Carroll, T.D., the leading parliamentary advocate women police supported the policy as an interim measure. She suggested that 'women wardens' be appointed to 'fulfil the many duties essential to the proper handling of women, young girls, and juvenile delinquents' pending the 'establishment of a women's police force'.[97] However, the JCWSSW criticised O'Carroll's suggestion as one that 'in no way meets the case', and contended that without 'the training, authority or status of police officers', the employment of such women would 'only be tinkering with a serious problem'.[98] The actual role performed by the Garda Woman Assistants lay somewhere between those conceptions. In addition to the escort work that was the principal basis for their employment, they regularly performed plainclothes patrol and detection work, and liaised between women and the police in some acute instances. The Women Assistants understood that the campaign championed by Mary Kettle, herself a widow, posed an indirect threat to their employment. However, the sub-formal policewomen remained in employment through the first decades of female membership of the Garda. Ban ghardaí (female gardaí) were few up to the late 1970s, and operated on a circumscribed basis. One feature that had implications for the escort and conveyance of young children by the Garda was that an no ban gharda was authorised to drive. Elements of the sexual politics that had been the basis of female policing in preceding decades, like the Garda Women Assistants, continued to operate for a lengthy period subsequent to technical female membership of the police.

NOTES

1. The author gratefully acknowledges a Government of Ireland Postgraduate Scholarship awarded by the Irish Research Council.

2. An Garda Síochána translates from Gaeilge as 'Guardians of the Peace'. The most recent history of the Garda is Vicky Conway, *Policing Twentieth-Century Ireland: A History of An Garda Síochána* (London: Routledge, 2014).

3. Author's interview with Mrs MB, former Garda Woman Assistant (hereafter GWA), June 2009.

4. Christopher Shepard, 'A liberalisation of Irish social policy? Women's organisations and the campaign for women police in Ireland, 1915–57', *Irish Historical Studies* (November 2009) 36, 4, pp.564–80.

5. *Report of the Committee of Public Accounts for 1927–28*, para. 1451–2.

6. *Report of the Committee of Public Accounts for 1948–49*, para. 359; *Report of the Committee of Public Accounts for 1949–50*, para. 428.

7. Commission to Inquire into Child Abuse, *Report* [hereafter *CICA Report*], (5 vols, Dublin, 2009) IV, pp.226, 237.

8. This was the historical legislative definition of the constitution of the Irish police, affirmed by references to the 'officers and men' of 'the amalgamated force' established by the Police Forces (Amalgamation) Act, 1925.

9. Carmel Quinlan, *Genteel Revolutionaries: Anna and Thomas Haslam and the Irish Women's Movement* (Cork University Press: Cork, 2002), pp.178–83.

10. Philippa Levine, '"Walking the streets in a way no decent woman should": Women Police in World War I', *Journal of Modern History* (1994), 66, pp.34–78; Angela Woolacott, '"Khaki Fever" and its Control: Gender, Class, Age, and Sexual Morality on the British Home Front in the First World War', *Journal of Contemporary History*, April 1994, 29, 2, pp.325–47.

11. Garda Archive, Women Police Box (hereafter GA), Deputy Commissioner to Commissioner, 26 April 1948.

12. GA, Deputy Commissioner to Commissioner, 26 April 1948.

13. Joan Lock, *The British Policewoman: Her Story* (London: Robert Hale, 1979) p.167; Frances Heidensohn, *Women in Control?: The Role of Women in Law Enforcement*

(Oxford: Oxford University Press, 1992), p.40. Louise Jackson, *Women Police: Gender, Welfare and Surveillance in the Twentieth Century* (Manchester: Manchester University Press, 2006) partially revised this characterisation.

14. National Archives of Ireland (NAI), Garda Commissioner's Memorandum to Criminal Law Amendment Committee, H247/41A.

15. NAI, Criminal Law Amendment Committee (1933), H247/41D.

16. Dáil debates, 19 April, 1944.

17. Liam McNiffe, *A History of the Garda Síochána: A Social History of the Force 1922-52, with an overview for the years 1952-97* (Dublin: Wolfhound Press, 1997), pp.57-8.

18. Edith Tancred, *Women Police 1914-1950* (London: National Council of Women, 1951), p.35.

19. NAI, Inter-Departmental Committee of Inquiry into An Garda Síochána, 1950-51, S7989c/2.

20. NAI, Garda Commissioner to Secretary, Justice, 29 December 1952, JUS 4/62/2.

21. *Irish Independent*, 18 November 1953.

22. NAI, Secretary Department of Justice to Minister for Justice, 4 March 1953, with Minister's note of 9 March 1953, JUS 4/62/2; Dáil debates, 22 April, 1953.

23. Caitriona Beaumont, 'Women & the politics of equality: the Irish women's movement, 1930-1943', in Maryann Gialanella Valiulis and Mary O'Dowd (eds), *Women & Irish History. Essays in Honour of Margaret MacCurtain* (Dublin: Wolfhound Press, 1997), p.179.

24. Linda Connolly, *The Irish Women's Movement: From Revolution to Devolution* (Basingstoke: Palgrave, 2002), p.81.

25. Mary Cullen, 'Women, emancipation and politics, 1860-1984', in J.R. Hill, *A New History of Ireland, Vol. VII, Ireland 1921-1984* (Oxford: Oxford University Press, 2003), p.872.

26. *CICA Report*, IV, p.234.

27. Mrs Mary Kettle (née Sheehy), B.A., Chairman of the Dublin Union 1930, Dublin City Councillor 1931-33, Member of the Commission of Inquiry into the Civil Service, 1932-34; daughter of David Sheehy, MP 1885-1918; m. Tom Kettle, MP 1906-1910, d.1916; sister of Hannah Sheehy-Skeffington.

28. NAI, JCWSSW Committee Minute Books, 98/14/5/1-4.

29. NAI, JCWSSW Committee Minute Book, Meeting 30 June 1948, 98/14/5/3.

30. GA, Appointment and Duty of Women Police, A68/234/26.

31. Margaret Cameron, *Women in Green* (Belfast: RUC Historical Society, 1993).

32. *Irish Times*, 5 November 1954.

33. NAI, Department of Justice memo for Minister, 9 November 1955, S16210.

34. Charles Callan and Barry Desmond, *Irish Labour Lives: A Biographical Dictionary of Irish Labour Party Deputies, Senators, MPs and MEPs* (Dublin: Watchword, 2010).

35. NAI, JCWSSW Minute Books, 98/14/5/3–4.

36. GA, Assistant Commissioner 'A' to Commissioner, 30 November 1955, with pencil note by Commissioner, A68/234/26.

37. NAI, Assistant Secretary Justice to Secretary Justice, 20 December 1955, JUS 4/62/1.

38. GA, Assistant Secretary Justice to Commissioner 20 January 1956, and Commissioner's reply 8 February 1956, A68/234/26.

39. NAI, Justice to Secretary Finance, 20 February 1956, JUS 4/62/1.

40. Kealan Elizabeth O'Keeffe, 'Women in An Garda Síochána', unpublished LLM dissertation, University College Cork (2002), p.32.

41. NAI, Minutes of Carrigan Committee, December 1930, JUS 90/4/2.

42. NAI, Justice memo, 12 September 1945, S13727; GA, Matrons in Bridewell, DMA, A 72/29/29.

43. Finola Kennedy, *From Cottage to Crèche: Family Change in Ireland* (Dublin, 2001), p.45.

44. Malcolm Young, 'Police Wives: a reflection of police concepts of order and control', in Hilary Callan and Shirley Ardener (eds), *The Incorporated Wife* (London: Croom Helm, 1984), p.78.

45. Interview with Mr M.M. and Mrs R.C., children of GWA Mrs J.M., October 2009; Interview with former GWA Mrs M.B., June 2009.

46. The Commissioner of An Garda Síochána and Donal J. O'Sullivan, *The Depot. A History of the Garda Síochána Deport at the Phoenix Park, Dublin* (Dublin: Navillus, 2007).

47. Eunan O'Halpin, *Defending Ireland: The Irish State and its Enemies Since 1922* (Oxford: Oxford University Press, 1999), p.116. The term 'Broy Harriers' was a play on the name of Eamon Broy, Garda Commissioner 1933–38, and the name of a Dublin running club.

48. *Irish Times*, 5 November 1954.

49. Lindsey Earner-Byrne, '"Parading their poverty...": Widows in Twentieth-Century Ireland', in Borbála Faragó and Moynagh Sullivan, *Facing the Other: Interdisciplinary Studies on Race, Gender, and Social Justice in Ireland* (Cambridge: Cambridge Scholars Press, 2008), pp.37–8. It was not an essential qualification for contributory pension under the Act.

50. GA, Chief Superintendent Farrell to Commissioner 'A', 27 April 1956, A68/234/26.

51. GA, GWA Mrs T.H. to Deputy Commissioner, 14 January 1956, A68/234/26.

52. Interview with Mr M.B., son of GWA Mrs M.B., April 2009.

53. GA, Chief Superintendent, DMA, 23 August 1958, B.880/58.

54. Private Collection, Notebooks of GWA Mrs T.H., 1954-1960s.

55. *CICA Report*, IV, pp.219–20.

56. Dáil debates, 7 November 1951, cited in *CICA Report*, IV, p.227.

57. Private Collection, Logbook of GWA Mrs M.B.; Private Collection, Notebooks of GWA Mrs T.H. This matter was referred to in *CICA Report*, IV, p.239.

58. Interview with Mr M.M. & Mrs R.C., children of GWA Mrs J.M., October 2009; Interview with Mr M.B., son of GWA Mrs M.B., April 2009.

59. *CICA Report*, I, 9, 'St. Joseph's Industrial School, Tralee'; II, 7, 'St. Vincent's Industrial School, Goldenbridge'; II, 9, 'St. Joseph's Industrial School, Clifden'.

60. *CICA Report*, II, p.416.

61. *CICA Report* IV, p.38. For McCarthy's misgivings, see also *CICA Report*, IV, p.338.

62. *CICA Report*, IV, p.218.

63. Ibid.

64. *CICA Report*, IV, p.236.

65. *CICA Report*, IV, p.235.

66. Interview with children of GWA Mrs J.M., October 2009.

67. Gene Kerrigan, *Another Country: Growing up in 1950's Ireland* (Dublin: Gill & Macmillan, 1998), p.83.

68. *Evening Mail*, 10 June 1954 [advertisement].

69. Private Collection, Logbook of GWA Mrs MB, 21 January 1957.

70. GA, 'Appointment of Women Assistants to An Garda Síochána', December 1953.

71. Major-General W.R.E. Murphy, Manual of Criminal Investigation (1946), p.148.

72. Thomas O'Malley, *Sexual Offences: Law, Policy and Punishment* (Dublin: Round Hall, 1996), p.8.

73. Ian O'Donnell, 'Sex Crime in Ireland: Extent and Trends', *Judicial Studies Institute Journal* (2003), 3, 1, p.95–6.

74. O'Donnell, 'Sex Crime in Ireland', pp.100–1.

75. Garda Commissioner, *Annual Report on Crime*, various years. See also Thomas O'Malley, *The Criminal Process* (Dublin, Round Hall, 2009), pp.257–67.

76. *Report of the Inter-Departmental Committee to establish the facts of State involvement with the Magdalen Laundries* (McAleese Report), 9.13, quoting Department of Justice 11 December 2012 to the Chair; *CICA Report*, V, p.67.

77. Private Collection, Logbook of GWA Mrs MB, 23 May 1956.

78. NAI, County and City of Dublin Circuit Criminal Court Trials Record Book for year 1956, V14/15/4; and Dublin Circuit Court State Files, October 1956, V14/8/17.

79. Private Collection, Logbook of GWA Mrs MB, 26 July 1956.

80. *Irish Independent*, 3 August 1956; and Interview with former GWA Mrs M.B., June 2009.

81. NAI, Deputy Commissioner Brennan to Department of Justice, November 1950, AGO 2002/17/25.

82. A similar association between poverty and sexual deviancy in this period was recalled by one of Jackson's RUC interviewees (Jackson, *Women Police*, p.154).

83. NAI, Note for Minister for Justice, 9 November 1955, S16210).

84. Kenneth Ferguson (ed.), *King's Inns Barristers, 1868–2004* (Dublin: Honorable Society of King's Inns in association with the Irish Legal History Society, 2005), p.235.

85. *Irish Times*, 9 March 1956.

86. *Irish Times*, 16 March 1956, 'Letters'. The Civic Guard was the title of the state police force 1922–3, until its re-constitution as An Garda Síochána in 1923. The *Irish Times* continued to use the former title of 'Civic Guard' to refer to the Garda, although this was not accurate nor an accurate translation of the official gaelic title.

87. NAI, *The People*, 11 March 1956 [cutting], JUS 4/62/2.

88. Fingal County Council Archive, *County Dublin County Council Minutes of Proceedings from 1st April 1955 to 31st March 1956*, p.185: [12 March 1956].

89. NAI, JCWSSW Minute Book, Meetings of 31 March 1955 and 27 October 1955, 98/14/5/3.

90. Private Collection, Papers of GWA Mrs M.B.; Private Collection, Papers of GWA Mrs J.H.

91. GA, Chief Superintendent, DMD, 23 August 1958, B.880/58.

92. GA, Assistant Commissioner to Deputy Commissioner, Dublin Castle, 17 September 1958, B.880/58.

93. NAI, P.A. Calleary, TD, to Minister for Justice, 13 June 1958, JUS 4/62/1; GA, Minister for Justice to Eugene Gilbride, TD, 20 November 1959 [copy], B.880/58. This description suggested the dead man's loyalty to the anti-Treaty, anti-Government side in the Irish civil war, 1921–3.

94. Conor Brady, *Guardians of the Peace* (Dublin: Gill and Macmillan, 1974), p.197.

95. Minister for Justice to Eugene Gilbride,TD, 20 November 1959, [copy], B.880/58.

96. GA, Inspector 'B' District to Chief Superintendent DMA, 14 June 1978, B.880/58; GA, Letter from GWA Mrs J.M., 15 December 1983, B.880/58; GA, GWA Mrs M.C. file.

97. Dáil debates, 24 May 1955.

98. *Evening Mail*, 28 May 1955.

6

SCHOOL-BASED SEX EDUCATION
IN IRELAND, 1996–2002:
THE PUBLIC DEBATE

Elizabeth Kiely

This chapter is derived from a more extensive study, which explored the politics of Irish school-based sex education provision from the 1960s onwards.[1] The first formal programme on Relationships and Sexuality Education (RSE) was introduced in the Irish schooling system in the late 1990s. An Expert Advisory Group, appointed by the Minister for Education, Niamh Bhreathnach, concluded as a result of its audit of formal sex education provision undertaken in Ireland in 1994 that relationships and sexuality education should be a required part of the curriculum in every primary and secondary school.[2] The introduction of the RSE programme stimulated media coverage and an active debate. TV, radio, as well as articles and the letters pages in the print media were key sites which facilitated the expression of public opinion on RSE. An RTÉ radio one programme 'The Godline', which broadcast an RSE panel debate on 21 February 1999 as well as the letters pages of two newspapers *The Irish Times* (1 January 1996–31 December 2002) and the *Irish Examiner* (1 July 1997–31 December 2002) provides the body of material for analysis in this chapter.[3] The key search terms 'Relationships and Sexuality Education' and 'RSE' were used to generate the archive of letters with the help of the newspapers' own online search facilities. Initially each letter was coded according to the criterion if it expressed opposition to the introduction of the programme or support for its introduction. However, it was very evident that in the fusion of sexuality and schooling prompted by the introduction of RSE, an opportunity was presented for programme opponents and proponents to elaborate their own set of regulatory ideals as they related to children, key figures in the production of the nation.

In articulating RSE programme opposition or support, competing discourses or understandings of four different sites (the child, the family, the school and the nation) were put forward in the letters. These were subsequently chosen as four key themes to organise and analyse the data. It is this analysis that is presented in this chapter but with consideration as to how the RSE debate impacted on programme implementation and opened up a space to discourse child and youth sexualities. Firstly, the development of the RSE programme is briefly outlined and its key characteristics elucidated.

THE RELATIONSHIPS AND SEXUALITY EDUCATION PROGRAMME

Prior to the early 1990s, there was no definitive action taken by any Irish government on the issue of school-based sexuality education. Kiernan reported in 1992 that Irish school-based sex education provision ranged from comprehensive programmes in a few Irish schools to limited or no provision in many other schools.[4] That a comprehensive, school-based sex education programme should be put in place was made explicit in the Green Paper in 1992 (Department of Education, 1992).[5] In 1993 the Fianna Fáil/Labour Programme for a Partnership Government (Fianna Fáil, 1993) stated its commitment to providing an adequate and comprehensive programme of sex education for second-level students.[6] This finally happened when in 1994 the Minister for Education Niamh Bhreathnach appointed an Expert Advisory Group, which produced a report calling for a national programme in sex education to be introduced in Irish schools.[7] Relationships and Sexuality Education (RSE) was perceived from the outset as a required part of the primary and post-primary curriculum and a key element of the Social and Personal Health

Education (SPHE) programme. The aims of RSE were identified as helping students to 'understand and develop friendships and relationships'. It set out to advance their 'understanding of sexuality' and to promote 'a healthy attitude to sexuality and to relationships'. It sought to advance students' 'knowledge of and respect for reproduction' and to enable them 'to develop attitudes and values towards their sexuality in a moral, spiritual and social framework'.[8] While the programme was compulsory and it had to be written into the school timetable, schools were allowed to choose what to teach in accordance with a set of resource materials, which consisted of six manuals providing a menu of options for class room lessons. Each manual included only those RSE themes considered appropriate for the developmental age of the targeted student group however, schools were encouraged to embed the programme by looking at how topics might be integrated into the teaching of other subjects where appropriate.[9] Each school was encouraged to develop its own school RSE policy, in accordance with its own school ethos and perceived student needs, to guide the teaching of the programme in that school.

Though very carefully steered from the beginning by programme planners, the introduction of the programme and its early implementation involved some trade-offs and resource commitments to keep religious bodies and the key educational stakeholders on board with programme implementation. For instance an opt-out clause was afforded to parents, who did not wish their children to participate and was also extended to teachers, who did not wish to teach the programme because of conscientious objection. The programme also prompted an extensive and costly in-service teacher training course and a sophisticated support infrastructure to aid its implementation.[10] The programme requirement that each school develop its own RSE policy facilitated religious schools to develop an RSE policy which fit with their particular ethos. As RSE came to be very gradually rolled out throughout the education system from the late 1990s onwards, it generated heated public debate, much of what was played out in the Irish media throughout this period.

DESCRIPTION OF THE ARCHIVE OF LETTERS EXAMINED AND ANALYSED

Of the total number of letters printed in the *Irish Examiner* on the subject of RSE, identified for the period studied, twenty-five were written in opposition to the programme and seven were written in support of the programme's introduction. Of those in opposition, a number of them were written by individuals who acknowledged their organisational affiliation (Positive Action for Children PACh, Parents and Teachers for Real Education PATRE, the Christian Democrats, the National Parent and Teacher Alliance and the National Party).[11] In contrast, of the supporting letters, only one was written by an individual who wrote it on behalf of a Dublin-based reproductive rights group. The period in which most of the letters were printed in the *Irish Examiner* was in the latter half of 1999, which may be explained by a growth in RSE programme activity in this period.[12]

In *The Irish Times*, there were nearly as many letters (16) categorised as having been written in support of the programme as in opposition to it (20), though it is important to point out that many of the contributions made, challenged opinions or points made by other letter writers without directly articulating support or otherwise for the programme. This indicates the extent to which the programme served as a vehicle for competing views about Irish society past and present. There were two letters written from individuals opposed to the programme representing organisations (PATRE, the Irish Family League) and one letter in support of the programme from the CEO of the Irish Family Planning Association.[13] A number of letter writers for and against the programme cited their credentials to contribute and these included parents, teachers, priests, psychologists, school principals and doctors. The majority of the contributions were made in the years 1997 and 1998, which coincided with the most concentrated attention being given to covering the RSE programme by journalists writing in *The Irish Times* as well as an intensive programme of in-service teacher training (1996–8) and the staging of a number of information sessions and public meetings on RSE (1997–8).[14]

COMPETING DISCOURSES ON THE CHILD/STUDENT

One of the key assumptions in letters written in opposition to RSE was that children of primary school age (approximately 4–12 years) were innocent and did not need to participate in a sex education programme. Innocence was presumed and conveyed to be a natural feature of childhood and RSE was a programme which according to one letter writer would 'rob our children of their childhood' or 'rob our youth of their innocence' according to another.[15]

In this context, a programme of sex education was perceived as having the potential to awaken prematurely a sexuality which was latent in the young child, but when awakened became disordered and dangerous. For instance C. wrote 'Many children have already experienced shock, embarrassment and even trauma by insensitive and ill-timed sex instruction' and N. drew attention to the '... conclusive evidence worldwide, to prove that classroom sex education had horrendous effects on children particularly in the latency period between six and twelve years of age'.[16] That sex education should not be given to children because it destroys their innocence is a longstanding discourse in Irish society and concern with the destruction of children's innocence was evident in the discursive opposition to Stay Safe, the Irish child abuse prevention programme introduced in the early 1990s in Irish schools and in more recent years in popular and official discourses concerned with the 'sexualisation' of children.[17] At the same time the ideal of childhood innocence and the discourse of adult protection it invokes has received much more critical attention in literature, particularly as qualitative and ethnographic studies have drawn attention to children's heterosexualised use of playground space, their use of sexual language and their engagement in homophobic and heterosexist harassment.[18] Such studies have challenged assumptions of children as asexual or as individuals with sexualities lying dormant rather they highlight pupil sexual cultures at work and schools as sites where sexualities are actively produced. It has also been argued that in the name of protecting childhood innocence, children's sexual subjectivities tend to be denied or pathologised and parents and other adults' protective action on behalf of children invoked, with at times negative implications for recognition of children's sexual rights and agency.[19] For instance Faulkner argues that with the adult idealisation of and preoccupation with the maintenance of childhood innocence, children are not encouraged or equipped to talk about sexual desire as they experience it or to negotiate risk.[20] In the context of sex education curricula, the protection of children's innocence involves the construction and parcelling out of discrete lessons over time, typically reflecting an 'adult formulated taxonomy of what pupils need to know and when' and obfuscating acknowledgement of students' own needs and experiences as sexual subjects.[21]

In contrast to RSE opponents, RSE programme supporters tended to construct children as sexual subjects. For instance T.C. wrote that receiving sex education 'was merely an acknowledgement of the fact that we are all sexual beings'.[22] Some letter writers argued that childhood innocence was used to keep children ignorant, but that ignorance could result in significant harm to children. For example O' S. viewed the RSE programme as reducing children's susceptibility to being sexually abused, when he wrote 'from whom would parents seek redress if their child suffered sexual abuse, particularly, which the child might have successfully countered, if it had received the relevant instruction via the RSE programme?'[23] The existence of births to teenagers and incidence of HIV among children were sufficient reasons for H. to question if it was right 'to keep young people in the dark in this day and age'.[24] S. also claimed that 'modesty will not protect our children. They must be given the skills and the appropriate language to report immediately such instances [of sexual abuse]'.[25] RSE proponents were more likely to construct children as sexual citizens in their contributions, albeit extending to them a restricted kind of sexual citizenship in the form of access to education and skills for their protection against exploitation and their responsible conduct.

COMPETING DISCOURSES ON THE FAMILY

In an analysis of the development of family policy in Ireland completed as a background paper for the *Commission on the Family Report* in 1998, Tony Fahey identified two contrasting policy paradigms, one which he called 'patriarchal familism' and he presented it as the dominant model up to the 1950s in Ireland. The other was 'egalitarian individualism' which emerged in the 1950s and according to Fahey, had gained ground since.[26] Patriarchal familism, as defined by Fahey, rested on the cultural ideal of family as a solidaristic mini-community, a foundation of social order and individual welfare. Roles for family members were well defined, differentiated and complementary as well as being hierarchically structured along gender and generational lines. Hence, the male household head was the dominant figure in the family household. In Fahey's analysis, public policy decisions as well as Catholic social and moral teaching were significant in elevating this patriarchal model of family life in twentieth-century Ireland. In contrast, with the emergence of Egalitarian individualism in the later part of the twentieth century (from the 1950s onwards) the importance accorded to family roles was reduced and greater significance was attributed to the needs, rights and obligations of individuals within families. According to Fahey, a mix of liberalism, secularism, humanism and feminism provided the ideological underpinnings of this new model. For instance the emergence of gender equality and children's rights as matters for public policy highlighted the ascendance of egalitarian individualism in more recent decades, but as Fahey pointed out, although the principles of this paradigm were more widely accepted, their implications for public policy were not at the time he was writing, fully worked out. Fahey argued that though egalitarian individualism was in the ascendant in family policy in Irish society, many aspects of patriarchal familism retained appeal and the model remained a potent influence.[27]

The assumptions, ideals and depictions about the family and state–family relations which underpinned patriarchal familism, were propagated in anti-RSE contributions. The anti-statist dimension of patriarchal familism was evident when DD. argued that by introducing RSE, 'the state in quiet collusion with select groups and interests has taken a deal of responsibility away from parents'.[28] Ní C. argued that the cross-curricular feature of RSE delivery in schools undermined the effective operation of the opt-out clause extended to parents, who did not wish their children to participate and essentially made 'a mockery of parents' rights'.[29] C. wrote 'For anybody outside of our family, to intrude into our family relationships in intimate matters, is totally unacceptable' and H. informed parents that if they wished to withdraw their children from RSE instruction in school that they had 'every right to do so'.[30] O' Flynn's anti-RSE letter constructed children as the property of their parents when she wrote 'remember parents, your children are yours and yours alone. You try to give them food for their bodies, remember their minds are much more important. ... Tell them what they need to know in the liberal world of today'.[31] W. was apprehensive that the RSE programme signalled a move too far away from familism towards individualism reflected in the promotion of a model of childhood autonomy underpinned by state protection: 'the notion of [parental] care and protection has almost gone in favour of the fatal illusion of children's autonomy together with state protection'.[32] McN also wrote about what she perceived as the dangers of individualism being promoted by a value relativist programme like RSE, which she likened to a child is being told '"Do your own thing darling" while he or she walks over a cliff'.[33] The patriarchal family based on marriage was idealised in contributions, which were critical of RSE for not placing enough emphasis on the marital union and for not being sufficiently condemnatory of lifestyles and practices, which fell outside of the patriarchal familist domain. MacK. argued that the unwanted outcome of RSE would be 'mums, unmarried, loads of' and O'S urged educators to 'teach more about marriage and the full-time care babies need, not just how to get pregnant'.[34]

Proponents of RSE tended to put less faith in parents abilities to carry out their responsibilities in the private sphere and they were much less likely to romanticise Irish family life then or in the past as idyllic. T. rather sarcastically responded to C.'s letter when she wrote that she hoped 'the sun always shines for her, up in *Seventh Heaven* on *Walton's Mountain*' but that RSE was needed in the real world where real families lived.[35] While some highlighted teenage pregnancies as evidence of parents' failings as sex educators and as justification for schools role in RSE, other letter writers thought it was important that the RSE programme be delivered in a manner that was sensitive to the needs of children and respected each child's family unit, regardless of its form.[36] Pro-RSE advocates unlike RSE opponents, tended not to argue for a revitalisation of patriarchal family values, though they were not necessarily supportive of alternative family forms either. Rather they viewed RSE as a more reliable and superior disciplinary technology than that which could be exercised in families. It could make up for those parents failing in their duties because it was delivered in school where students are a captive audience.

COMPETING DISCOURSES ON SCHOOLING

The school as an appropriate site for sex education generated conflicting views. Letter writers opposed to the RSE programme articulated their resistance to any kind of sex education being imparted in the school context. For instance T. wrote 'There is no right way to give explicit sex education in a classroom setting'.[37] K. was concerned that because children learn skills which they are expected to practice (e.g. reading, writing and spelling) in school 'it would follow that for them sex education is also for now, not for the future'.[38] Indeed ideas that providing sex education encourages sexual activity or that it is proven to be effective or ineffective are also persistent and are supported or challenged by findings of studies on the impact of sex education instruction on students, which tend to be mixed.[39] Reductions or increases in the 'problems' associated with children's sexualities (e.g. teenage pregnancy) tend to be attributed to the success or otherwise of sex education provision.[40]

Pro-RSE contributors recognised the positive features of the classroom setting for sex education lessons. For instance T.C. argued that 'the group setting of a school is ideal for reinforcing standards and utilising peer support', opportunities which were limited in the family setting.[41] RSE opponents tended to valorise the common-sense knowledge of parents and their intimate relationship with their children to argue that sex education should stay within the private family domain. For instance McK. used a food analogy to make her appeal to parents to resist RSE. She argued that if a team of well-trained chefs were to go around to schools, they would make parents feel inadequate as food providers, but she reminded parents that '...we know that most of the time most parents are able to provide food, it may be rough and ready as part of our work as parents. That analogy holds true for RSE. We, the parents love and care for our children and we are able to help our children in these areas simply because we are parents'.[42] Similarly K. argued that sex was not such '...a complicated matter that it takes the whole 13 years of school life to impart it', rather it should be left to parents, which by comparison to a lengthy school-based programme, is much more expedient and practical.[43] One contributor highlighted that teachers' expertise was in imparting discrete subject knowledge not sex education and '...that teachers just don't want to spend their time in a classroom discussing sex with children'.[44] In contrast, K., a teacher, drew the activity of RSE inside teachers' professional competence and he advised parents to '...trust teachers' who he claimed were working with them in imparting RSE, not against them.[45]

RSE proponents tended to cast doubt on parents' abilities to consistently respond to children's sex education needs and thus, their contributions were more likely to validate teacher knowledge, professionalism and competence above that of parents, who were at times constructed as ignorant, incompetent and careless. C. asserted that 'not all children are fortunate enough to have clear-headed parents, who are completely comfortable with all aspects of sexuality, a reality made manifest by commonplace examples of ignorant remarks', and H. wrote 'Is it not better that children are educated about sex from teachers who can give them the facts in a delicate and educating manner?'[46] The resource materials distributed to schools to guide teachers delivering the RSE programme, which included a list of supplementary materials, were likened by one anti-RSE contributor to the kind that 'only a sadist or a psychopath might be able to feign comfort with'.[47] Similarly, another contributor objected to 'at least one grossly objectionable pro-abortion book cited as a resource for junior cert'.[48] The employment of defensive techniques by teachers who wish to avoid parent upset or controversy in an area like sex education, which is perceived 'risky' as well as the fear of any whiff of controversy, which pervades school communities has been documented in the literature on sex education.[49] Presumably in the event that they would not succeed in achieving programme withdrawal their ultimate goal, anti-RSE contributors sought to exercise some control over teachers' use of resources, their scripts and classroom interactions. Notwithstanding some significant barriers impacting on RSE implementation, there is evidence of slow implementation of RSE and indicators of defensive RSE teaching at work, which may in some small part, be attributable to the publicity achieved by RSE opponents.

COMPETING DISCOURSES ON THE NATION

Discursive differences were evident in the letters pages, which related to the perceived origins of the RSE programme and the success (or otherwise) of similar programmes in other jurisdictions. These generated another competing discourse about the 'imagined community' of Ireland, as articulated by pro and anti-RSE proponents.[50] RSE opponents presented the programme as a creation of the International Planned Parenthood Federation and its affiliate the Irish Family Planning Association. Ní C. claimed that the Minister for Education was 'helping to further the agenda of International Planned Parenthood' an organisation which 'supported abortion, contraception, sterilisation and perverted sexual practices'.[51] Similarly M. argued that the RSE programme and its materials were 'the pernicious products of the International Planned Parenthood Federation (and its affiliate, the Irish Family Planning Association) aided and abetted by the Irish Education and Health Departments'.[52]

Proponents of RSE contested the notion that RSE was not an Irish programme. For instance, F. welcomed the programme and viewed it as the product of the coming together of different representative bodies in Irish education.[53] Anti-RSE contributors presented themselves as protectors of an Irish way of life, which they perceived to be under threat by the introduction of foreign secularist programmes like RSE. Ní C. posed the question in her letter on RSE: 'Now that we have entered the post-Christian era in Ireland, must we be apologetic for being grateful and proud of our Irish Christian heritage?'[54] O' M. railed against the convergence of culture and lifestyle characteristic of a more globalised world, of which RSE was yet another marker: 'It seems that Americanism has completely swamped our people so that all we do, say and think in the big cities and towns is under American influence.'[55] Anti-RSE proponents selected some countries with longstanding sex education programmes such as the US and Britain as having active, excessive, promiscuous and dangerous sexualities and they issued apocalyptic warnings as to what would happen in Ireland. O'F pleaded with parents in Ireland to familiarise themselves with RSE because 'so many other countries where this type of programme has been introduced have found themselves – with an increase in crime, violence, promiscuity, teenage pregnancies, venereal diseases etc. Don't accept "assurances" that the Irish RSE programme is not like those in other countries. It is like them.'[56] In a significant number of letters written by those opposed to RSE, certain social problems served as potent metaphors for the destruction of the social fabric, which would result from the teaching of RSE. By equating the 'outside' with the proliferation of such social problems, the 'inside' or the familial nation was constructed as the space of heterosexual normalcy in need of protection.

However, letter writers in support of RSE countered arguments that school-based sex education produced disastrous results in other countries. T.C., who explained she was a dual American and Irish citizen, advocated for the programme on the basis of the perceived benefits of school sex education in the US: 'In the US ... the schools near us do an admirable job of giving students the understanding needed to make them morally responsible teenagers, as well as giving them enough knowledge to assist in making confident decisions about right and wrong. Do Irish children deserve less?'[57] The 'imagined community' of Ireland constructed in anti-RSE contributions was challenged in other letters.[58] It was argued that the social problems projected on to other countries existed in Ireland and P. cited statistics in evidence: 'With 60 teenagers under 16 giving birth and 26 cases of HIV in children under 12, we simply cannot afford not to give our youngsters sex education.'[59] References to the existence of clerical abuse and sexual abuse within families in pro-RSE contributions in a sense exposed Irish society's underbelly, which was used to counter the assumption that Irish society was morally superior any time in its history. They disputed the binary oppositions in anti-RSE letters of insider / outsider, safety / dangerousness, health / disease, sexual normalcy /

sexual abnormality.[60] The existence of the pregnant teenager or the child with sexual infection inside Irish boundaries justified the need for a disciplinary technology such as RSE according to its proponents.

CONCLUSION

It remains difficult to assess the impact of this public debate on RSE and its implementation. While there are indicators of defensive teaching and teacher discomfort with the teaching of the programme and the rate of implementation has been slow over time, undoubtedly this cannot all be attributed to the public debate the programme generated in the 1990s and early 2000s. Mark Morgan in his evaluation of programme implementation, which at the time was very tardy, found that teachers gave much less importance to 'vigorous objections by people against RSE being part of the curriculum' than other factors such as the overcrowded curriculum in explaining what hindered RSE implementation.[61] O' Carroll and Szalacha, who in their study of RSE, made reference to a teacher who thought it her best option not to cover anything about sexual orientation, because otherwise she would have to present the Catholic Church's official teaching on homosexuality, a requirement in a school with a Catholic ethos or run the risk of getting into trouble.[62] They found it extremely difficult to identify any school addressing the topic on sexual orientation. Their research led them to express the view that 'the extent of opposition to the RSE programme is impossible to determine, but clearly it is active and will have an impact on the implementation of the programme.'[63] Another study of implementation identified a number of significant facilitators and barriers to RSE implementation in schools, which could not be directly attributed to the public debate on RSE, because it happened more than ten years previous.[64] However, teacher discomfort was identified as a barrier connected to factors including fears about parents' views or misgivings about RSE and their anxieties about what can be safely addressed. In a study of SPHE and RSE implementation, which surveyed students and was conducted by Dáil na nÓg (Irish Youth Parliament), delegates found even lower rates of implementation at post-primary level than in other studies.[65] The main recommendations put forward by survey participants were mandatory RSE classes and a wider curriculum, with more detailed coverage of topics and better trained teachers to deliver RSE. It is interesting that 'Understanding sexual orientation' was found to be the least emphasised theme in the RSE curriculum according to students surveyed.

As shown in this chapter, the RSE programme generated considerable attention, particularly in the print news media. The letters pages of newspapers provided an obvious target for anti-RSE proponents to present their concerns in the public sphere and to galvanise any opposition to the programme that might be present in the wider society. Opposition to RSE never succeeded in forcing programme withdrawal, which was the intention of those opposed to the programme. Anti-RSE contributions prompted reaction from those, who took issue with arguments made and who succeeded in ensuring that pro-RSE arguments also found their way into the public repertoire to exert influence. Though I characterised contributions as anti- or pro-RSE, this categorisation is problematic to the extent that a perspective on RSE was not always proffered, rather it served as a vehicle in many instances for the expression of competing views on the child, the family, the school and the nation. Indeed many letter-writers may not have been familiar with anymore than the broad outline of the programme but could still have made contributions under the rubric of RSE.

What is worthy of note, is that none of the letters included in the corpus analysed showed any signs of the emergence of a radical counter-discourse, capable of dramatically transcending the limits set by either anti-RSE or pro-RSE contributions. For example, there was nothing in letters favourable to the programme's introduction to suggest that anything other than nominal improvements of a regulatory kind was envisaged as a result of programme participation. In letters promoting or advocating for RSE, an increase in sexual knowledge was considered important for the purpose of reducing sexually transmitted infections and pregnancies among young people. Dominant constructions of sexuality for the most part remained uncontested in letters and there was no indication that the programme's value was perceived in the potential it might have to open up spaces for students to explore limited sexual subjectivities and their associated practices. The consistent message from both sides of the RSE debate was that sexually responsible, heterosexual citizens had to be produced with the help of RSE, even if there were variations in the definitions of such citizens and different perspectives on their production.

NOTES

1. E. Kiely, '"Sexing the Curriculum"; A Poststructuralist Interrogation of the Politics of Irish Sexuality Education 1960–2002' (PhD Thesis in Social Policy, University College Cork, 2004). This study, supported by the Irish Research Council, drew extensively on poststructuralism, which ascribes a crucial role to discourse and its connections with forms of power and it employed critical discourse analysis to provide the tools to explore these connections. For more discussion of poststructuralism, see M. Peters, *Poststructuralism, Politics and Education* (Connecticut and London: Bergin and Garvey, 1996) and for an account of critical discourse analysis, see S. Titscher, M. Meyer, R. Wodak and E. Vetter, *Methods of Text and Discourse Analysis* (London: Sage, 2000).

2. Government of Ireland, *Report of the Expert Advisory Group on Relationships and Sexuality Education* (Dublin: Stationery Office, 1995).

3. I commenced the search from the date each online newspaper archive was launched, hence the different starting date for each newspaper search. However, after finding and reading a number of other letters on RSE on microfilm held in the library in University College Cork, the different starting date did not seem to raise any issues worthy of consideration.

4. K. Kiernan, 'School Sex Education in Ireland – Towards a Feminist Perspective' (M.Phil Thesis in Women's Studies, Trinity College Dublin, 1992).

5. Department of Education, *Education for a Changing World* (Green Paper) (Dublin: Stationery Office, 1992) p.131.

6. Fianna Fáil, *Fianna Fail, Labour Programme for a Partnership Government 1993–1997* (Dublin, 1993) p.31.

7. Government of Ireland, *Report of the Expert Advisory Group*, 1995.

8. Ibid., p.17.

9. See Kiely, 'Sexing the Curriculum' p.170.

10. RSE involved the most extensive and costly in-service teacher training course ever undertaken in the state up to this period, see J. Walshe, *A New Partnership in Education: From Consultation to Legislation in the Nineties* (Dublin: Institute of Public Administration, 1999). An RSE training support service was established at Drumcondra Education Centre and an RSE co-ordinator and ancillary staff appointed. There existed an RSE implementation group and a project management

group. For a more extensive account of RSE infrastructure, see Kiely, 'Sexing the Curriculum', p.200–2.

11. The National Party was a minor political party founded in 1995 by Nora Bennis, an active Catholic conservative campaigner and it later became known as the Christian Democrats. This party is now inactive and it never exercised any electoral success. Little is known about the other organisations, which were undoubtedly Catholic conservative in motivation and seemed to organise specifically against the introduction of RSE in Irish schools.

12. The growth in RSE programme activity was noted by Mark Morgan, *Relationships and Sexuality Education, An Evaluation and Review of Implementation* (Dublin: Stationery Office, 2000).

13. The Irish Family League is a Catholic conservative group, which was relatively active in the 1980s and it organised to oppose anything perceived to threaten its vision of Irish society as a Catholic society for Catholic people. The Irish Family Planning Association, a national voluntary organisation, was initiated in 1969 when a number of health professionals came together in an inconspicuous manner to provide more comprehensive family planning services than what was on offer from Catholic controlled clinics in Irish maternity hospitals. It has subsequently developed its services and became a strong campaigner for the extension of women's reproductive rights in Ireland.

14. See Kiely, 'Sexing the Curriculum', p.228.

15. J., *The Irish Times*, 14 May 1997; T., *The Irish Times*, 10 March 1999.

16. *Irish Examiner*, 29 April 1999; *The Irish Times*, 30 March 1998.

17. See Kiely 'Sexing the Curriculum', p.157 for evidence of this and E. Kiely, D. Ging, K. Kitching, M. Leane, G. Harold and C. Keane, Report on the Commercialisation and Sexualisation of Children, An Exploratory Study, (Ireland: commissioned by the Department of Children and Youth Affairs, Ireland, forthcoming).

18. See, for example, Walsh, S. 'A Different Kind of Learning: Relationships and Sexuality Education', *Irish Educational Studies*, 18, (1999), pp.223–33; A. Wallace A. and J. VanEvery, 'Sexuality in the Primary School', in *Sexualities*, 3, 4 (2000), pp.409–23; see E. Renold, *Girls, Boys and Junior Sexualities* (Oxford: Routledge Falmer, 2005).

19. R.D. Egan and G.L. Hawkes, 'The Problem with Protection: Or Why We Need to Move Towards Recognition and the Sexual Agency of Children', *Journal of Media*

& *Cultural Studies* 23, 3 (2009) pp.389–400; J. Faulkner, 'The Innocence Fetish: The Commodification and Sexualisation of Children in the Media and Popular Culture', in *Media International Australia*, 135, (2010), pp.106–17. K.H. Robinson, 'Difficult Citizenship: The Precarious Relationships Between Childhood, Sexuality and Access to Knowledge', *Sexualities*, 15 No. 3/4, (2012), pp.257–76.

20. Faulkner, 'The Innocence Fetish', 2010, p.115–16.

21. M.J. Kehily, *Sexuality, Gender and Schooling, Shifting Agendas in Social Learning* (Routledge Falmer, London, 2002).

22. *The Irish Times*, 8 August 1997.

23. *The Irish Times*, 6 June 1998.

24. *Irish Examiner*, 14 March 2000.

25. *Irish Examiner*, 20 October 1998.

26. T. Fahey, 'Family Policy in Ireland – A Strategic Overview, Background Papers for the Commission on the Family', *The Commission on the Family, Final Report to the Minister for Social, Community and Family Affairs, Strengthening Families for Life* (Dublin: Government of Ireland, 1998), pp.384–403.

27. Fahey, 'Family Policy in Ireland', p.386.

28. *Irish Examiner*, 5 February 2000.

29. *The Irish Times*, 8 May 1997.

30. *Irish Examiner*, 29 April 1999 and *Irish Examiner*, 13 December 1999.

31. *Irish Examiner*, 19 September 1999.

32. *The Irish Times*, 24 October 1998.

33. *The Irish Times*, 3 February 1999. Anti-RSE contributors viewed the RSE programme to be value relativist because they argued that it did not do enough to state what was right and wrong in accordance with Catholic moral precepts.

34. *The Irish Times*, 23 June 1997 and *Irish Examiner*, 23 March 1999.

35. *Irish Examiner*, 6 May 1999 and 6 April 1999. 'Seventh Heaven' and 'The Waltons' are two American TV dramas where families confront challenges and tribulations but overcome them to become stronger and more united. Both programmes could be perceived as romanticising family life.

36. C., *The Irish Times*, 30 May 1997 and S., *Irish Examiner*, 20 October 1998.

37. *The Irish Times*, 20 March 1999.

38. *The Irish Times*, 18 August 1997.

39. See, for example, P.A., Cavazos –Rehg, M.J. Krauss, E.L. Spitznagel, M. Iguchi, M. Schootman, L. Cottler, F.A. Grucza, L.J. Beirut, 'Associations Between Sexuality Education in Schools and Adolescent Birthrates, A State-Level Longitudinal Model', *Archives of Pediatrics and Adolescent Medicine*, 166, 2 (2012), pp.134–40.

40. For example, in discussing the results of a study commissioned by a pharmaceutical company of persons in Ireland between the ages of 18 and 45 years, which revealed a low rate of contraceptive use and a high degree of sexual risk taking, Katherine Holmquist, a journalist asked 'where is all this supposed sex education getting us?' and she also cited a representative from Cherish, who claimed that '...the RSE programmes in schools are obviously not working'. See K. Holmquist, 'Tendency to Take Chances on Pregnancy is Alive and Well', *The Irish Times*, 24 November 2001.

41. *The Irish Times*, 8 August 1997.

42. RTÉ radio programme 'The Godline' broadcast on the 21 February 1999.

43. *The Irish Times*, 18 August 1997.

44. B., *The Irish Times*, 28 August 2000.

45. *The Irish Times*, 16 May 1997.

46. *The Irish Times*, 19 August 1997 and *Irish Examiner*, 14 March 2000.

47. D.D., *Irish Examiner*, 5 March 1999.

48. D.H., *Irish Examiner*, 12 January 2000.

49. See, for instance, D. Cooper 'Governing Troubles: Authority, Sexuality and Space', *British Journal of Sociology of Education*, 18, 4 (1997), pp.501–17, and D. Epstein 'What's in a Ban? The Popular Media, Romeo and Juliet and Compulsory Heterosexuality', in D.L. Steinberg, D. Epstein and R. Johnson (eds), *Border Patrols, Policing The Boundaries of Heterosexuality* (London: Cassell, 1997) pp.183–203. Both highlight and discuss the case of one school in London which because of the actions of the principal, generated media attention and public controversy. See M.H. Whatley, 'Whose Sexuality is it Anyway?', in J.T. Sears (ed.), *Sexuality and The Curriculum* (New York: Teachers College Press), pp.78–84 and B.N. Trudell, *Doing Sex Education, Gender Politics and Schooling* (New York: Routledge, 1993) who both discuss the impact of the Moral Right on teachers who engage in self-censorship, defensive teaching and narrowing sex education content to avoid controversy.

50. B. Anderson, *Imagined Communities: Reflections on the Origins and Spread of Nationalism* (London: Verso, 1983).

51. *The Irish Times*, 8 May 1997.

52. *Irish Examiner*, 16 December 1999.

53. *The Irish Times*, 3 May 1997.

54. *The Irish Times*, 5 June 1997.

55. *Irish Examiner*, 10 April 2000.

56. *The Irish Times*, 28 May 1996.

57. *The Irish Times*, 8 August 1997.

58. F., *The Irish Times*, 3 May 1997; P., *Irish Examiner*, 16 December 1999.

59. *Irish Examiner*, 16 December 1999.

60. Binary oppositions as associated with the writings of Jacques Derrida, form the basis of Western thought systems. They exist in violent interdependence, as one term is the primary or dominant one and the other, through its opposition, the secondary or subordinate one. The process of deconstruction can involve reversing or disrupting binary oppositions. See J. Derrida, *Positions* (Trans. A. Bass) (Chicago: University of Chicago Press, Chicago, 1981).

61. Morgan, *Relationships and Sexuality Education*, p.46.

62. I. O' Carroll and L. Szalacha, *A Queer Quandary: The Challenges of Including Sexual Difference Within The Relationships and Sexuality Education Programme* (Dublin: LOT/ LEA, 2000).

63. O' Carroll and Szalacha, *A Queer Quandary*, p.30.

64. P. Mayock, K., Kitching and M. Morgan, *RSE in the Context of SPHE: An Assessment of the Challenges to Full Implementation of the Programme in Post-Primary Schools* (Dublin: Crisis Pregnancy Agency, 2007).

65. S. Roe (in co-operation with Dáil na nÓg), *Life skills matter not just points: A survey of implementation of Social, Personal and Health Education (SPHE) and Relationships and Sexuality Education (RSE) in second-level schools* (Dublin: Office of the Minister for Children and Youth Affairs, 2010).

7

BREAKING THE SILENCE: PRO-CHOICE ACTIVISM IN IRELAND SINCE 1983

Mary Muldowney

This chapter will consider the change in Irish attitudes to abortion from the perspective of pro-choice activists in the various campaigns on the issue that took place between 1983 and 2002.[1] It will present extracts from oral history interviews with people who participated in the Anti-Amendment Campaign in 1983, the widespread protests about the X Case in 1992 and the campaigns associated with the 1992 and 2002 Referenda, as well as campaigns on other 'hard cases' and various initiatives to promote the inclusion of abortion in reproductive health services in Ireland. The socially conservative forces that were so influential in 1983 have mainly modified their agendas to coincide with public sympathies or have retreated from the stage. To what extent that can be attributed to the efforts of the campaigners featured in this chapter will be considered. While it is not manifest that the Irish people would be ready yet to overturn the Eighth Amendment to the Constitution in order to allow the legalisation of abortion services in Ireland, what is demonstrated by successive Referenda and opinion polls is that Irish political leaders have been considerably less compassionate than the voters in their response to women with crisis pregnancies.

ABORTION AND CONTRACEPTION IN IRELAND
BEFORE 1983

The 1983 Referendum on abortion followed nearly a quarter century of unprecedented economic, political and social change in Ireland. The 1950s witnessed the real start of the transformation of the Irish population from being predominantly rural to mainly urban with 60 per cent of the population living in large towns and cities at the end of the twentieth century. The 1960s saw the introduction of various modernising influences such as television, free secondary education and a much faster pace of internal migration from the countryside to Dublin. It was not until the 1970s that Ireland began to see the pace of social change really start to speed up, but women's reproductive rights were not high on many agendas.

> I suppose pro-choice politics and campaigning only really appeared in Ireland in about 1980. Prior to that there had been individuals, most notably, Noel Browne, the Labour and subsequently the Socialist Labour Party TD[2] who did on several occasions call for what he described as therapeutic abortion to be available in Ireland but no, essentially it wasn't an issue that was talked about and didn't really figure onto anybody's radar until 1980 when a small group formed in Dublin, the Women's Right to Choose Group, with the intention of beginning to break the silence and force the issue into the public domain.[3]

Many of the older pro-choice activists had previously been involved in campaigns for the legalisation of contraception,[4] among other social justice issues.

The legal situation forced the adoption of a range of imaginative measures to get around the law. In 1971 members of the Irish Women's Liberation Movement travelled by train from Belfast to Dublin in the so-called 'Contraceptive Train' initiative so that they could consciously break the law and draw attention to the issue.

The tactic of breaking the law; this probably sounds bizarre now but I was at the opening of this thing on the contraception issue. It kind of reached a log jam in, I think it was 1977 or 1978 in that contraception was becoming more widely available but it was still strictly illegal. You had these inventive but strange procedures going on in the clinics in Merrion Square.[5] Where you'd go down there, they always had a supply of pencils which were very expensive pencils and depending on the particular pencil you got, you got the right contraceptives and condoms and whatever because it was illegal to sell contraceptives but legal to buy them.[6]

Contraceptives that were illegal in the Republic of Ireland could be legally purchased across the Border in Northern Ireland. Sandra was born in Belfast but she and her husband moved to Cork in the 1970s.

When I was in College people were always asking about contraceptives and could you bring them from the North. When I came here I was on the Pill and I brought it with me; you know I'd get six month's supply and I'd bring it down.[7] Then when I had my first child I realised that all you had to do was ask the doctor for a prescription [laughs].[8]

In 1979, Charles Haughey was Minister for Health when he introduced the Health (Family Planning) Act 1979 that made contraceptives available (by medical prescription only) 'for the purpose, bona fide, of family planning or for adequate medical reasons'. It gave physicians and pharmacists who had moral objections to contraception the right to refuse to write prescriptions or to fill them.

It was an era when teachers in schools were being discriminated against and in a couple of cases actually lost their jobs on account of their personal relationships or marital circumstances.[9] ... It was also the era in which legislation was introduced by Charlie Haughey that would allow you to get condoms on prescription and this was heralded as a great advance. ... I think it was probably the first – it's gone into the vernacular since – but I think it was the first time you had that phrase 'An Irish Solution to an Irish Problem' being used at the time.[10]

THE 1983 'PRO-LIFE' REFERENDUM

The process of industrialisation in Ireland in the second half of the twentieth century was accompanied by increasing urbanisation and demographic change. The growth of modern media, particularly television, improved communications, increased foreign travel, greater employment opportunities for women and expanded education all contributed to major cultural change.[11] The forces that influenced the holding of the 1983 Referendum and the embedding of the anti-abortion position in the Constitution have often been portrayed as the assertion of traditional values in the defence of Irish culture. The role played by the Catholic Church and its devotees was an intrinsic element of that defence. Archbishop Kevin MacNamara of Dublin was the author of a pamphlet published as part of the Pro-Life Amendment Campaign's literature:

> A vote in favour of the Amendment (i.e. a 'Yes' vote) will be a vote that some unborn children in the future will not be put to death, but allowed to be born and live. A vote against the Amendment, or failure to vote at all, will be – whether one intends it or not – to opt for leaving the existing legal protection of the unborn child at risk, and open to an unrelenting and ever-increasing attack.[12]

The anti-Amendment campaigners were portrayed and for the most part saw themselves as the harbingers of a more open, liberal society in which traditional authority figures would be replaced by political representatives who thought outside the old certainties of nationality and religion. The debate about abortion that still continues is now much more about the practicalities than the principles but the issue is still central to any analysis of women's status in twenty-first-century Ireland. The referendum result in 1983 suggests that an overwhelming majority of the electorate rejected abortion, which had been presented to them as inherently evil, anti-Catholic and there were even suggestions that it was anti-Irish. A 1981 banner featured the slogan 'the abortion mills of England grind Irish babies for blood that cries to the Heavens for vengeance' reinforcing the notion of Irishness as encompassing moral rectitude, from which women were tempted to stray by alien forces.

Within I'd say two weeks of coming to live in Cork someone asked me if I knew how to get an abortion, where to go to get an abortion. It was somebody I'd met and they asked me, I think it was for their daughter, and it was all very hush, hush but the assumption was that because I was English that I must know all about these things and I found that quite shocking too.[13]

The 1983 pro-amendment campaign was conducted on emotive lines that played effectively to an electorate that was still operating within a framework shaped by the Catholic Church's influence on the legislature.

Several of the interviewees referred to the ambivalence of some campaigners on the substantive issue and the reluctance to discuss abortion openly. Open Door Counselling had been offering advice and referrals to abortion clinics in England since 1980[14] but there was no clear demand for abortion rights and the focus of the Anti-Amendment Campaign was simply on securing a rejection of the Eighth Amendment, in which it was notably unsuccessful.[15] Table 1 shows the final results.

Table 1. 1983 Referendum Results, 7 September 1983.
Referendum on Eighth Amendment of the Constitution Bill 1982
(The Right to Life of the Unborn).

Total electorate	Total poll	Percentage poll	For the proposal	Against the proposal	Spoiled votes
2,358,651	1,265,994	53.7	841,233	416,136	8,625

It is clear from research subsequent to the 1983 Referendum that at that time Irish women had been travelling to England in significant numbers to access the abortion services made available by the passing of the 1967 Abortion Act.[16] Nevertheless, discussion of the issue was not encouraged and when it did occur, as Eilís recalled, it was often in an atmosphere that was not conducive to open debate.

It came to about fifth year in school and we were looking at issues in the context of religion class or civics class and that – and I went to a predominantly, it was a strong Catholic school, the Sisters of Mercy, it was all female, all girls and at one stage we had a priest teaching our religion class. ... We all wanted to talk about issues like abortion and divorce and those kinds of issues that were topical or social. I remember he came into the class and he said well you wanted to talk about abortion so we're going to talk about it today. Then he just proceeded to relay this anecdotal case of this woman who was wanton and had loads of abortions and by a certain age had her tubes tied and then untied. ... Then when we started questioning anyway he got very rattled and angry – I remember him at one stage shouting at one of the girls in the class to shut up, just shut up.[17]

One interviewee recalled that the Workers Party produced a leaflet in 1983 advocating a 'No' vote in which abortion was not mentioned once. Even more significantly, neither were women mentioned.

Some individuals and groups tried to raise public consciousness about abortion in the context of women's rights and they felt the 1983 Referendum offered the opportunity to make arguments that might not otherwise be possible. John was involved in the publication of a pamphlet *No More Chains! Why You Should Oppose the Constitutional Ban on Abortion*,[18] knowing that what they were doing was in contravention of the law, specifically the laws on censorship which actually prohibited discussion of the issue.[19]

I remember that I typed it out on an electric typewriter that I got a loan of ... There were other people involved who contributed bits and pieces to it. We deliberately put in the middle ... it was a diagram or drawing of how an abortion takes place; it was full of drawings of genitalia and things like this and S. was joking that it must have been the first pamphlet she was involved with that had dirty pictures in it. ... Our thing was use this, we're more than likely going to lose this referendum but we might as well use the opportunity to get the information out and make it sort of obvious to people that this was what was happening.[20]

After the passing of the Eighth Amendment, pro-choice groups continued to use the tactic of provocation. This was done to help women with crisis pregnancies as much as it was to challenge the law.

We thought we should do a mixture of a sort of a campaigning pamphlet and an information pamphlet and the Defend the Clinics Campaign brought out an information pack around 1990 I think, giving details of abortion clinics and how to get on to them and all of that sort of stuff. We incorporated that into this, which was *Censored: Ireland's Abortion Reality – including a Guide to Services for Irish Women*.[21]

The group was unable to get the pamphlet printed in Cork and they brought it to Dublin to a sympathetic printer in Temple Bar who agreed to do the printing but without putting his company name on it so that he would not fall foul of the law on publishing information on abortion. Various initiatives were undertaken in the years between 1983 and 1992 to get information out to women who needed it.

This was probably done most publicly by handing out leaflets, practically every Saturday, in Dublin city centre, for several years, containing information with a telephone number of, I suppose we'd have to call it an underground, guerrilla abortion information service that had been set up in Dublin called the Women's Information Network where anybody could phone up and could arrange to meet someone, could arrange to get information, non-judgemental, hard information on all the options available to them. ... completely illegal.[22]

ATTITUDES TO ABORTION

Two of the questions that were asked of the interviewees were about the attitudes of their close family and friends to abortion generally and specifically to their own role as pro-choice activists. The interviewees who had been active in the 1983 Anti-Amendment Campaign mainly came from families who believed that the existing position was adequate and there was no need for a Referendum to outlaw a procedure that was already illegal. Others believed that the measure was sectarian and were preparing to vote against it to maintain the *status quo*. During this and later campaigns, there seems to have often been a tacit agreement with friends and workmates not to discuss the issue overtly, although there were instances, particularly during the X Case in 1992 when that was not the case. One or two interviewees reported significant differences with family members that reflected the experience of many activists when canvassing for a pro-choice position, especially in 1983.

> My father had died a year or two years previously and his sister was a nun. She's still alive. She's in her late nineties now so I suppose she would have been in her late sixties then. ... So we were standing in Daunt Square and I happened to be handing out those Anti-Amendment leaflets and I was standing under a poster, it was a SPUC (Society for the Protection of the Unborn Child) poster of a graphic foetus, you know the whole abortion picture. ... Well she came along with this smile and she went 'oooh' as if I'd been sort of rescued from everything she assumed I was.... Even though she would have known I was vaguely politically active and long-haired and not quite pious this was beyond her comprehension because when I handed her the leaflet and said 'vote no to the Amendment' and so on, she completely freaked and her face was contorted into hatred and she said 'your father would be ashamed and your father's not cold in his grave' and she ripped up the leaflet and threw it in my face. Now everyone else assumed it was just another mad nun, you know, but it was my aunt.[23]

While there was very little possibility of any meeting of minds from the opposing sides, the Referendum campaign in 1983 was particularly marked by the violence exhibited by some of the pro-amendment activists. This trend continued through the subsequent decades but it resulted in a split between the more extreme elements of the anti-choice groups and those who presented themselves as representing the views of the majority of the Irish people.

THE X CASE AND THE 1992 REFERENDUM

The response to the X Case[24] in 1992 illustrated perhaps the most dramatic change in public perception of abortion in the extent to which ordinary people took to the streets to register their support for the young girl at the centre of the case.

> I remember being in a pub in Wexford Street and this big bruiser of a man came up to me. We were collecting signatures in a pub and him saying 'are you pro-abortion?' and me swallowing very hard and going kind of 'yes'. And he said 'grand' and signed away.[25]

The activists who were involved in organising the big demonstration in Dublin in February 1992 were taken by surprise by the numbers who appeared and by the number of protest marches that took place in Ireland and around the world.

The appeal to traditional values that was so successful in 1983 was now tempered by the consciousness that the issue was not as clear cut as had been claimed. All the interviewees believed that the fact that a 14 year-old was at the centre of the controversy was hugely significant because the amendment had been sold on the basis of protecting children and here was a child who was suffering because of that amendment and the state's insistence on upholding it.

> I remember reading, I think it was the *Evening Herald* at the time, it had the front page on the X Case in my kitchen on a Wednesday and just reading the headline and feeling really depressed and kind of going this is just awful and nothing is going to happen. ... the group I was involved in, we had a very quick meeting and saying ... we have to have a response ... so we called a march to have on the next immediate Saturday.[26] Leading up to that, there were other groups who were also doing things so there were small demos at the Dáil and pickets and I just seem to remember there was a period of a week when there seemed to be constantly something every day, some sort of demo or demonstration.[27]

After the Supreme Court delivered its judgement on X and the young girl at the centre of the case was given permission to travel to England for an abortion,[28] the government was under pressure to make constitutional change in recognition of the complex situation that now existed because of the X Judgement. Another outcome of the X Case was its impact on the determination of some activists to start openly demanding the right to abortion and be absolutely clear about their message.

> I remember we were getting signatures for a petition, outside Clerys I think it was, either that Saturday or the following Saturday and this woman came up, kind of late middle age, kind of elderly woman say up from the country doing her shopping in Clerys or whatever, and at

that stage we were certainly open about being pro-choice but we didn't particularly think the term pro-abortion was accurate so if people said 'are you pro-abortion?' we would always have said 'no, we're pro-choice'. But this woman came up and she said 'listen, are ye pro-abortion?' and I went into this thing and she said 'listen, do you think that little girl should be allowed to have an abortion?' and I said 'yes' and she said 'well, so do I'.[29]

The 1992 Referendum campaign was dogged by confusion, not least because there were three propositions and the campaign also coincided with a General Election. The first proposal was intended to reverse the X Judgement while the second and third referred to the right to travel from Ireland to have an abortion and the right to secure information and counselling about abortion in Ireland. By 1992 the Pro-Life Amendment Campaign had evolved into the Pro-Life Campaign and continued to work against any possibility of relaxing the ban on abortion. They found themselves arguing for a rejection of the Twelfth Amendment but on diametrically opposed grounds to those put forward by the pro-choice advocates. They rejected the government's wording because they said it would leave the assessment of risk to the life of the mother to doctors and they believed that some doctors might give in to the temptation to carry out abortions.

Youth Defence emerged after a split in the anti-choice movement. They were mainly young people who believed that the Pro-Life Campaign was not militant enough in its approach to campaigning. They launched themselves publicly on the radio show run by Father Michael Cleary, who used it as a platform to oppose the liberalisation of Irish society.[30] Youth Defence consistently adopted confrontational and occasionally violent approaches to campaigning, resulting in increasing distance being placed between it and other anti-choice groups. They used extreme forms of rhetoric in well-funded advertisements and were involved in referendum and election campaigns under the banner of related organisations such as Cóir and the Mother and Child Campaign. In 1992 Youth Defence mobilised their first 'Rally for Life' which brought 10,000 people on to the streets of Dublin, most of them from areas outside the city. The abortion issue has consistently reflected a rural/urban divide in Ireland, although cities like Cork and Galway had predominantly 'pro-life' patterns of voting in each Referendum.

I remember males who were very conservative thinkers and I knew them from courses and just being around the place. They had pikes and they were dressed up in devil gear and such like and shouting at people and ranting as they were going down to vote and if they knew you had a different view were really aggressive and hostile towards you. ... They were so conservative on a range of issues and patriarchal as well in their thinking about women.[31]

In the event the Referendum result was a victory for the pro-choice side in that the attempt to overturn the Supreme Court ruling on X was voted down and the rights to travel and obtain information were accepted and later enshrined in the Thirteenth and Fourteenth Amendments to the Constitution.

Table 2 sets out the results of the 1992 Referendum. The turnout was much higher than it had been for the 1983 Referendum, suggesting that the nature of the X Case had undermined the certainties postulated in the earlier campaign and many voters had been shaken by the effect that the Eighth Amendment could have in practice.

Table 2. 1992 Referendum Results, 25 November 1992.

Twelfth Amendment of the Constitution Bill (Referendum on Right to Life) 1992.

Total electorate	Total poll	Percentage poll	For the proposal	Against the proposal	Spoiled votes
2,542,841	1,733,309	68.2	572,177	1,079,297	81,835

Thirteenth Amendment of the Constitution Bill (Right to Travel) 1992.

Total electorate	Total poll	Percentage poll	For the proposal	Against the proposal	Spoiled votes
2,542,841	1,733,821	68.2	1,035,308	624,059	74,454

Fourteenth Amendment of the Constitution Bill (Right to Information) 1992.

Total electorate	Total poll	Percentage poll	For the proposal	Against the proposal	Spoiled votes
2,542,841	1,732,433	68.1	992,833	665,106	74,494

Politicians were very afraid of the issue. CWPA[32] was getting going more at the time of the Referendum ... and in that organisation I suppose there were women who were responding more specifically to their shock around the X Case and what had been done to that girl. ... They were a layer of Irish society that I wouldn't really have had so much contact with prior to involvement in the CWPA and it was interesting to have that sense of women, some of whom were involved in political parties, who took a position quite opposite to the position taken by the men in their parties. ... They simply thought what was happening was wrong and at the time of Maastricht when it came out that the government had made arrangements to make it impossible to change the law on abortion in this country many of those women who were involved in that organisation were absolutely appalled that something so anti-women could have been dealt with in such a secretive way.[33]

HARD CASES AND DESPERATE STRAITS

There was a relatively muted public response to the C and D Cases in 1997 and 2007 respectively when again two young women were faced with the might of the state refusing them the right to travel abroad for an abortion.[34] The interviewees felt this was due to the belief that the courts would 'do the right thing' and permit them to leave, which of course was what happened, rather than indifference to their plight. This confidence in the safety valve offered by abortion services in other countries was also evident in the response to the Women on Waves initiative mounted by a coalition of pro-choice activists in 2001.[35] Despite the media frenzy when it was announced that a Dutch ship would be bringing a portable surgery to Ireland in which abortions could be carried out in international waters, the event had very little impact on national sensibilities. Given that more than 300 women called the helplines organised by the Irish activists requesting termination of crisis pregnancies and that they were clearly prepared to go on board a ship to be taken to international waters for that procedure, the level of desperation evident in those calls was strangely unacknowledged.

> I know there were all sorts of difficulties about it but I still think it very much laid the groundwork for the campaign for the 2002 referendum in that a network of activists was established, people who knew they could work and relate to each other and knew what the various institutional supports were and all that.[36]

THE 2002 REFERENDUM

The role of the Catholic Church has come under particular scrutiny in recent years in the aftermath of the paedophile scandals and the reaction of the Irish episcopate to revelations of their role in covering up abuse. The influential role played by the Catholic Church in 1983 was impossible to repeat in 2002 when the Fianna Fáil/Progressive Democrat coalition tried to overturn the X judgement. The evolution of the anti-choice position in line with developments in public sympathy manifested quite dramatically during the 2002 Referendum campaign, when the Pro-Life Campaign's support for the Government's proposition required them to concede that abortion might actually be necessary in some cases. The pro-choice side was represented by the Alliance for a No Vote, who argued against the proposal because it would remove even the limited protection offered by the X Judgement for suicidal pregnant women.

> I was in NUI Galway at the time and a very, very conservative college and it was interesting that William Binchy[37] had been invited in to speak on the Referendum; they didn't have anyone from the pro-choice side coming up and he was in one of the largest lecture halls in Galway at the time and it was absolutely packed. There was maybe eight or nine of us who went down to leaflet it beforehand, and we went into the meeting and we were just not given the opportunity to speak. ... It was much harder in Galway than it had been in Dublin.[38]

Table 3. 25th Amendment (Protection of Human Life in Pregnancy Bill) 2001, 6 March 2002.

Total electorate	Total poll	Percentage poll	For the proposal	Against the proposal	Spoiled votes
2,923,918	1,254,175	42.9%	618,485	629,041	6,649

The voter turnout was roughly 50 per cent in the 1983 Referendum, in the high 60s in 1992 and much lower in 2002, varying between 48 per cent in Dublin and as low as 37 and 38 per cent in Connacht and Ulster. To what extent this represented voter fatigue with a difficult issue or complacency about the safety valve represented by the right to travel is one of the questions that should be explored in more depth.

Opinion polls in recent years certainly suggest that a majority of Irish people would be in favour of abortion being made available in this country, albeit on limited grounds. Whether there is support for more than legislating on the basis of the X Judgement is not clear although one interviewee who is involved in policy development in the area is convinced that the Irish government's inconclusive interventions in the European Court A, B and C cases and in submissions to the United Nations Convention on the Elimination of Discrimination Against Women were evidence of their ambivalence and the intention to allow abortion by default rather than initiating legislation.[39] The government responded to the European Court's ruling by appointing an Expert Group to study the options[40] but the outraged national and international response to the tragic death of Savita Halappanavar[41] on 28 October 2012 forced the issue. The Irish abortion ban and the failure of successive governments to legislate for abortion as required by the X Judgment, left doctors with no legislative framework for dealing with complications in a pregnancy that threatened the life of the mother. The Fine Gael/Labour government delivered the Protection of Human Life in Pregnancy Act 2013 as their solution, finally legislating for the limited terms of X after more than twenty years. In discussion with some of the interviewees about the parliamentary debates leading up to the passing of the 2013 Act, the view was expressed that some of the arguments posed by opponents of the legislation had not changed since the early 1980s and did not reflect at all the significant changes in the general public's attitude to the role of abortion in women's reproductive health choices in Ireland.

CONCLUSION

There's been a huge sea change because I think there's been more openness. I mean with the changes, the radical changes that happened – you know ...accessibility to contraception, you can travel now to have an abortion and you won't be prosecuted if you're gay, there's an acceptance that society isn't all mammy, daddy, two children, car, cat, dog and budgie, you know what I mean, that there's not that nuclear family?[42]

How does a historian assess the kind of social change represented by the difference in public reaction to the arguments made in 1983, in 1992 and in 2002 that was clearly marked by the results of the referenda in those years? In one sense it is easy to measure – one only has to compare the ballot results.

Table 4. Comparison of Voting Patterns in Abortion Referenda, 1983–2002.

Year	Referendum Title	Turnout in numbers and as percentage of electorate	Percentage in favour of the proposal	Percentage against the proposal
1983	The right to life of the unborn	1,265,594 (53.7)	66.4	32.9
1992				
(i)	Right to Life	1,733,309 (68.2)	33.0	62.3
(ii)	Right to Travel	1,733,821 (68.2)	59.7	35.9
(iii)	Right to Information	1,732,433 (68.1)	57.3	38.4
2002	Protection of Human Life in Pregnancy	1,254,175 (42.9)	49.3	50.2

While it is not evident that the Irish people would be ready yet to overturn the Eighth Amendment in order to allow the legalisation of abortion services here in Ireland, what is demonstrated by successive Referenda and opinion polls is that their political leaders have been considerably less imaginative in their response to women with crisis pregnancies. The forces of reaction that were so influential in 1983 have mainly modified their agendas to coincide with public sympathies or have retreated from the stage altogether. What is clear is that the silence about abortion is now of a very different nature than it was in 1983 although women's human rights in Ireland are still restricted.

> I was contacted by a woman I work with that one of her clients had borrowed money from a loan shark in order to go to Britain to have an abortion and then she came back and she got beaten black and blue because she couldn't afford to pay the loan shark. So she had contacted me knowing I was involved in the movement to see if we could, if there was any way we could raise money together. Now it was me putting an email out over the list to people I knew were going to give me twenty quid towards this woman and they do every single time so no, I don't think it's moved on. I still think it's behind closed doors; it's not a subject that people want to talk about because you're not sure who your audience is going to be.[43]

Other interviewees were more positive, not least because of the anger among young people that followed the death of Savita Halappanavar that resulted in new activist formations and renewed determination to give women in Ireland a choice about how they deal with crisis pregnancies that reflects the reality of their lives.

Oral history offers an opportunity to explore the many issues that arise, with the huge advantage that so many of the actors are still on the stage. The recollection of their pro-choice activity for the interviews referred to in this chapter prompted the interviewees to reflect on their experiences. The majority of them believe that their activity during the several Referenda and the other campaigns was worthwhile, although progress has been very slow. The majority also felt that it will be sooner rather than later when the Eighth Amendment to the Constitution is repealed because an Irish government finally catches up with the belief of most Irish people that abortion as a solution to a crisis pregnancy should be available to women who want to make that choice.[44] On the other hand, because of the silence that still shrouds the experiences of so many women who have had to avail of abortion services outside this country it may be some time before the full story is told.

NOTES

1. Brief biographical information about the interviewees is contained in Appendix I.

2. Noel Christopher Browne (1915–97) was a public representative who managed to be a TD (Member of the Irish Parliament) for five different political parties (two of which he co-founded). He introduced the Mother and Child Scheme in 1951 when he was Minister for Health. It was opposed by both the Catholic Church and the medical profession and Browne resigned when he was not supported by the government, although many of the reforms that he proposed were adopted by later governments.

3. Interview with Alan MacSimóin, 16 July 2010.

4. Sections 16 and 17 of the Censorship of Publications Act 1929 banned the printing, publishing, distribution, or sale of publications advocating contraception or abortion as a means of birth control, and defined the advertising of 'drugs, medicines, appliances, treatment, or methods for procuring abortion or miscarriage or preventing conception' as 'indecent or obscene'. Section 17 of the Criminal Law Amendment Act 1935 prohibited the import and sale of contraceptives.

5. The Fertility Guidance Company Limited opened its doors in Merrion Square in Dublin in March 1969. It changed its name to the Irish Family Planning Association in July 1973, after it had opened a second clinic in Mountjoy Square, on the other side of Dublin city.

6. Interview with John Meehan, Dublin, 24 July 2010.

7. It was quite a common practice at the time for general practitioners to prescribe the Pill for 'menstrual irregularities' rather than as a contraceptive.

8. Interview with Sandra MacAvoy, Cork, 21 February 2012.

9. In 1982, schoolteacher Eileen Flynn was dismissed from her job in a Catholic secondary school when she became pregnant as a result of her relationship with a man who was separated from his wife. Her court case against the dismissal was unsuccessful.

10. Interview with Frank Vaughan, Dublin, 8 November 2010.

11. J.P. O'Carroll, 'Bishops, Knights – and Pawns? Traditional Thought and the Irish Abortion Referendum Debate of 1983' in *Irish Political Studies*, 6, 1991, pp.53–71.

12. Bishop Kevin McNamara, *The Pro-Life Amendment to the Constitution* (Bray: Irish Messenger Publications, 1983) pp.21–2.

13. Interview with Glenys Spray, Cork, 22 February 2012.

14. In the early 1980s Open Door Counselling took over the operation of the Irish Pregnancy Counselling Centre (IPCC) which had been set up in 1979 to offer non-directive pregnancy counselling and referral to Britain for legal abortions there. In 1980 the Director of Public Prosecutions confirmed that the service was legal under the criminal law. The IPCC had financial difficulties and Open Door was set up in 1983.

15. Nearly 67 per cent of the valid poll (53.67 per cent of the electorate) voted for the Eighth Amendment. 'Referendum Results 1937 to 2009'. http://www.environ.ie/en/LocalGovernment/Voting/Referenda/PublicationsDocuments/FileDownLoad,1894,en.pdf (accessed 20 March 2010).

16. 'The UK Department of Health releases statistics each year on the number of women and girls who gave Republic of Ireland addresses at abortion clinics in England and Wales. It is important to note that these numbers are an underestimation as not all women resident in the Republic of Ireland will provide their Irish address for reasons of confidentiality. Furthermore, some Irish women will give addresses in the UK at which they are not resident in order to obtain abortion care paid for by the NHS. Between 1980 and 2011 at least 152,061 women living in Ireland have travelled to England and Wales to access safe abortion services.' Irish Family Planning Association website, http://www.ifpa.ie/Hot-Topics/Abortion/Statistics (accessed 4 September 2012).

17. Interview with Éilis [name changed at interviewee's request], Cork, 22 February 2012.

18. *No More Chains! Why You Should Oppose the Constitutional Ban on Abortion* (Belfast and Dublin: A People's Democracy Pamphlet, 1983.)

19. The Censorship of Publications Act 1929 was applicable until the 1992 Fourteenth Amendment to the Constitution removed the prohibition on the publication of information about abortion.

20. John, Dublin, July 2010.

21. Interview with Donal Ó Drisceoil, Cork, 22 February 2012.

22. Alan, Dublin, 16 July 2010.

23. Donal, Cork, 22 February 2012

24. In February 1992 the case of a 14 year-old girl who had been raped by a neighbour came to public knowledge when the Attorney General, Harry Whelehan sought an injunction to prevent her having an abortion in England. The Attorney General had been informed of the girl's intention when her family approached the Gardaí about collecting DNA from the foetus to identify the rapist. The case was appealed to the Supreme Court where a majority judgement held that the girl's suicidal condition presented 'a real and substantial risk' to her life and an abortion could therefore be permitted within the terms of Article 40.3.3 of the Constitution.

25. Interview with James Kingston, Dublin, 27 July 2010.

26. The Dublin Abortion Information Campaign organised demonstrations in Dublin between 17 and 22 February 1992 at which tens of thousands of people protested the treatment of Miss X and demanded the right to information on abortion.

27. Interview with Aileen O'Carroll, 16 July 2010.

28. The girl miscarried before the abortion could be carried out.

29. James, Dublin, 27 July 2010.

30. Michael Cleary was a Catholic priest who had a very high national profile in the 1970s and 1980s, partly on account of his development work in Dublin's inner-city communities, where he raised the issue of poverty but also because of his frequent appearances on radio and television. After his death it was revealed that he had fathered two children with his housekeeper who had been only 17 when their relationship commenced. The first child was adopted and the second was raised by the couple without Cleary acknowledging him as his son.

31. Éilis, Cork, 22 February 2012.

32. Cork Women's Political Association.

33. Sandra, Cork, 21 February 2012.

34. The C Case involved a 13 year-old girl who was raped. She was placed in the care of the Local Authority and a successful court case was taken on her behalf to seek permission for her to travel to Britain for an abortion, on the grounds of her suicidal state. The D Case also involved a young girl (aged 17) who became pregnant while in the care of the Local Authority. Her foetus was diagnosed as anencephalitic with no chance of surviving outside the womb and again the court ruled that she should be permitted to travel to Britain for an abortion.

35. Women on Waves was set up in 1999 in The Netherlands by Dr Rebecca Gomperts with the aim of preventing unsafe abortions and unwanted pregnancies by providing sexual health services including early medical abortions with pills, on board a Dutch ship outside the territorial waters of countries where abortion is illegal. They were invited to Ireland and came in June 2001 but the Dutch government said the ship would not be licensed and any medical procedures that took place on board would not be covered by Women on Waves' insurance.

36. John, Dublin, 24 July 2010.

37. Professor William Binchy is a barrister and Regius Professor of Laws at Trinity College Dublin. He is the legal adviser to the Pro-Life Campaign.

38. Siân Muldowney, Dublin, 19 July 2010.

39. In 2005 three women, known as A, B and C, challenged Ireland's restrictive abortion laws at the European Court of Human Rights. All three women had been forced to travel abroad for abortions. In December 2010 the Court unanimously found that Ireland's failure to provide life-saving abortion services was a breach of Ms. C's human rights. She had found she was pregnant while she was receiving treatment for cancer. The Court ruled that all three women had experienced stigma and isolation, and that the necessity to travel to the UK for abortions caused them significant psychological, financial and physical hardship. The Court also found that there had been an interference with the rights of Ms. A and Ms. B under the European Convention on Human Rights.

40. The expert group was tasked with resolving three central issues:
    1. To examine the A, B and C v Ireland judgment of the European Court of Human Rights;
    2. to elucidate its implications for the provision of health care services to pregnant women in Ireland;
    3. to recommend a series of options on how to implement the judgment taking into account the constitutional, legal, medical and ethical considerations involved in the formulation of public policy in this area and the overriding need for speedy action.
    Government of Ireland Action Report on A, B and C v. Ireland, 13 January 2012. http://health.gov.ie/wp-content/uploads/2014/03/Action_Report1.pdf (accessed 3 January 2015).

41. Savita Halappanavar was a young Indian woman living in Galway with her husband when she became pregnant. When she developed sepsis the medical

staff at Galway University Hospital would not terminate the pregnancy because a foetal heartbeat could still be heard. Savita died shortly afterwards. When the story broke in the national and international media, it was followed by mass protests in Ireland and other countries, including India.

42. Interview with Rhonda Donaghy, Dublin, 19 July 2010.

43. Siân, Dublin, 19 July 2010.

44. In June 2013 *The Irish Times* commissioned a poll of 1,000 voters in face-to-face interviews in all constituencies on attitudes to abortion. They found that 75 per cent were in favour of the government's then proposed legislation (the *Protection of Life during Pregnancy Bill 2013*), with 14 per cent opposed and 11 per cent undecided. Furthermore, 89 per cent felt that abortion should be allowed when the woman's life is at risk, 83 per cent felt that abortion should be allowed whenever the foetus cannot survive outside the womb, 81 per cent felt that abortion should be allowed in cases of rape or abuse, 78 per cent felt that abortion should be allowed when the woman's health is at risk, 52 per cent felt that abortion should be allowed where the woman is suicidal as a result of the pregnancy, and 39 per cent felt that abortion should be provided when a woman deems it to be in her best interest. This was in stark contrast to the results of a similar poll commissioned 16 years earlier by *The Irish Times* in 1997, which found that 18 per cent believed that abortion should never be permitted, 77 per cent believed that it should be allowed in certain circumstances (35 per cent felt that an abortion should be allowed in the event that the woman's life is threatened; 14 per cent if her health is at risk; 28 per cent that 'an abortion should be provided to those who need it') and 5 per cent were undecided. See www.irishtimes.ie (accessed 26 January 2014).

BIBLIOGRAPHY

Connolly, L. and T. O'Toole, *Documenting Irish Feminisms. The Second Wave* (Dublin: The Woodfield Press, 2005).

Hesketh, T., *The Second Partitioning of Ireland?: The Abortion Referendum of 1983* (Dublin: Brandsma Books, 1990).

Kingston, J. and A. Whelan, with Ivana Bacik, *Abortion and the Law* (Dublin: Round Hall Sweet & Maxwell, 1997).

Mahon, E., C. Conlon and L. Dillon, *Women and Crisis Pregnancy: A Report Presented to the Department of Health and Children* (Dublin: Government Stationery Office, 1998).

Morgan, O.K., and H. McGee, *Irish Contraception and Crisis Pregnancy Study 2010 (ICCP-2010) A Survey of the General Population* (Dublin: HSE, 2010).

O'Carroll, J.P., 'Bishops, Knights – and Pawns? Traditional Thought and the Irish Abortion Referendum Debate of 1983', in *Irish Political Studies*, 6, 1991, pp.53–71.

Riddick, R., *The Right to Choose: Questions of Feminist Morality* (Dublin: Attic Press, 1990).

Ruane, M., *The Irish Journey: Women's Stories of Abortion* (Dublin: Irish Family Planning Association, 2000).

Smyth, A. (ed.), *The Abortion Papers Ireland* (Dublin: Attic Press, 1992).

Smyth, L., *Abortion and Nation: The Politics of Reproduction in Contemporary Ireland* (Aldershot: Ashgate Publishing, 2005).

Spreng, J., *Abortion and Divorce Law in Ireland* (North Carolina: MacFarland & Company, 2004).

APPENDIX I
BIOGRAPHICAL INFORMATION ON INTERVIEWEES
QUOTED IN THIS CHAPTER

Alan has been very actively involved in campaigning for abortion rights since 1989, although he was very aware of previous campaigns and was a member of the Contraception Action Campaign. He has also been a trade union activist and a political campaigner on a number of economic and social issues, from employment rights and anti-racism to opposition to water, refuse and household taxes. Alan was one of the organisers of the X March in Dublin in February 1992.

Aileen first became involved in pro-choice activity when she was a student in Trinity College Dublin. She has been a spokesperson for a number of campaigns for abortion rights and was also one of the organisers of the Dublin X March. She was not an organiser in the 2002 Referendum Campaign although she distributed leaflets and canvassed for a 'No' vote.

Donal also became active in pro-choice activity and other political engagement when he was a student in University College Cork. He was one of the organisers of a series of pro-choice campaigns in Cork, most notably on the 1992 Referendum and the Women on Waves initiative in 2001. He has been less active in recent years but remains committed to promoting an equitable Irish society.

Eilís had been pro-choice in outlook since her secondary school days but she did not become politically active until the Women on Waves visit to Cork and the 2002 Referendum campaign. Eilís was raised in a small rural town where the population was predominantly Catholic and socially conservative.

Frank worked as an education officer with the IFPA during the 1980s when he was responsible for trying to enlighten people about contraception and training for health professionals and youth workers in particular. He was very conscious of the need at the time to be very circumspect about discussing abortion as an option in reproductive health services. As a student he had been a member of the Contraception Action Campaign.

Glenys was born in England and she was involved with left-wing political groups during the 1970s, before moving to Ireland and eventually settling in Cork. She was one of the founders of a women's group in Cork who advocated for women's rights in a number of areas, including access to contraception. She was also active in the Cork Women's Political Association before becoming one of the founding members of the Cork Women's Right to Choose Group.

James is another activist who came to a pro-choice position in university and he was one of the organisers of the response to the SPUC injunction against the students' unions. He remembers that he was prepared to go to prison if SPUC had been successful in their case. He campaigned in the 1992 and 2002 referendum campaigns and was actively engaged in the Women on Waves initiative in 2001.

John has the longest record in pro-choice activity of all the interviewees to date. He was involved in campaigning for access to contraception in the 1970s, particularly when he was a student in University College Dublin and he has advocated full abortion rights for women in Ireland since the 1983 Referendum. Since the 1970s he has also been involved in left-wing political groups and organised on issues such as opposition to the privatisation agenda of the EU, to the Government proposition in the 2003 Citizenship Referendum and other human rights issues.

Rhonda was a trade union activist from a young age and a few months before the X Case she had proposed that her union should fight against the legal position in Ireland that forced women to travel abroad for abortions. The conference occurred around the time the X Case became public and she became the centre of controversy within the union, although the motion was carried. She now works as a full-time union official but she has consistently campaigned for abortion rights and for other socially modernising measures, such as divorce, civil partnership and other human rights issues.

Sandra was born in Belfast and studied history in Trinity College Dublin (TCD). In the 1970s she and her husband moved to Cork where she had her children, before undertaking postgraduate work in University College Cork (UCC). Her involvement in a Women's Studies course had ignited her interest in politics through the Cork Women's Political Association and subsequently in pro-choice activity, as a result of the X Case. She has been a member of the National Women's Council for some years and continues to campaign actively on abortion rights and to make submissions to national and international bodies concerned with the issue.

Siân was fifteen when the X Case broke in 1992 and she went with friends to join the Dublin marches against the position adopted by the Attorney General. She maintained her interest in pro-choice activity after that and as Women's Rights Officer in the TCD Students Union was one of the organisers of the student protests outside the Four Courts when the final stage of the SPUC case against the students unions was heard in 1997. Her campaigning work continued through the C Case in 1997, the Women on Waves initiative in 2001 and the Referendum in 2002. As a postgraduate student in NUIG she was one of two young women who unsuccessfully challenged the constitutionality of the Referendum in the High Court.

APPENDIX II
UK DEPARTMENT OF HEALTH STATISTICS OF
IRISH WOMEN ACCESSING

Abortion Services in England and Wales 1980–2010

Year	All ages	Under 16	16-17	18-19	20-24	25-29	30-34	35-39	40 and over	Not stated
2011	4,149	37	111	295	1,109	1,051	755	534	257	
2010	4,402	41	115	303	1,181	1,137	789	565	271	
2009	4,422	38	155	291	1,234	1,164	759	523	258	
2008	4,600	27	140	344	1,296	1,232	841	499	221	-
2007	4,686	47	147	350	1,387	1,282	790	474	209	-
2006	5,042	39	194	419	1505	1370	824	491	200	-
2005	5,585	39	173	482	1759	1451	860	541	280	-
2004	6,217	49	209	540	1963	1663	951	607	235	-
2003	6,320	42	242	552	2090	1597	954	579	264	-
2002	6,522	54	245	615	2258	1604	928	552	263	1

Year	All ages	Under 15	15	16-19	20-24	25-29	30-34	35-39	40-44	45 and over	Not stated
2001	6,673	12	29	903	2,404	1,685	875	508	239	18	-
2000	6,391	10	17	857	2,243	1,631	853	549	216	15	-
1999	6,226	8	25	894	2,301	1,519	749	502	196	31	1
1998	5,891	7	20	871	2,137	1,489	686	462	195	23	1
1997	5,340	10	30	782	1,986	1,235	645	448	178	26	-
1996	4,894	6	22	738	1,871	1,107	608	351	171	19	1
1995	4,532	7	18	673	1,763	943	561	382	162	23	-
1994	4,590	9	28	591	1,856	987	545	387	172	15	-
1993	4,402	9	28	622	1,678	924	561	372	186	22	-
1992	4,254	5	15	696	1,610	855	529	372	156	16	-
1991	4,154	7	14	679	1,511	845	521	385	174	18	-

Year	All ages	Under 20	20-34	35+	Unstated
1990	4,064	667	2,881	516	-
1989	3,721	588	2,624	509	-
1988	3,839	556	2,768	514	-
1987	3,673	512	2,671	490	-
1986	3,918	569	2,858	491	-
1985	3,888	574	2,827	487	-
1984	3,946	556	2,904	484	2
1983	3,677	559	2,680	435	3
1982	3,650	555	2,697	397	4
1981	3,603	556	2,655	375	17
1980	3,320	495	2,494	326	5

Year	Recorded Number of Women Accessing Abortion Services in the Netherlands
2005	42
2006	461
2007	451
2008	351
2009	134
2010	31

Source: Irish Family Planning Association, http://www.ifpa.ie/Hot-Topics/Abortion/Statistics (accessed 4 September 2012).

8

BUILDING BODIES: A LEGAL HISTORY OF INTERSEX IN IRELAND

Tanya Ní Mhuirthile

This chapter examines the impact which laws changing conception of corporeality has had on people with intersex bodies. Historically, in medieval and renaissance times, the law recognised three types of bodies as conferring legal status: male, female and hermaphrodite. Contemporaneous to increased specialisation in medical knowledge about hermaphroditic conditions during Victorian times, the laws governing the registration of persons were introduced. Intersex is notable in its absence from these legal provisions. This coincidence of events is analysed and it is argued that it signals the beginning of the erosion of intersex from legal consciousness. Such a contention is further strengthened by an examination of case law which has directly addressed the categorisation of bodies as either male or female. The results of this consideration reveal the disappearance of 'intersex' from legal consciousness.

The continuing importance of the dual role of the birth certificate as both a historical 'snapshot' of events at a particular moment and as a crucial and current identification document becomes apparent. It is argued that adherence to a binary understanding of gender actively discriminates against intersex people. Finally, the chapter considers the re-emergence of the historical paradigm of self-declaration of gender identity for intersex people.

INVESTIGATING INTERSEX

The question of how the legal gender of a person ought to be determined has received considerable attention over the past decade in Ireland. There have been two High Court decisions, a Declaration of Incompatibility with Ireland's obligations under the law of the European Convention on Human Rights (ECHR), an advisory group report to Government, two Private Members Bills introduced in the Oireachtas and the publication of the general scheme of a Government sponsored piece of legislation which has been subjected to Joint Oireachtas Committee scrutiny prior to official drafting.[1] This analysis has revealed that, currently, the law categorises bodies as either male or female. Yet, the existence of intersex in the natural world is commonly accepted. There are many plant and animal species that exhibit intersex traits.[2] That there are also intersex people is unsurprising.[3]

As a term, 'intersex', is becoming more familiar yet it is often misconstrued as referring to ambiguous sexual orientation or the transition period between one gender and the other for transgender people. Intersex describes those bodies that cannot be categorised as either male or female as their sexual or reproductive anatomy does not fit the typical definitions of those categories. It is not always immediately apparent when a body is intersex. Thus while some people are identified as intersex in early childhood due to ambiguous genitalia, others are recognised at a later stage in development. It is not unusual for intersex to become manifest at puberty, when seeking assistance with fertility difficulties or even on autopsy when intersex at a genetic level can become obvious.

When discussing intersex, language becomes loaded. Therefore it is appropriate to pause to explain the linguistic choices taken in drafting this chapter. Historically the term 'hermaphrodite' was employed, however due to the associations with the myth of Hermaphroditus and consequent resonance of fantasy, this term has fallen out of favour. Thus intersex was preferred.[4] The linguistic difficulty with the term intersex is that it presupposes that there are two defining sexes and that this third category is a hybrid which exists between the two. This kind of assumption is limited and eschews recognising the complexity of sex, gender and identity. Since 2006, the term 'disorder of sexual development' (DSD) has been used in addition to or in place of intersex for the very reasons outlined above.[5] This latest term can be contested as it presumes an underlying disorder and that there is something intrinsically wrong with the intersex body requiring it to be fixed as either male or female.[6] It can be argued that using this term perpetrates the medicalisation and problematisiation of something which is not inherently medically problematic.[7] Generally this chapter will use the term intersex save where it is more appropriate, particularly in a historical context, to employ another term such as hermaphrodite.

HISTORICAL HERMAPHRODITES

Intersex is not a new or recent phenomenon. There have always been intersex individuals in human society. Through an exploration of how society, the law and the medical profession have interacted with intersex people throughout the ages, the repositioning of hermaphrodites, largely unnoticed and unremarked in history as, from the time of the Enlightenment, objects for close scrutiny will be highlighted. Increased interest caused hermaphrodites to be treated as curios both for the paying public at shows and fairs, as well as for the medical community.[8] This visibility contrasts sharply with the virtual invisibility of intersex people in the twentieth century until the advent of the intersex advocacy movement in the mid-1990s. In relating the history of hermaphrodites and situating it within the context of the history of sexuality, the chapter attempts to tease out why these changes in visibility occurred.

THE AGE OF ANTIQUITY

The word hermaphrodite originates from the story of Hermaphroditus. This story was told by Ovid in his book *Metamorphoses*. When the nymph Salmacis saw Hermaphroditus, the son of the gods Hermes and Aphrodite, swimming in her lake she fell rapturously in love with him and implored the gods that they never be separated. The gods, with their usual sardonic sense of humour, took her at her word and their two bodies were fused into one: 'They two were two no more, nor man, nor woman – One body then that neither seemed and both.'[9]

Hermaphrodites were more than mere myths. Hippocrates, the father of western medicine held that a uterus had seven cells.[10] If a foetus gestated in one of the three cells on the left it would develop as a male. If it developed in one of the three cells on the right it would be a female. Finally, if it developed in the middle cell, it would be a hermaphrodite and combine traits of both males and females. Therefore, Hippocrates considered that hermaphrodites were a third sex in a spectrum of sexes. Aristotle, by contrast, viewed males and females as polar opposites without any intermediate forms. His explanation for the existence of hermaphrodites was as follows; extra sexual organs, like extra fingers or toes, result from an excess of generative matter, too much for one embryo and not enough for two.[11]

MEDIEVAL AND RENAISSANCE ATTITUDES

In Medieval and Renaissance times being either a man or a woman affected one's legal status in society. Men were entitled to own property and to vote, women were not. On the issue of the hermaphrodite, Henry de Bracton wrote that mankind could be classified as male, female or hermaphrodite and that a hermaphrodite is classified with male or female according to the predominance of the sexual organs.[12] This was still the legal position during renaissance times when Lord Coke writing on succession laws noted: 'Every heire is either a male, or female or an hermaphrodite, that is both male and female. And an hermaphrodite (which is also called Androgynous) shall be heire, either as male or female, according to that kind of the sexe which doth prevaile.'[13] Maimonides, a Jewish rabbi, doctor, theologian and lawyer, provides in his *The Book of Women* a detailed diagnostic procedure for determining whether a person was a man, woman or a hermaphrodite.[14] According to Maimonides, a hermaphrodite could become betrothed to marry either a man or a woman. Such an engagement, being suspect, would require a judgment before the marriage could take place.

Although in theory this appears inclusive, as if it would enable a hermaphrodite to declare himself male, for example, and then to live his life without interruption from the State, the reality for hermaphrodites could be different. Daston and Park recount the tale of Marie/Marin from Renaissance France.[15] Raised as a female, in her late teens Marie changed her name to Marin and began living as a man. Marin became engaged to marry a fellow maidservant Jeanne. Both Marin and Jeanne were charged with female sodomy, with having committed lesbian acts. Furthermore Marin was charged with usurping masculine name and dress. At the trial, in 1601, medical examiners testified that Marin had female genitalia and his employers further bore witness to his regular menstrual periods. Jeanne, however, who was widowed with two children, testified that Marin had satisfied her sexually as much if not better than her deceased husband. Marin too testified that he became erect when aroused, but he declined to demonstrate this to the court.

Both Jeanne and Marin were found guilty of unnatural acts. Marin was sentenced to be hanged and burned. Jeanne was sentenced to watch the execution, be whipped in public for three days, have her possessions confiscated and then be banished from Normandy. Following the trial one of the medical examiners examined Marin using a different method. He became convinced Marin possessed a penis when, following extensive rubbing, thick masculine semen was ejaculated, from what had previously been considered a clitoris. The doctor reported his findings to the court. The original sentence was lifted from both Marin and Jeanne. Instead Marin was sentenced to dress as a woman and to refrain from sex with either men or women for four years. Ten years later, Marin was spotted wearing men's clothes and sporting a thick beard.[16]

If, as indicated by the dicta of de Bracton, Coke and Maimonides, hermaphroditism was accepted in society why was Marie/Marin brought before the court when s/he had chosen to marry in the male role and presumably intended to live in that role? Examining the alternative sentences handed down at the original trial and once the evidence of the post-trial examination had been adduced to court, sheds light on the matter. At the original trial, evidence of Marie's menstrual cycle was deemed sufficient to determine her sex as female. Thus the proposed marriage was between two women and hence sufficiently offensive to the law to mandate a death sentence. However, once the evidence of the post-trial examination was admitted to court, the fact of ejaculation was considered sufficient to call into question the sex of Marie/Marin and thus, potentially, the relationship between the accused persons was uncontroversial and heterosexual. Viewed from this perspective, it was Marie/Marin's suspected lesbianism and not the fact of her hermaphroditism which was the cause of societal concern. An alternative reading of the case could be to do with Marie/Marin's gender performance rather than her sexual orientation which was the cause for concern.[17] Either way what is clear is that once the anxiety concerning gender/sexuality transgression was eliminated the punishment was reduced enormously.

Prior to the French Revolution, sodomy was a serious crime handled by the religious courts but it was not outlawed by the civil law of the land.[18] This was reflected in the codification of the law, as neither the Penal code of 1791 nor the Napoleonic Code of 1810, mentions or criminalises private sexual acts between consenting adults over 21 years of age. In England and Ireland, the civil law adopted this offence under canon law in 1533 when the first civil law outlawing sodomy, the statute 25 Hen. VIII c. 6, was enacted.[19] Under this statute acts considered sodomy were classed as felonies punishable by hanging. Prosecution under this Act was not solely confined to homosexual acts but to anal intercourse in general, as well as to acts of bestiality.[20]

Michel Foucault offers as an explanation for this sudden interest in regulating sexuality the contention that changes made to the sacrament of penance by the Council of Trent (1545–63), lead to increasing discourse on sexuality and hence that which had previously been confined to the private realm, became public.[21] The increase in discourse about sex and sexuality became evident in the eighteenth century. The study of demographics began as a means of regulating the population. The sex lives of citizens became an important object of public scrutiny, as statistics regarding birth rates, fertility rates, illegitimate births and so on became important for public use.[22] Thus, sexuality became a matter of public interest. Sex became something to be studied rationally, to be analysed, classified and understood as a statistical phenomenon. Laws prohibiting certain kinds of sex became tighter,[23] studies of sex became more frequent, and the general awareness of sexuality was heightened leading to even more talk about sex.[24]

THE NINETEENTH CENTURY AND THE AGE OF GONADS

The publication of Charles Darwin's *The Origin of the Species* greatly perturbed society in the nineteenth century.[25] His theory of evolution held that males and females existed purely for procreative purposes and were naturally selected to ensure the survival of the fittest and the continuation of the species. Thus the polarisation of males and females is the foundation on which life itself was based. The heterosexual male and female were prioritised by society as the highest form of humanity as, uniquely, they were in a position to ensure the survival of the species through procreation.[26] It can be argued that the prioritisation of a binary gender paradigm in an organised and intentional manner dates from this time.[27] It was during the Victorian era that the recording of statistics relating to the births, marriages and deaths of the population was put on a statutory footing.[28] The first definition of marriage as something exclusively the preserve of heterosexual men and women was handed down by a court.[29] The law outlawing sodomy was restated afresh and reinterpreted as a prohibition on homosexuality and although the death penalty was removed as a punishment, the crime was punishable by up to life imprisonment.[30] Furthermore, the erasure of the hermaphrodite from both recognised civil society and from the public consciousness began.

Foucault argues that the attempt to regulate sexuality and to eliminate degeneracy through natural selection resulted in society becoming concerned with the instability of political–sexual identities, hence the increase in prosecutions for homosexuality.[31] Simultaneously, doctors were beginning to specialise, and gynaecology, which previously had been almost exclusively the preserve of the midwife, was becoming a specialisation in its own right.[32] Doctors began to discover and report in medical journals a number of physically hermaphroditic subjects. This can partly be attributed to the rise of gynaecology and, as Dreger argues, 'anxiety of sex roles probably also contributed to the rapid rise in medical reports of hermaphrodites by making physicians sensitive to their patients' sexual identities, anatomies and practices.'[33]

In an attempt to curtail hermaphroditism lest it amplify the social sexual confusion, biomedical experts sought a stable definition of male and female. In 1896, Blacker and Lawrence published an article in which they argued that it is the gonadal tissue, revealed as either testicular or ovarian upon microscopic examination, which is the true indicator of an individual's sex, regardless of any other anatomical factor.[34] This argument received widespread acceptance by the medical community.[35] Consequently a person who possessed testes would be labelled a male-pseudo-hermaphrodite regardless of how feminine they might be. This led to some cases of extreme social nonsense, such as that of L.S., a Parisian fashion model with testes, who was described as 'frankly homosexual' by doctors because she exclusively sexually desired men.[36]

Therefore all people could be labelled as male or female even if 'apparently and falsely' hermaphroditic. It was only upon microscopic inspection of the gonads by many teams of experts that an individual could be declared a 'true hermaphrodite'. Given that biopsies and exploratory surgery were extremely rare occurrences, in practice the only true hermaphrodite tended to be the dead and autopsied hermaphrodite.[37] As a result of this new test, far fewer people met the criteria for diagnosis as a hermaphrodite regardless of what other 'apparently' hermaphroditic traits they might possess. Thus the erasure of the hermaphrodite from society began.

SURGICAL SOLUTIONS

With the advent of live biopsies in the early twentieth century it was no longer sustainable to adopt a gonadal definition of sex. William Blair Bell advanced the idea that when determining the sex of an apparent hermaphrodite, each case should be considered as a whole and the focus should not be exclusively on the gonads.[38] He also suggested that in addition to determining the sex of an individual with ambiguous biology, doctors should help that diagnosis along: '[S]urgical procedures should in these special cases be carried out to establish more completely the obvious sex of the individual.'[39]

Thus surgeons began to 'disappear' intersex individuals from society by surgically altering their physical appearance such that it more closely resembled the appearances of males or females. Advances in medicine, particularly surgical techniques and hormonal treatments, made it possible to eradicate the external evidence of intersexuality and to 'make' an individual either male or female. The most prolific proponent of this approach was Dr John Money, who specialised in the psychology of sex at the Gender Identity Clinic of Johns Hopkins Hospital in Baltimore, Maryland. He believed that in the nature versus nurture debate, the latter is paramount. Therefore, sexual identity is not a matter of biology, but rather a learned process. Any child can be taught to have a male or female identity, regardless of biological fact. So when treating an intersexed child, the assignment of sex is inconsequential, so long as the child is raised clearly and unequivocally as either male or female.[40] Surprisingly his argument was, to a large extent, based on the study of one individual known as the John/Joan case.[41]

John was one of a set of identical twins born in 1965. At eight months old his penis was severely burned and completely lost during a routine circumcision. With little hope that it could be repaired, the parents ultimately turned to Dr Money who suggested a gender change. In July 1967, John underwent gender re-assignment surgery and was sent home as Joan. Her parents were under strict instruction from Money and the treatment team to keep her original sex a secret and to constantly reaffirm her feminine identity. The twins were cared for by a local psychiatric team under Money's direction and were brought to Baltimore annually to be evaluated.[42] Money reported that although she did exhibit some tomboyish traits, Joan's parents were now successfully raising her as a typical girl.[43] The John/Joan case was proclaimed a triumph, conclusive proof of the supremacy of nurture over nature. The existence of John's twin, a genetically identical control who was a typical boy, convinced doctors that gender was a fiction of society. Intersex children could be raised as either male or female, providing the gender was assigned before the crucial identity gate was reached. Thus genital normalisation and sexual assignment surgery became the standard treatment for intersex individuals.

Following the US example, other countries also began to practise routine gender assignment surgery on intersexed infants. The reconstruction of these children as either male or female contributed to the disappearance of intersex from the social consciousness. For decades the success of the John/Joan case was unquestioned despite the lack of any other corroborative research.[44] No follow-up studies were ever done on adult intersex individuals who underwent such surgery as children.[45] In the late 1990s, researchers attempting to challenge Money's theories began to search for Joan, whom Money had reported was 'lost to research'. The boy who was raised as a girl was now living as a man. Diamond and Sigmundson published an article in 1997 refuting the results of Money's famous research.[46] It was the publication of the eventual outcome of the John/Joan story that caused some practitioners to begin to reconsider the approach to the medical management of intersexuality they had been following.[47]

INTERSEX IN MODERN IRELAND

Intersex has been the subject of very little official discussion since the creation of the Irish State. In fact prior to 2009 there was no mention of either intersex or hermaphrodite in any official text or sources from any public body. Where intersex has been mentioned the consideration thereof has been cursory at best. The first mention of intersex was in a case before the High Court S v An Bord Uchtála in 2009.[48] The case concerned a child born with an intersex condition who was the subject of a foreign adoption order and consequently noted in the Register of Foreign Adoptions as female. Upon closer medical examination when the child was brought to Ireland it was determined that he would most likely identify as male and thus his family decided to raise him as a boy. In support of this decision they sought to have the gender marker on the Register of Foreign Adoption amended as the certificate therefrom would operate as a foundational identification document for their son especially as regards registration for school and so on. An Bord Uchtála was of the opinion that, given the historical importance of the register, to change the record was beyond their power and refused to do so resulting in judicial review proceedings. The Court issued a ruling ordering the requested change be made. While this was the desired outcome for the individual litigants it is unsatisfactory for intersex individuals in general. The lack of a carefully considered judgment reduced the precedential value of the S case. Thus it is uncertain whether the legal recognition afforded to S would extend to another intersex person and it is less clear whether it might encompass someone who identifies outside the binary male/female gender paradigm.

The only legal cases to consider the parameters of legal gender identity in Ireland have occurred in the context of a transgender woman reeking to have her birth certificate altered to reflect her preferred identity as female.[49] Dr Lydia Foy lost her first case in 2002, the Court emphasising the importance of the register of births as a historical record, a snapshot of a moment in time.[50] Subsequent to a unanimous decision from the European Court of Human Rights, in the case of Goodwin v UK, that the persistent failure of English law to recognise the preferred gender identity of a transwoman amounted to a violation of her right to respect for her private and family life under Article 8 of the ECHR, Dr Foy brought fresh proceedings.[51] Although she lost on the domestic legal points, Dr Foy won her argument that, based on Goodwin, Irish law violated her Convention right to respect for her private life. The ruling of the Court was historic as it was the first time that an Irish Court had issued a Declaration of Incompatibility between Irish law and the State's legal obligations flowing from the ECHR under the European Convention on Human Rights Act, 2003.[52]

What is interesting about the Foy case is that it adopted into Irish law the decision of the English High Court as to how legal gender ought to be determined. In Corbett v Corbett (1970) it was held that the legal gender of an individual was determined by the congruence of the chromosomes, gonads and genitals at birth.[53] Thus the test has both biological and temporal aspects. In cases where this congruence is not present at birth the judge held that the genital sex ought to be determinative.[54] However, given the importance of the birth moment in determining legal gender such a preference for genital appearance is reductive as it may restrict the gender category available to an intersex person whose condition is only discovered later in life or who does not identify with the gender the genital appearance might suggest. Consequently, in W v W (2000) the English High Court was willing to develop the Corbett test to find that advances in medical technology would enable Mrs W to be accepted as female in modern times, given she had asserted a female identity since the time she was able to choose her gender, that this ought to be acknowledged.[55] The Irish court in the Foy cases was silent on whether this variation on the Corbett test might be applicable in the context of Irish intersex individuals, although, given the practical resolution of the S case, it is reasonable to presume it would be persuasive if advanced in legal argument.[56]

The first mention of intersex from an official source in Ireland, not a court report, was contained in the Report of the Gender Recognition Advisory Group (GRAG) published in 2011.[57] The Group had been convened to advise the Minister for Social Protection as to how best to introduce gender recognition legislation to Ireland. The Group declined to recommend that space to acknowledge intersex lived experience be created within any proposed legislative scheme as to do so was both beyond its remit and required more research and medical expertise than was available to it.[58] Thus the report amounts to a knowing refusal to engage with the complex challenge intersex poses for the law. The various legislative proposals currently before the Oireachtas make that more meaningful engagement. Both the private members bills, the Gender Recognition Bill 2013 and the Legal Recognition of Gender Bill 2013, adopt a self-declaration model.[59] In this model individuals inform the State as to their preferred gender of legal recognition where that differs from that registered on the birth certificate. No additional proof is needed to ground an application for recognition. These bills propose a return to the historical method of self-declaration as evidence in the writings of Coke. Such a self-declaration model is in accordance with best practice in international human rights discourse as evidenced in the Argentinian law on gender recognition.[60]

Contrastingly, the General Scheme for the Gender Recognition Bill 2013 proposed by the Minister for Social Protection would require applicants (who must be at least 18 years of age) to provide a supporting statement from their primary treating physician confirming that they have transitioned or are transitioning to their 'acquired gender'.[61] In restricting the ambit of the recognition rights to those over 18, the Government's proposed scheme would exclude intersex children from amending their official identification documentation, which was the very defect the S case was brought to address. On a related note, the language of transition strongly implies that the rights in the legislation will be framed in a binary context and those seeking recognition outside this paradigm will be unsuccessful. It was the lacuna leaving intersex children out of the ambit of the potential rights under the proposed legislative scheme outlined by the Government that prompted most discussion on intersex inclusion therein. The Report of the Joint Oireachtas Committee on their examination of the scheme identifies these concerns repeatedly.[62] In particular it notes the concerns raised by the Ombudsman for Children's Office (OCO) in its report to the committee.[63] The OCO report detailed the State's obligations under international human rights law in this regard and concluded that any right to recognition enjoyed by an adult under Article 8 ECHR extended equally to children.[64]

As a result of these investigations the Committee recommended that the age limit for applicants be reduced to 16 years with provisions to address the day-to-day concerns of those under that age. It also recommended that the criterion concerning evidence of transition be reconsidered in order to ensure that it does not stigmatise applicants.[65] Although the recommendations of the Committee do not specifically address intersex, read together with the discussions contained in their report, they do suggest a more inclusive acknowledgment of the lived reality of intersex lives than has existed in previous Government sponsored discourse. Whether these recommendations will become part of the final draft legislation remains to be seen.

CONCLUSION

This chapter has traced the evolving response of law to the existence of intersex individuals. It demonstrates that, historically, law acknowledged the legitimacy of hermaphrodites. The chapter argues that as medical knowledge and interest in regulating bodies and sexuality increased, intersex identity was rendered illegitimate. The requirement in birth registration legislation that all children be declared to the State as being either male or female shortly after birth caused the law to be complicit in the erasure of intersex from legal and social consciousness. Cases such as S and W demonstrate that a practical and pragmatic approach by the courts can alleviate the difficulties of a system of gender recognition stymied by the prioritisation of the moment of birth as definitive in the determination of a person's legal gender. Nonetheless, it is in legislation that the true transformative potential of the law lies. Intersex identity was delegitimised by the introduction of birth registration legislation and it is through the introduction of rights realising gender recognition legislation that intersex identity can be re-legitimised.

NOTES

1. *Foy v Ant Ard Chláraitheoir (No 1)* (2002) IEHC 166 and *Foy v An tArdChláraitheoir (No 2)* (2007) IEHC 470; the first Declaration of Incompatibility between Irish Law and Ireland's obligations under the ECHR was handed down in *Foy (No 2)*, this was the first such Declaration to be issued under the *European Convention on Human Rights Act, 2003; Report of the Gender Recognition Advisory Group* (Dublin: Department of Social Protection, 2011); The *Gender Recognition Bill, 2013* was introduced in the Dáil by Aengus Ó Snodaigh, TD on 23 May 2013 and the *Legal Recognition of Gender Bill, 2013* was introduced by Senator Katherine Zappone in the Seanad on 27 June 2013; *General Scheme of the Gender Recognition Bill 2013* Available online at https://www.welfare.ie/en/downloads/Gender-Recognition-Bill-2013.pdf (accessed 11 February 2014), Joint Committee on Education and Social Protection *Report on the General Scheme of the Gender Recognition Bill 2013* (Dublin: House of the Oireachtas, 2014). Available online at https://www.welfare.ie/en/downloads/Gender-Recognition-Bill-2013.pdf (accessed 11 February 2014).

2. P.E. Howard & D.E. Bjorling, 'The Intersexual Animal: Associated Problems', *Problems in Veterinary Medicine*, 1, 1 (Jan–March 1989), pp.74–84; A. Spivey, 'Prelude to Intersex in Fish: Identifying a Sensitive Period for Feminization', *Environmental Health Perspectives*, 113, 10 (October 2005), A686.

3. W.P. Bemis, & G.B. Wilson, 'A New Hypothesis Explaining the Genetics of Sex Determination', *Journal of Heredity*, 44, 3 (1953), pp.91–5.

4. R. Goldschmidt, 'Intersexuality and the Endocrine Aspect of Sex', *Endocrinology*, 1, 4 (October 1917), pp.433–56.

5. C.P. Houk, I.A. Hughes, P.A. Lee, & S.F. Ahmed, in collaboration with the participants in the International Consensus Conference on Intersex organised by the Lawson Wilkins Endocrine Society and the European Society for Paediatric Endocrinology, 'Consensus Statement on the Management of Intersex Conditions', *Pediatrics*, 118, 2 (August 2006), pp.753–7. See also S. Groveman Morris, *DSD But Intersex Too: Shifting Paradigms Without Abandoning Roots.* Available online at http://www.isna.org/node/1067 (accessed 11 February 2014).

6. M. Diamond & H. Beh, 'Variations of Sex Development Instead of Disorders of Sex Development: Letter to the Editor in response to Houk et al', available online at http://adc.bmj.com/cgi/eletters/91/7/554 (accessed 15 July 2013). See also E. Reis, 'Divergence or Disorder: The Politics of Naming Intersex', *Perspectives in Biology and Medicine*, 50, 4 (Autumn 2007), pp.535–43.

7. G. Boulos, 'The DSD: Letter to the Editor in response to Houk et al', available online at http://adc.bmj.com/cgi/eletters/91/7/554 (accessed 15 July 2013) See further all the letters to the editor regarding this publication. See also A.D. Dreger & A.M. Herndon, 'Progress and Politics in the Intersex Rights Movement: Feminist Theory in Action', *GLQ: A Journal of Lesbian and Gay Studies*, 15, 2 (2009) pp.199–224.

8. The Bearded Lady of circus sideshow fame is an example of hermaphrodites treated as curios. While in the medical community in 1888, Fancourt Barnes famously presented his 'living specimen of hermaphroditism' at a meeting of the British Gynaecological Society. See further A.D. Dreger, *Hermaphrodites and the Medical Invention of Sex* (Cambridge, Mass.: Harvard University Press, 1998), p.59.

9. Ovid, *Metamorphoses*, translated by A.D. Melville (Oxford: Oxford University Press, 1986), p.85.

10. G.E.R. Lloyd, *Science, Folklore and Ideology: Studies in the Life Sciences in Ancient Greece*, (Cambridge: Cambridge University Press, 1983), p.176.

11. Aristotle, *On the Generation of Animals* (trans. A.L. Peck) (Cambridge, Mass: Loeb Classical Library, Harvard University Press, 1979).

12. H. de Bracton, *On the Laws and Customs of England* (1268) (Cambridge, Mass: Harvard University Press, 1968).

13. Sir E. Coke, *The First Part of the Institutes of the Law of England* (Philadelphia, Penn.: Robert H. Smith, 1853), p.225.

14. Maimonides, *The Code of Maimonides, Book 4 The Book of Women* (New Haven, Conn: Yale University Press, 1972).

15. L. Daston & K. Park, 'Hermaphrodites in Renaissance France', *Critical Matrix*, 1, 5 (1985), pp.1–19.

16. For a discussion of interpretation of masculinity in the Marie/Marin case amongst others see C. McClive, 'Masculinity on Trial: Penises, Hermaphrodites and the Uncertain Male Body in Early Modern France', *History Workshop Journal*, 68, 1 (2009), pp.45–68.

17. See P. Simmons, *The Sex of Men in Premodern Europe: A Cultural History* (Cambridge: Cambridge University Press, 2011); M. Schaus (ed.), *Women and Gender in Medieval Europe: An Encyclopedia* (New York: Routledge, 2006).

18. See further G. Ferguson, *Queer (Re)readings in the French Renaissance: Homosexuality, Gender, Culture* (Farnham: Ashgate Publishing, 2008), p.271. Ferguson argues that in Renaissance France, penetration was not central to the offence of female sodomy rather it was a synecdoche for gender transgression and for the usurpation by women of prerogatives reserved for men.

19. This Act is also known as the *Buggery Act of 1533*. Until the passing of this Act, the only sexual behaviour between consenting adults which attracted the attention of the civil law was adultery. The Act was briefly repealed during the reign of Queen Mary, but was re-instated by Queen Elizabeth I in 1563. The first person to be executed under the 1533 Act was Walter Hungerford, the First Baron Hungerford of Heytesbury.

20. *King* v. *Wiseman* [1718] 92 Eng. Rep. 774.

21. M. Foucault, *The History of Sexuality: Volume 1 The Will to Knowledge* (trans. R. Hurley) (London: Penguin Books, 1998), Part II Chapter 1.

22. Foucault, *The History of Sexuality*, pp.24–7.

23. In the UK the punishment for sodomy of the death penalty was altered to life imprisonment by the *Offences Against the Person Act, 1861*. The *Criminal Law (Amendment) Act, 1885* raised the age of consent, and delineated the penalties for sexual offences against women and minors, and strengthened the legislation prohibiting prostitution.

24. Foucault, *The History of Sexuality*, pp.31–2.

25. C. Darwin, *The Origin of the Species*, (1859).

26. For a discussion of homosexuality and Darwin, see J.H. Barkow, *Darwin, Sex, and Status: Biological Approaches to Mind and Culture* (Toronto: University of Toronto Press, 1989); J. McKnight, *Straight Science?: Homosexuality, Evolution and Adaptation* (London: Routledge, 1997).

27. See further M. Foucault, *The History of Sexuality*.

28. The *Registration of Births and Deaths Acts 1863*.

29. *Hyde v Hyde* [1866] LR 1 P & D 130.

30. *Offences Against the Person Act, 1861* and *Criminal Law (Amendment) Act, 1885*.

31. Foucault, *The History of Sexuality*, pp.30, 44–5, and 105. See also M. Cook, *London and the Culture of Homosexuality, 1885–1914* (Cambridge: Cambridge University

Press, 2003); N.M. Goldsmith, *Worst of Crimes: Homosexuality and the Law in Eighteenth-Century London* (Farnham: Ashgate, 1998).

32. The Obstetrical Society of London was founded in 1854, the break-away society the British Gynaecological Society was founded in 1884. Eventually these two societies merged in 1929 to form the British College of Obstetricians and Gynaecologists. The College was granted the title 'Royal' in 1938, but did not receive its royal charter until 1947, after World War II.

33. A.D. Dreger, 'A History of Intersex: From the Age of Gonads to the Age of Consent', in A.D. Dreger (ed.), *Intersex in the Age of Ethics* (Hagerstown, Md: University Publishing Group, 1999), pp.5–22.

34. G.F. Blacker, & T.W.P. Lawrence, 'A Case of True Unilateral Hermaphroditism with Ovotesis Occuring in Man, with a Summary and Criticism of the Recorded Cases of True Hermaphroditism', *Transaction of the Obstetrical Society of London*, 38 (1896) p.265.

35. The growing interest in laboratory-based medicine and the influence of eminent German pathologists like Theodor Klebs, are two possible explanations for the scale of the acceptance. See further A.D. Dreger, *Hermaphrodites and the Medical Invention of Sex* (Cambridge, Mass: Harvard University Press, 1998), pp.151–4.

36. Dreger, *Hermaphrodites and the Medical Invention of Sex*, pp.7–9.

37. Dreger, 'A History of Intersex: From the Age of Gonads to the Age of Consent', p.9.

38. W.B. Bell, 'Hermaphroditism' (1915) 35 *Liverpool Medico-Chirurgical Journal*, 35 (1915), p.291.

39. Ibid., p.292.

40. J. Money, & A.A. Ehrhardt, *Man and Woman, Boy and Girl: Differentiation and Dimorphism of Gender* (Baltimore: Johns Hopkins University Press, 1973); J. Money, *Sex Errors of the Body and Related Syndromes: A Guide to Counselling Children* 2nd Revised Edn (Baltimore: Brooks Publishing, 1994).

41. John/Joan is the pseudonym given to David Reimer by M. Diamond &K. Sigmundson in their 1997 follow-up article 'Sex Reassignment at Birth; Long-term Review and Clinical Implications', *Archive of Pediatric & Adolescent Medicine* 151, (1997) pp.298–304. Although his biography by Colapinto identifies John as David Reimer, born Bruce, whose name was changed to Brenda, and then David, to

avoid confusion he shall be referred to throughout this article as John when male and Joan when female. See J. Colapinto, *As Nature Made Him; The Boy Who was Raised as a Girl* (New York: Perennial, 2001).

42. Ibid., p.79.

43. Ibid., p.68.

44. Colapinto, *As Nature Made Him*, Chapter 4, A. Fausto-Sterling, *Sexing the Body: Gender Politics and the Construction of Sexuality* (New York: Basic Books, 2000), pp.66–71.

45. Constitutional Court of Colombia in its case No.SU-337/99. Available online at www.isna.org/node/116 (accessed 11 February 2014).

46. Diamond & Sigmundson, 'Sex Reassignment at Birth'.

47. For an introduction to various methods of medical management of intersex, see T. Ní Mhuirthile, 'Realising Gender Reocgnition: Rendering the Vulnerable Visible or Further Vulnerabilising the Invisible?' *UCD Working Papers in Law, Criminology and Socio-Legal Studies Research Paper No 41/2010.* Available online at http://papers.ssrn.com/sol3/papers.cfm?abstract_id=1680899

48. *S v An Bord Uchtála* (unreported High Court, December 2009).

49. *Foy v An tArd Chlaraitheoir (No 1)* and *Foy v An tArd Chlaraitheoir (No 2)* supra n1.

50. *Foy (No 1), supra* n1, at para 170.

51. *Goodwin v UK* [2002] EHRR 588.

52. Under the European Convention on Human Rights Act 2003, Irish courts are for the first time obliged to be cognisant of the decision made by the Strasbourg court. Thus the judge in Foy was obliged to follow the ruling in Goodwin that to refuse to recognise Foy's preferred gender identity was to violate her right to privacy as guaranteed by Article 8 of the Convention. The Declaration of Incompatibility was intended to ensure that notice of this dissonance between domestic law and the States international legal obligation was brought to the attention of the legislature. The Declaration obliged the Taoiseach to read the court order into the Oireachtas records within twenty-one working days of it being made. This should then prompt the Oireactas to rectify the incompatibility. It has been of limited practical use in Ireland and as of the time of publication, a Heads of Bill, or a mere outline for how such recognition might be achieved was finally introduced before the cabinet in July 2013 but no draft legislation has yet been forthcoming.

53. *Corbett v Corbett* [1970] 1 All ER 33.

54. *Corbett v Corbett*, p.48.

55. *W v W* [2001] 1 FLR 324.

56. For a more in-depth discussion on the *Foy* cases and the introduction of gender recognition legislation to Ireland see T. Ní Mhuirthile, 'Legal Recognition of Preferred Gender Identity in Ireland: An Analysis of Proposed Legislation', in M. Leane and E. Keily (eds), *Sexualities and Irish Society: A Reader* (Dublin: Orpen Press, 2014), pp.127–48.

57. *Report of the Gender Recognition Advisory Group* (Dublin: Department of Social Protection, 2011).

58. *Report of the Gender Recognition Advisory Group*, p.35.

59. *Gender Recognition Bill, 2013* and the *Legal Recognition of Gender Bill, 2013*.

60. *Gender Identity Law, 2012* (Argentina) available online from http://globaltransaction. files.wordpress.com/2012/05/argentina-gender-identity-law.pdf

61. *General Scheme of the Gender Recognition Bill 2013*, at Head 6(vi).

62. *Report on the General Scheme of the Gender Recognition Bill 2013*, p. 30–31.

63. Ibid., p.25.

64. Ibid.

65. Ibid., p.37.

SELECT BIBLIOGRAPHY

Anderson, B., *Imagined Communities: Reflections on the Origins and Spread of Nationalism* (London: Verso, 1983).

Anon., *Manners and Rules of Good Society: Or Solecisms to be Avoided by a Member of the Aristocracy* (first published London: Warne & Co., 1911: repr. London: Elibron Classics, 2004).

Barton, A., 'Wayward Girls and Wicked Women: Two Centuries of "Semi-penal" Control', *Liverpool Law Review*, 22 (2000), pp.151–71.

Beaumont, C., 'Women and the Politics of Equality: The Irish Women's Movement, 1930–1943', in M. Valiulis and M. O'Dowd (eds), *Women & Irish History: Essays in Honour of Margaret MacCurtain* (Dublin: Wolfhound Press, 1997), pp.173–88.

Bell, W.B., 'Hermaphroditism', *Liverpool Medico-Chirurgical Journal*, 35 (1915), pp.272–92.

Blacker G.F. & T.W.P. Lawrence, 'A Case of True Unilateral Hermaphroditism with Ovotesis Occuring in Man, with a Summary and Criticism of the Recorded Cases of True Hermaphroditism', *Transaction of the Obstetrical Society of London*, 38 (1896), pp.265–317.

Bracton, H. de., *On the Laws and Customs of England* (Cambridge, MA: Harvard University Press, 1968).

Brady, C., *Guardians of the Peace* (Dublin: Gill and Macmillan, 1974).

Bretherton, G., 'Irish Inebriate Reformatories, 1899–1920: A Small Experiment in Coercion', *Contemporary Drug Problems*, 13 (1986), pp.473–502.

Butler, J., *Bodies That Matter: On the Discursive Limits of 'Sex'* (New York and London: Routledge, 1993).

Callan, C. and B. Desmond, *Irish Labour Lives: A Biographical Dictionary of Irish Labour Party Deputies, Senators, MPs and MEPs* (Dublin: Watchword, 2010).

Cameron, M., *Women in Green* (Belfast: Royal Ulster Constabulary Historical Society, 1993).

Casella, E.C., '"Doing Trade": A Sexual Economy of Nineteenth-Century Australian Female Convict Prisons', *World Archaeology*, 32, 2 (Autumn 2000), pp.209–21.

Casella, E.C., 'Bulldagers and Gentle Ladies: Archaeological Approaches to Female Homosexuality in Convict-Era Australia', in R.A. Schmidt & B.L. Voss (eds), *Archaeologies of Sexuality* (London: Routledge, 2000), pp.143–59.

Coke, E., *The First Part of the Institutes of the Law of England* (Philadelphia, MD: Robert H. Smith, 1853).

Colapinto, J., *As Nature Made Him: The Boy Who was Raised as a Girl* (New York, NY: Perennial, 2001).

Connolly, L. and T. O'Toole, *Documenting Irish Feminisms: The Second Wave* (Dublin: Woodfield Press, 2005).

Connolly, L., *The Irish Women's Movement: From Revolution to Devolution* (Basingstoke: Palgrave, 2002).

Conway, V., *Policing Twentieth-Century Ireland: A History of An Garda Síochána* (London: Routledge, 2014).

Cooper, D., 'Governing Troubles: Authority, Sexuality and Space', *British Journal of Sociology of Education*, 18, 4 (1997), pp.501–17.

Cousins J. and M. Cousins, *We Two Together* (Madras: Ganesh, 1950).

Cullen, M., 'Women, Emancipation and Politics, 1860–1984', in J.R. Hill (ed.), *A New History of Ireland, Vol. VII, Ireland 1921–1984* (Oxford: Oxford University Press, 2003), pp.826–91.

Cullen, M. *Telling it Our Way: Essays in Gender History* (Dublin: Arlen House, 2013).

Damousi, J., *Depraved and Disorderly: Female Convicts, Sexuality and Gender in Colonial Australia* (Cambridge: Cambridge University Press, 1997).

Daniels, K., 'The Flash Mob: Rebellion, Rough Culture and Sexuality in the Female Factories of Van Diemen's Land', *Australian Feminist Studies*, 8, 18 (1993), pp.133–50.

Daniels, K., *Convict Women* (St Leonard's NSW: Allen & Unwin, 1998).

Daniels, K. and M. Murnane, *Uphill All the Way: A Documentary History of Women in Australia* (St Lucia: University of Queensland Press, 1980).

Datson, L. and K. Park, 'Hermaphrodites in Renaissance France', *Critical Matrix*, 1, 5 (1985), pp.1–19.

Diamond M. and K. Sigmundson, 'Sex Reassignment at Birth: Long-term Review and Clinical Implications', *Archive of Pediatric & Adolescent Medicine*, 151 (1997), pp.298–304.

Dreger, A.D., 'A History of Intersex: From the Age of Gonads to the Age of Consent', in A.D. Dreger (ed.), *Intersex in the Age of Ethics* (Hagerstown, MD: University Publishing Group, 1999), pp.5–22.

Dreger, A.D. and A.M. Herndon, 'Progress and Politics in the Intersex Rights Movement: Feminist Theory in Action', *GLQ: A Journal of Lesbian and Gay Studies*, 15, 2 (2009), pp.199–224.

Dreger, A.D., *Hermaphrodites and the Medical Invention of Sex* (Cambridge, MA: Harvard University Press, 1998).

Earner-Byrne, L., '"Parading their poverty...": Widows in Twentieth-Century Ireland', in B. Faragó and M. Sullivan (eds), *Facing the Other: Interdisciplinary Studies on Race, Gender, and Social Justice in Ireland* (Cambridge: Cambridge Scholars Press, 2008), pp.32–46.

Earner-Byrne, L., 'Child Sexual Abuse, History, and the Pursuit of Blame in Modern Ireland', in K. Holmes & S. Ward (eds), *Exhuming Passions: The Pressure of the Past in Ireland and Australia* (Dublin, Irish Academic Press, 2011), pp.51–70.

Earner-Byrne, L., 'Reinforcing the Family: Understandings of Gender and Sexuality in the Irish Welfare Debate, 1922–44', *History of the Family: International Quarterly Journal*, 13, 4 (2008), pp.360–9.

Earner-Byrne, L., '"Aphrodite Rising from the Waves"?: Women's Voluntary Activism and the Women's Movement in Twentieth-Century Ireland', in Thane, P. and E. Breitenbach (eds), *Women and Citizenship in Britain and Ireland* (London: Continuum Books, 2010) pp.95–112.

Egan, R.D. and G.L. Hawkes, 'The Problem with Protection: Or Why We Need to Move towards Recognition and the Sexual Agency of Children', *Journal of Media & Cultural Studies*, 23, 3 (2009), pp.389–400.

Egan, R.D. and Hawkes, G.L., 'Endangered Girls and Incendiary Objects: Unpacking the Discourse on Sexualization', *Sexuality and Culture*, 12, 4 (2008), pp.291–311.

Epstein, D., 'What's in a Ban? The Popular Media, Romeo and Juliet and Compulsory Heterosexuality', in D.L. Steinberg, D. Epstein and R. Johnson (eds), *Border Patrols, Policing The Boundaries of Heterosexuality* (London: Cassell, 1997), pp.183–203.

Fahey, T., 'Family Policy in Ireland – A Strategic Overview, Background Papers for the Commission on the Family', in *The Commission on the Family, Final Report to the Minister for Social, Community and Family Affairs, Strengthening Families for Life* (Dublin: Government of Ireland, 1998), pp.384–403.

Farrell, E. (ed.), *'She said she was in the family way': Pregnancy and Infancy in Modern Ireland,* (London: Institute of Historical Research, 2012).

Faulkner, J., 'The Innocence Fetish: The Commodification and Sexualisation of Children in the Media and Popular Culture', *Media International Australia*, 135 (2010), pp.106–17.

Fausto-Sterling, A., *Sexing the Body: Gender Politics and the Construction of Sexuality* (New York, NY: Basic Books, 2000).

Ferguson, K. (ed.), *King's Inns Barristers, 1868–2004* (Dublin: Honorable Society of King's Inns in association with the Irish Legal History Society, 2005).

Ferriter, D., *Occasions of Sin: Sex and Society in Modern Ireland* (London: Profile Books, 2009).

Foucault, M., *The History of Sexuality: Volume 1 The Will to Knowledge*, R. Hurley, trans, (London: Penguin Books, 1998).

Frost, L., 'Eliza Churchill Tells...' in L. Frost & H. Maxwell-Stewart (eds), *Chain Letters: Narrating Convict Lives* (Melbourne: Melbourne University Press, 2001), pp.79–90.

Gay, P., *The Bourgeois Experience: Victoria to Freud* (Oxford: Oxford University Press, 1984).

Gerard, J., *Country House Life: Family and Servants, 1815–1914* (Oxford: Blackwell Press, 1994).

Goldschmidt, R., 'Intersexuality and the Endocrine Aspect of Sex', *Endocrinology*, 1, 4 (October 1917), pp.433–56.

Government of Ireland, *Report of the Expert Advisory Group on Relationships and Sexuality Education* (Dublin: Stationery Office, 1995).

Haslam, T.J., *The Marriage Problem* (Dublin, 1868).

Haslam, T.J., *The Women's Advocate* (Dublin, 1874).

Hayes, A., 'Afterword: A Feminine Occupation for a Female Audience?: A Future for Irish Women's History', in A. Hayes and D. Urquhart (eds), *Irish Women's History* (Dublin: Irish Academic Press, 2004), pp.199–202.

Heidensohn, F., *Women in Control?: The Role of Women in Law Enforcement* (Oxford: Oxford University Press, 1992).

Hesketh, T., *The Second Partitioning of Ireland?: The Abortion Referendum of 1983* (Dublin: Brandsma Books, 1990).

Jackson, L., *Women Police: Gender, Welfare and Surveillance in the Twentieth Century* (Manchester: Manchester University Press, 2006).

Jalland, P. and J. Hooper, *Women From Birth to Death: The Female Life Cycle in Britain, 1830–1914* (Atlantic Highlands, N.J., 1986).

Jalland, P., *Women, Marriage and Politics: 1860–1914* (Oxford: Oxford University Press, 1988).

Kehoe, E., *Fortune's Daughters, The Extravagant Lives of the Jerome Sisters: Jennie Churchill, Clara Frewen and Leonie Leslie* (London: Atlantic Books, 2004).

Kennedy, F., *From Cottage to Crèche: Family Change in Ireland* (Dublin, 2001).

Kerrigan, G., *Another Country: Growing up in 1950's Ireland* (Dublin: Gill & Macmillan, 1998).

Kiely, E., 'Sexing the Curriculum: A Poststructuralist Interrogation of the Politics of Irish Sexuality Education 1960–2002' (University College Cork: PhD Thesis, 2004).

Kiernan, K., 'School Sex Education in Ireland – Towards a Feminist Perspective' (Trinity College Dublin: M.Phil. Thesis in Women's Studies, 1992).

Kingston, J, A. Whelan with I. Bacik, *Abortion and the Law* (Dublin: Round Hall Sweet & Maxwell, 1997).

Lane, L., *Rosamund Jacob: Third Person Singular* (Dublin: University College Dublin Press, 2010).

Levine, P., '"Walking the streets in a way no decent woman should": Women Police in World War I', *Journal of Modern History*, 66 (1994), pp.34–78.

Lock, J., *The British Policewoman: Her Story* (London: Robert Hale, 1979).

Luddy, M., 'The Problem of Equality: Women's Activist Campaigns in Ireland, 1929–40', in T.E. Hachey (ed.), *Turning Points in Twentieth-Century Irish History* (Dublin: Irish Academic Press, 2011), pp.57–76.

Luddy, M., 'Women and Work in Nineteenth and Early Twentieth-Century Ireland: An Overview', in B. Whelan (ed.), *Women and Paid Work in Ireland, 1500–1930* (Dublin: Four Courts Press, 2000), pp.44–56.

Luddy, M. *Matters of Deceit: Breach of promise to marry cases in nineteenth- and twentieth-century Limerick.* (Dublin: Four Courts Press, 2011).

MacCurtain, M. and Ó Corráin, D. (eds), *Women in Irish Society: The Historical Dimension* (Dublin: Arlen House, 1978).

MacCurtain, M., O'Dowd, M. and Luddy, M., 'An Agenda for Women's History in Ireland, 1500–1900', *Irish Historical Studies*, 28, 109 (1992), pp.1–37.

MacPherson, D.A.J. and Hickman, M. (eds), *Women and Irish Diaspora Identities: Theories, Concepts and New Perspectives* (Manchester: Manchester University Press, 2014).

Mahon, E, C. Conlon and L. Dillon, *Women and Crisis Pregnancy: A Report Presented to the Department of Health and Children* (Dublin: Government Stationery Office, 1998).

Maimonides, *The Code of Maimonides, Book 4 The Book of Women* (New Haven, CT: Yale University Press, 1972).

Malcolm, E., *The Irish Policeman, 1822–1922: A Life* (Dublin: Four Courts Press, 2006).

Mayock, P., Kitching, K. and M. Morgan, *RSE in the Context of SPHE: An Assessment of the Challenges to Full Implementation of the Programme in Post-Primary Schools* (Dublin: Crisis Pregnancy Agency, 2007).

McAvoy, S., 'Before Cadden: Abortion in Mid-Twentieth Century Ireland', in D. Keogh, F. O'Shea and C. Quinlan (eds), *The Lost Decade: Ireland in the 1950s* (Cork: Mercier, 2004), pp.147–63.

McCormick, L., 'Filthy Little Girls: Controlling Women in Public Spaces in Northern Ireland during the World Wars', in G. McIntosh and D. Urquhart (eds), *Irish Women at War* (Dublin: Irish Academic Press, 2010), pp. 103–19.

McCormick, L, *Regulating Sexuality: Women in Twentieth-Century Northern Ireland* (Manchester: Manchester University Press, 2010).

McNiffe, L., *A History of the Garda Síochána: A Social History of the Force 1922–52, with an overview for the years 1952–97* (Dublin: Wolfhound Press, 1997).

Meaney, G., O'Dowd, M. and B. Whelan, *Reading the Irish Woman: Studies in Cultural Encounters and Exchange, 1714–1960* (Liverpool: Liverpool University Press, 2013).

Money, J. and A.A. Ehrhardt, *Man and Woman, Boy and Girl: Differentiation and Dimorphism of Gender* (Baltimore, MD: Johns Hopkins University Press, 1973).

Morgan O.K. and H. McGee, *Irish Contraception and Crisis Pregnancy Study 2010: A Survey of the General Population* (Dublin: HSE, 2010).

Morgan, M., *Relationships and Sexuality Education, An Evaluation and Review of Implementation* (Dublin: Stationery Office, 2000).

Morrison, B., 'Controlling the Hopeless: Re-visioning the History of Female Inebriate Institutions c. 1870-1920', in H. Johnston (ed.), *Punishment and Control in Historical Perspective* (London: Palgrave Macmillan, 2008), pp.135–76.

Ní Mhuirthile, T. 'Legal Recognition of Preferred Gender Identity in Ireland: An Analysis of Proposed Legislation', in M. Leane and E. Keily (eds), *Sexualities and Irish Society: A Reader* (Dublin: Orpen Press, 2014), pp.127–48.

Ní Mhuirthile, T., 'Realising Gender Recognition: Rendering the Vulnerable Visible or Further Vulnerabilising the Invisible?' *UCD Working Papers in Law, Criminology and Socio-Legal Studies Research Paper No 41/2010.* Available at http://papers.ssrn.com/soI3/papers.cfm?abstract_id=1680899

O'Carroll, J.P. and L. Szalacha, *A Queer Quandary: The Challenges of Including Sexual Difference Within The Relationships and Sexuality Education Programme* (Dublin: LOT/ LEA, 2000).

O'Carroll, J.P., 'Bishops, Knights and Pawns? Traditional Thought and the Irish Abortion Referendum Debate of 1983', *Irish Political Studies*, 6 (1991), pp.53–71.

O'Donnell, I., 'Sex Crime in Ireland: Extent and Trends', *Judicial Studies Institute Journal*, 3, 1 (2003), pp.89–106.

O'Dowd, M. and S. Wichert (eds), *Chattel, Servant or Citizen: Women's Status in Church, State and Society* (Belfast: Institute of Irish Studies, Queen's University of Belfast, 1995).

O'Halpin, E., *Defending Ireland: The Irish State and its Enemies since 1922* (Oxford: Oxford University Press, 1999).

O'Malley, T., *Sexual Offences: Law, Policy and Punishment* (Dublin: Round Hall, 1996).

O'Malley, T., *The Criminal Process* (Dublin: Round Hall, 2009).

O'Riordan, M., 'Home, Family and Society: Women of the Irish Landed Class, 1860–1914: A Munster Case Study', Unpublished PhD thesis, University College Cork, 2014.

Offen, K. (ed.), *Globalizing Feminisms, 1789–1945* (London: Routledge, 2010).

Paseta, S., *Irish Nationalist Women 1900–1918* (Cambridge: Cambridge University Press, 2013).

Peterson, M.J., 'No Angels in the House: The Victorian Myth and the Paget Women', *American Historical Review*, Vol. 89, No. 3 (Jun. 1984), pp.677–708.

Peterson, M.J., *Family, Love and Work in the Lives of Victorian Gentlewomen* (Bloomington, In.: Indiana University Press, 1989).

Quinlan, C., *Genteel Revolutionaries: Anna and Thomas Haslam and the Irish Women's Movement* (Cork University Press: Cork, 2002).

Radzinowicz, L. and R. Hood, *A History of English Criminal Law, Vol. 5: The Emergence of Penal Policy* (London: Stevens, 1986).

Reid, K., *Gender, Crime and Empire* (Manchester: Manchester University Press, 2007).

Reiner, R., *The Politics of the Police* (Oxford: Oxford University Press, 2010).

Reis, E., 'Divergence or Disorder: The Politics of Naming Intersex', *Perspectives in Biology and Medicine*, 50, 4 (Autumn 2007), pp.535–43.

Renold, E., *Girls, Boys and Junior Sexualities* (Oxford: Routledge Falmer, 2005).

Riddick, R., *The Right to Choose: Questions of Feminist Morality* (Dublin: Attic Press, 1990).

Robinson, K.H., 'Difficult Citizenship: The Precarious Relationships between Childhood, Sexuality and Access to Knowledge', *Sexualities*, 15, 3/4 (2012), pp.257–76.

Robinson, L., *Palette and Plough: A Pen-and-Ink Drawing of Dermod O'Brien* (Dublin: Brown and Nolan, 1948).

Roe, S. (in co-operation with Dáil na nÓg / Children's Parliament) *Life Skills Matter Not Just Points: A Survey of Implementation of Social, Personal and Health Education (SPHE) and Relationships and Sexuality Education (RSE) in Second-Level Schools* (Dublin: Office of the Minister for Children and Youth Affairs, 2010).

Ruane, M., *The Irish Journey: Women's Stories of Abortion* (Dublin: Irish Family Planning Association, 2000).

Schneid Lewis, J., *In the Family Way: Childbearing in the British Aristocracy, 1760–1860* (New Brunswick, N.J.: Rutgers University Press, 1986).

Shepard, C., 'A Liberalisation of Irish Social Policy? Women's Organisations and the Campaign for Women Police in Ireland, 1915–57', *Irish Historical Studies*, 36, 4 (November 2009), pp.564–80.

Smith, B., *Australia's Birthstain: The Startling Legacy of the Convict Era* (Crow's Nest, NSW: Allen & Unwin, 2008).

Smith, B.A., 'Ireland's Ennis Inebriates' Reformatory: A Nineteenth-Century Example of Failed Institutional Reform', *Federal Probation*, 53 (1989), pp.53–6.

Smyth, A. (ed.), *The Abortion Papers Ireland* (Dublin: Attic Press, Dublin, 1992).

Smyth, L., *Abortion and Nation: The Politics of Reproduction in Contemporary Ireland* (Aldershot: Ashgate Publishing, 2005).

Spreng, J., *Abortion and Divorce Law in Ireland* (North Carolina: MacFarland & Company, 2004).

Tiernan, S. and M. McAuliffe (eds), *Sapphists and Sexologists: Histories of Sexualities Volume II* (Newcastle: Cambridge Scholars Publishing, 2009).

Tiernan, S. and M. McAuliffe (eds), *Tribades, Tommies and Transgressives: Histories of Sexualities Volume I* (Newcastle: Cambridge Scholars Publishing, 2008).

Trudell, B.N., *Doing Sex Education, Gender Politics and Schooling* (New York: Routledge, 1993).

Valiulis, M. (ed.), *Gender and Power in Irish History* (Dublin: Irish Academic Press, 2008).

Wallace A. and J. Van Every, 'Sexuality in the Primary School', *Sexualities*, 3, 4 (2000), pp.409–23.

Walsh, O., *Anglican Women in Dublin: Philanthropy and Education in the Early Twentieth Century* (Dublin: University College Dublin Press, 2005).

Walsh, S., 'A Different Kind of Learning: Relationships and Sexuality Education', *Irish Educational Studies*, 18 (1999), pp.223–33.

Weinberger, B., 'A Policewife's Lot Is Not a Happy One: Police Wives in the 1930s and 1940s', *Oral History*, 21, 2 (Autumn, 1993), pp.46–53.

Weinberger, B., *The Best Police in the World: An Oral History of English Policing from the 1930s to the 1960s* (Aldershot: Scolar Press, 1995).

Whatley, M.H., 'Whose Sexuality is it Anyway?', in J. T. Sears (ed.), *Sexuality and The Curriculum* (New York: Teachers College Press), pp.78–84.

Whelan, B. (ed.), *Women and Paid Work in Ireland, 1500–1930* (Dublin: Four Courts Press, 2000).

Wilson, D., *Women, Marriage and Property in Wealthy Landed Families in Ireland, 1750–1850* (Manchester: Manchester University Press, 2009).

Woolacott, A., '"Khaki Fever" and its Control: Gender, Class, Age, and Sexual Morality on the British Home Front in the First World War', *Journal of Contemporary History*, 29, 2 (April 1994), pp.325–47.

Young, M., 'Police Wives: A Reflection of Police Concepts of Order and Control', in H. Callan and S. Ardener (eds), *The Incorporated Wife* (London: Croom Helm, 1984), pp.67–78.

Young, M., *An Inside Job: Policing and Police Culture in Britain* (Oxford: Clarendon, 1990).

INDEX